Theories of the Sign
in Classical Antiquity

Advances in Semiotics
Thomas A. Sebeok, General Editor

Theories of the Sign
in Classical Antiquity

•••••••••••••••••

GIOVANNI MANETTI

Translated by Christine Richardson

This publication was made possible through the cooperation of *Biblioteca Italia*, a Giovanni Agnelli Foundation programme for the diffusion of Italian culture.

INDIANA UNIVERSITY PRESS
Bloomington and Indianapolis

© 1993 by Indiana University Press

First published as *Le teorie del segno nell'antichità classica* by Giovanni Manetti, © 1987 Gruppo Editoriale Fabbri, Bompiani, Sonzongo, Etas S.p.A., Milan. This translation is issued with permission of the original Italian-language publisher.

The paper used in this publication meets the minimum requirements of American National Standard for Information Sciences—Permanence of Paper for Printed Library Materials, ANSI Z39.48-1984.

Manufactured in the United States of America

Library of Congress Cataloging-in-Publication Data

Manetti, Giovanni.
    [Teorie del segno nell'antichità classica. English]
    Theories of the sign in classical antiquity / Giovanni Manetti : translated by Christine Richardson.
        p.   cm. — (Advances in semiotics)
    Includes bibliographical references.
    ISBN 0-253-33684-8 (alk. paper)
    1. Semiotics—History.   2. Language and languages—Philosophy—History.   3. Philosophy, Ancient.   I. Title.   II.Series.
    P99.M34513   1993
    302.2—dc20   92-28924

1   2   3   4   5   97   96   95   94   93

Contents

Contents

Acknowledgments

I would like to thank the many friends who have read and discussed the various parts of the present text with me. I particularly appreciate the critical response and advice of Mario Bernardini, Silvana Borutti, Giuliana Crevatin, Paolo Fabbri, Paola Manuli, Costantino Marmo, Andrea Tabarroni, Mario Vegetti, and Patrizia Violi. The study owes much with respect to general form and ideas to Umberto Eco, who has followed and encouraged my work from the very beginning. Special thanks go to Amedeo G. Conte, who revised an earlier form of the text and who provided me with countless valuable suggestions. As far as any mistakes or imprecisions are concerned, I am the sole culprit. This book is dedicated to my students.

Introduction

In *Semiotics and the Philosophy of Language* (1984a), Umberto Eco observed that during the present century, precisely at the moment it is emerging from marginality and being accepted as a discipline and when its role as paradigmatic science is being recognized, semiotics has become the final term of reference in a series of statements announcing the death, or at least the crisis, of the sign. This is hardly a novel situation, Eco comments, for the history of Western thought may be read as a history of elimination and repression of semiotics as a science, despite (and notwithstanding) the many announcements, projects and hypotheses of a theory of signs which, so often, have marked theoretical reflection during the last two and a half millennia. Eco suggested that what was needed was the development of a current project of semiotics which could be fitted into the space between recent negations of semiotics and the undeniable presence of semiotics in the past. This would mean that semiotics must retrace the path of history and become an archaeology of knowledge about signs. In this way, it would be possible to go beyond the linguistic impasse which lies at the base of current definitions of the sign, definitions which criticize its format as either too restrictive or too wide and which are not able to apply the model outside of verbal systems.

This study may be seen as an attempt to take up Eco's suggestion: it aims to investigate both semiotic practices from the origins and the theoretical considerations of the sign which were developed in the ancient world and which have come down to us through the literary, philosophical, medical, historical and rhetorical traditions.

The aim therefore is to rediscover a thread which may be traced through the classical world from its origins to the fourth century A.D., forming a concept of the sign which is significantly different from that proposed in the twentieth century.

Most twentieth-century theories of the sign—both those stemming from linguistics, from Saussure's *Cours de linguistique générale* onwards, and those which have been developed from a more purely semiological approach—are based on two presuppositions which form no part whatsoever of the classical considerations of the sign. Firstly, that the model of the sign used, the model on which the whole semiological investigation is based, is that of the linguistic sign; secondly, that the relationship postulated as existing between the two components of the sign, the signifier and the signified, is that of equivalence ($p \cong q$). It is because of this that the most widely held notion of meaning in semantic theories up until very recently was that which considered meaning as synonymy or as essential definition. From Hjelmslev's structuralism onwards, up until the componential and interpretative semantic theories of generative linguistics, the individual linguistic term, or rather the form of expression of the sign, has been seen as equivalent to a series of content figures or semantic markers, in their turn expressed metalinguistically by an equivalent number of linguistic forms: for example |woman| $\cong$ "animate being" + "human" + "female" + "adult".

An investigation of the way in which classical antiquity treated and developed considerations of the sign will enable us to discover that, with respect to the first point noted above, not only is there no homologization of the different types of sign under the general representative example of the linguistic sign, but that the two theories (the semantic theory of language and the theory of the non-linguistic sign) proceed rather in parallel without ever being interconnected. A clear example of this may be seen in the way that Aristotle uses the term *sýmbolon* to indicate the linguistic sign whereas he uses the terms *sēmeîon* and *tekmḗrion* to indicate the non-linguistic sign.

The blending of the two types of sign occurs only much later, with Augustine, but even here it is the linguistic sign which is subsumed into the general category already covering the non-linguistic sign.

With respect to the second point considered above, both the areas using signs which have come down to us through tradition and the classical theories are based on a function of the sign which works from *implication* ($p \supset q$) rather than *equivalence*. A well-known example of a paradigmatic sign which re-appears throughout the classical tradition from Aristotle to Quintilian by way of the Stoic philosophers is "If a woman has milk in her breasts, then she has recently given birth". We can already see here a fascinating contrast with later sign theories. The implicative classical model is not only more interesting than the equivalence model, but it is even more "modern". The most recent research in sign theory is in fact attempting to revise the paradigm of the sign and to go beyond "dictionary" semantics (which functions according to the equivalence model) to focus rather on an "encyclopedia" semantics (which functions according to the implicative model).

However, the interest of such a work of reconstruction of semiotic theories from classical antiquity by no means lies only in the recovery of forgotten material with the aim of forming a picture to contrast with that of contemporary theories. There is undoubtedly an intrinsic interest also in observing how semantic fields and their associated terminology gradually came to be distinguished and how they took form from situations of linguistic use which were originally much more diverse and much less clearly distinguished. Here too it is Aristotle who first set precise limits on terms and concepts which had previously been used (up until the end of the fifth century B.C., and even beyond—for example, in the texts of the *Corpus Hippocraticum*) with a considerable semantic laxity.

Before Aristotle tightened definitions and classifications, expressions such as *sēmeîon*, *aitía*, *próphasis*, *tekmḗrion* and *eikós* not only formed a field of related terms but also of terms which often overlapped and allowed a certain interchangeability (cf. Lloyd, 1979). In the same way, the cultural references of certain expressions were various and diverse before Aristotle. *Sēmaínō*, for example, as may be seen in the Heraclitus fragment 93 (Diels-Kranz), was the verb used to indicate the enigmatic pronouncements of the god at Delphi; *tekmaíromai*, on the other hand, denoted the general sense of proceeding by means of rational conjecture but was nonetheless used by the tragic dramatists and the lyric poets to refer to the practice of divinatory interpretation; *sēmeîon* (or its Homeric variant, *sêma*) was the most complex term of all, for it was used to indicate a wide range of phenomena, from evidence to distinguishing features to divine portents, even being used as the general term for the divinatory sign (cf. Bloch, 1963; Benveniste, 1969).

It was above all in the spheres of divination and astrology, and through these to the art of navigation, that theoretical considerations of the sign were first applied.

This connection may be seen in Alcman's cosmogony, in which the sea goddess Thetis appears at the beginning of the world with three divine beings: *Póros* ("the way") and *Tékmōr* ("the signal, the point of reference") on one side and *Skótos* ("darkness") on the other. As Marcel Detienne and Jean-Pierre Vernant (1974) point out, *Tékmōr* has a role of primary importance: "In the original confused darkness (*skótos*) of the sky and the sea, he brings distinct differentiated ways (*póroi*) which make visible on the surface of the sky and the sea the various directions of space, giving direction to a surface which was previously devoid of all markings and of all points of reference, *áporon kaì atékmarton"*. Thus, sailors construct a bridge between the visible and the invisible.

With Aristotle, the terms of the semiotic vocabulary which had previously maintained an exclusive reference to the realm of the sacred (as they would continue to do even after Aristotle in areas apart from philosophy and rationalism) were turned to a strictly secular use (cf. Lanza, 1979, p.107). However, even if the original sacred character of the terminology is lost, some trace of it remains and can be seen through later forms, and if Aristotle, in his delimitation of conceptual fields, limits the expression *sēmeîon* to signs which are not certain and which can be misleading (whereas he reserves the term *tekmērion* for the reliable sign), what we have with Aristotle's work of clarification and tightening of definitions is the transformation of the ambiguous sign of divine revelation into the ambiguous sign of the rationalist cognitive model.

Even if the roots of the semiotic paradigm are to be found in the "non-scientific" practices of divination and magical medicine, in the course of the centuries such origins are nonetheless purified of all traces of the irrational and the unconfirmable (even if outside of philosophical theorizations the paradigm will continue to be used in many diverse and irrational ways, as may be seen, for example, in Artemidorus of Daldis' and Aelius Aristides' works on dream signs).

Bearing this in mind, it is not so surprising that the propositional and implicative form which the Stoics give to the sign ("If there is a scar, there has been a wound") may be found in Mesopotamian divinatory tablets from the third millennium B.C.

The ancient Babylonians also expressed the sign by means of a hypothetical period formed by a *protasis*, introduced by the connective *šumma* (the equivalent of the Greek *ei*, which was used to introduce the Stoic conditional), and by an *apodosis*. These two clauses translate into linguistic propositions the sign and its interpretation, respectively ("If the lung is reddish on the right and on the left—there will be a fire") (Bottero, 1974).

Among the Greeks, a blending of the divinatory sign and the logical form of implication can be seen in one of the Delphic dialogues of Plutarch, *De E apud Delphos*. This work contains the debate of several prestigious thinkers on the meaning of an object, shaped like the letter E, included among the votive offerings in the temple at Delphi. Theon proposes an interpretation of the "E" which rests on the name given to this letter in the ancient language, that is, *eî*. He draws the parallel between this name and the hypothetical connective *ei* ("if") and shows that this connective has an essential role in dialectics in that it is used to express the logical relationship *par excellence*, that found in conditionals of the type "If it is day, it is light" (one of the most classical examples of Stoic semiotic logic). Theon finally points out the fact that the Delphic god, Apollo, is a god who "favors dialectics", so much so that the oracles themselves take the form of the conditional, $p \supset q$, which is the very form taken by universal phenomena (which leads to the Stoic theory of "universal harmony").

What Plutarch's text (probably written at the beginning of the second century A.D.) seems to imply is that, at most, the Stoic theory of Fate and divination was based on logic (that destiny consisted of an interconnected series of conditionals). But could it not be that it is in fact quite the reverse? Could it not be that the bare, ascetic, rational tool of logic in reality originates from the sphere of divination? This seems to be demonstrated by the strict connection which exists between logic, signs and divination in Stoic thought (cf. Goldschmidt, 1953, p.80; Verbeke, 1978, p.402).

Nonetheless, a large step has been taken from the Babylonian divinatory texts to Stoic logic. The propositional form remains the same, but with the Stoics it has been purified not only of all sacred traces but also of any content-based element. For the Stoics it is there solely for propositional calculation. The ancient Mesopotamians, on the other hand, used the content of the protasis to infer the content of the apodosis by means of more or less complex processes of analogy and tropic relations (the redness of the lung allowed them to infer "a fire" through a common semantic marker).

Last but not least, an investigation of classical semiotic considerations enables us to discover that the debate on signs and on their nature and classification took place at the very highest levels of philosophical speculation, as is the case with the discussion of conditionals which took place within the Stoic school (between Diodorus, Philo and Chrysippus) and the dispute between the Stoics and the Epicureans on the relationship between antecedents and consequents in signs (a debate reflected in the *De Signis* of Philodemus).

Discussion of semiotic issues in the classical world always took place with reference to, or was explicitly identified with, the more general, fundamental sphere of the problem of knowledge.

In the Roman world, these aspects of cognitive problems were applied to the more pragmatic levels of judicial knowledge. The problem of signs became identified with the problem of the methodology of assigning greater or lesser value of proof to evidence presented at a trial. In this way, semiotics was put to the service of the art of detection and thus rather surprisingly prefigured one of the most fascinating aspects of contemporary interest in evidential paradigms (cf. Eco and Sebeok [eds.], 1983).

The theory of the sign was finally linked to the theory of language only with Augustine in the fourth century A.D., thereby enabling the inclusion of verbal signs in a single category along with non-verbal signs.

Theories of the Sign
in Classical Antiquity

ONE

Mesopotamian Divination

1.0 DIVINATION IN
MESOPOTAMIAN CULTURE

The Mesopotamians were recognized as masters in the field of divination by all the ancient cultures.

Despite such ancient appreciation, the attitudes held by more contemporary culture with respect to this sphere of activity tend to be considerably more negative. Contemporary evaluations place the divinatory paradigm in a position exactly opposite on the scale of values from that of the scientific paradigm. However, there are at least two reasons which should prompt us to look at Mesopotamian divination in a more positive and appreciative light.

First of all, as Carlo Ginzburg (1979) has suggested, we must reconsider the relationship between the "divinatory" paradigm and the "scientific" paradigm and see it as a much more complex relationship than might be generally supposed and as a relationship which does not necessarily work to the detriment of the divinatory. For Ginzburg, the divinatory paradigm (variously defined—according to the contexts in which it appears—as "evidential", "semeiotic" or "hunting") is a model of specific knowledge which is characterized by its qualitative nature; it is based on an individual's knowledge and is reached by means of conjecture. This quality enables the divinatory paradigm to achieve notable effects in the principal areas of its use (not only in religion but also in medicine, philology and so on, right up to criminology, connoisseurship and psychoanalysis), even if it carries with it an inevitable chance element. This paradigm represents in fact the type of knowledge that Peirce (1980, 1984) defines as "abductive", in contrast to the quantitative model of knowledge, which uses deduction as the means of reasoning.

The second point in favor of the divinatory paradigm is that divination in Mesopotamia underwent a long and complex process of evolution which moved from an initial tendency to infer causes from effects (the typical procedure of abduction) to an increasing accentuation of generalizing and *a priori* tendencies, thus setting the foundations for a true scientific method of the abstract type (cf. Bottero, 1974).

From the point of view of a historical reconstruction of the discipline of semiotics, the most significant aspect of Mesopotamian divination is that it is centered precisely on a distinctive and individual notion of the *sign*, which is a scheme of inferential reasoning that allows particular conclusions to be drawn from particular facts.

It is interesting to note how the sign becomes central in the whole Mesopotamian cognitive universe; starting out from the sphere of divination, it reaches into other cultural practices and disciplines, such as medicine and law and eventually brings all areas of knowledge into its unifying model. We therefore reach the point in Mesopotamia where, at the basic levels, knowledge works according to the unified and formal scheme of the divinatory sign even if differentiated contents can be found elaborated within the scheme. It is already possible to map out the form taken by the model of the sign in Mesopotamian culture (we shall discuss this form in greater detail below): a hypothetical period in which a certain conclusion is given in the apodosis as being derived directly from the state of things given in the protasis. In other words, a model in which the protasis is the "sign" of the apodosis.

This kind of sign model ("If p, then q") is very close to what has come down to us from Greek thought at the height of its semiotic maturity. In particular, the model of the sign elaborated by the Stoic school functions according to this type of implicative scheme. However, we must make a certain distinction here: the way the sign is used in Mesopotamian divination, it is generally *material* (or content-linked) elements which permit the passage from protasis to apodosis, whereas, in Stoic semiotics, inferences are made possible solely through *formal* elements.

Nonetheless, even taking into consideration these significant differences and without confronting the problem of possible debts of influence owed to Mesopotamian culture by Greek culture in this respect,[1] it is extremely interesting to note the presence of the same sign scheme, $p \supset q$, running through two civilizations (Greek and Mesopotamian) and two spheres of cultural activity (divination and philosophy) which otherwise have little in common with one another.

1.1 DIVINATION AND WRITING

The fact that Mesopotamia was a civilization based on writing provides a basis for understanding both the type of divination which developed there and the reasons for its far-reaching influence. In Mesopotamia, writing formed the model for a whole series of intellectual activities, not the least among which was the interpretation of signs sent by the gods.

In Mesopotamia, reading the future and gaining knowledge of hidden things were not achieved through direct divine inspiration but rather through the same process which operates in the interpretation of written signs.

It is in fact due to the great importance given to writing in this culture that *technical divination* represents the dominant model of divination, that is, divination based on the interpretation of signs which are to be seen in the external world and which require specialist assistance for their explanation (cf. Bouché-Leclercq, 1979–82, vol. 1, pp. 111, 274).

The differences in divinatory tendencies in writing-based and oral-based cultures may be clearly illustrated by the comparison of the civilizations of Mesopotamia and of ancient Greece. The latter, as is well known, was an essentially oral culture in which writing was developed in a relatively recent period and, rather than being an autonomous system with respect to speech, was its reproduction in phonetic characters.

As a direct consequence of the oral nature of its culture, *inspirational divination* formed the dominant divinatory model in ancient Greece. Inspirational divination is the form of divination in which the god speaks to humanity through a prophet who is selected as his or her voice, as in the famous example of oracle divination practiced by the Pythia at Delphi. It is thus hardly by chance that in ancient Greece there was no formation and constant presence of a priestly class specialized in the interpretation of both writing and divinatory signs as was, in contrast, the case in Mesopotamia. In Mesopotamia, writing was both a relatively ancient phenomenon and a structure containing mechanisms which were largely autonomous with respect to speech.

The first traces of cuneiform writing date back to the period between the end of the fourth millennium and the beginning of the third millennium.[2] In its primitive form, this writing is pictographic in that it is made up of signs which are intended to designate what they depict. For example, the representation of a bovine head, formed by an outline which was nonetheless identifiable, indicated in the first instance "ox". However, through a kind of semantic amplification or inflation of the sign, it also indicated "cow" and "large domestic herd animal". In the same way, the schematic design of a foot also had the meaning "to stand" and, as a result, could in addition mean "immobile", "to walk" and "to leave", up to the point of being used also to mean "to carry off" or "to take away".

As may be seen, the pairing of signifiers and signifieds is neither exclusive nor arbitrary. A fairly complex interpretative effort is required to check the inflation and the reduction or compression of the signifieds for an individual sign.

The extension of meanings becomes more complicated with new associations derived from the juxtaposition of different signs. For example, the sign for bread written next to that for mouth creates the semantic product "to eat"; the sign for water next to the sign for eye means "tear", whereas next to the sign for sky it produces "rain". A more curious case is shown when the sign for mountains is placed next to the sign for woman to give the sense "slave girl". This meaning comes about because mountains formed the northern and eastern boundaries of the Mesopotamian lands and thus a woman brought into the region from a place beyond the mountains was necessarily a foreigner destined to be a slave.

There are therefore complicated encyclopedic mechanisms which govern the interpretation of written signs.

However, it may also be seen that, in its oldest form, cuneiform writing is a *writing of things* (cf. Bottero, 1974), as it does not need to pass through spoken language to designate real objects. The complete autonomy of cuneiform writing from spoken language means that its signs can be understood by people who speak different languages, and in fact these signs were pronounced differently in each of these different languages in much the same way that Arabic numerals are in the modern world. The Mesopotamians remained very attached to their "writing of things" and refused to abandon it even when significant advances towards phonetic-based expression were made with the invention of syllabic writing.

Roughly a century after their first development, the signs of pictographic writing began to undergo a process of dislocation from the *things* they designated and began to be linked more directly to the *words* with which the spoken language designated the same objects. The process was favored by the monosyllabic nature of many words and the high percentage of homonyms. An interesting example of the phenomenon, and also the earliest, is shown by the sign for arrow (Figure 1.1). This sign came to

$$\triangleright\!\!-\!\!\triangleleft\,\Upsilon\!\!-\!\!\triangleleft$$

Figure 1.1

mean not only "arrow" but also "life" due to the homonymity of the two words which designated the two concepts, both pronounced |ti| in the Sumerian language.[3] The process may be illustrated as shown in Figure 1.2. At this point it would have been sufficient to eliminate all the ideo-

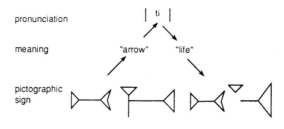

Figure 1.2

grams which indicated words, thus leaving merely the syllable signs to create a fully syllabic alphabet, a minimal unit which could have been used and re-used in an infinite number of ways and combinations. However, the Mesopotamians preferred to retain the signs that were understood according to their earlier pictographic value in parallel with signs that were understood according to their phonetic, syllable-related value.

There are two very important consequences for divination of this organization of writing. First of all, and most importantly, as the examples showed, pictographic writing has the essential characteristic of weaving a subtle, complex web of relationships between things. It trains the mind to see secret relationships and unexpected links in things. It encourages a mental attitude that sees the objects of the real world as containing triggers of an analogous semiotic process. Thus not only does the linking of the pictograms for mountain and for woman indicate "slave girl", but the same linking in real life or in a dream will also lead to an analogous inference. It is exactly this type of inferential mechanism which lies at the heart of divination.

The second consequence is linked to the specialized knowledge required for the interpretation of writing. Cuneiform characters are by no means accessible to all, as they have a highly complex system of codification. A sort of aristocracy of experts capable of interpreting the signs of writing therefore had to be formed. In the same way, the caste of *bârû* soothsayers was formed for the interpretation of the signs sent by the gods. Interestingly, the *bârû* guild had as its emblem the writing table and the stylus.

1.2 THE WRITING OF THE GODS

As Jeannie Carlier (1978, p.1227) has pointed out, talking about a writing of the gods is not a metaphor in Mesopotamia. Mesopotamian culture projected into the theological field precisely the same model of organization as operated in the field of civic bureaucracy. Just as the king spread his power from the center to the edges of the state through a highly developed capillary administrative network which transmitted his written orders to his subjects, so the gods used writing to make known to humanity the fate which they had fixed for each individual. For the gods, however, the only writing tablet large enough for their expression was the universe itself (*ibid.*).

Šamaš and Adad, the gods of divination, can be compared to the king who notifies his subjects of his will by means of written messages, yet they can also be compared to the judge who, having made a decision, ratifies it on the writing tablet in order to give it validity and to make it public.

The world, therefore, is a huge writing tablet, made up of objects which serve as material support for the omens from which oracles are drawn. Such a conception is illustrated in a hymn of Assurbanipal to Šamaš which states: "You examine in the light (of) your (gaze) the whole earth like (so many) cuneiform signs".

The Babylonians talked of the position of the stars as "sky writing" which was "read" by astrologers. It frequently happened that an omen consisted literally of a writing sign traced in the folds of the liver of a sacrificial animal or in the lines of a person's forehead.

1.3 AN "ANTE LITTERAM" SEMIOLOGY

Now that we have established the deep affinity which may be seen between the cuneiform system of writing and divination understood as the writing of the gods, we shall move on to look at the internal structure of the divinatory sign. Thanks to the numerous divinatory tracts which have come down to us, we can form a fairly clear idea of this structure. These tracts consist of lengthy lists of complex propositions, each made up of a protasis and an apodosis. The protasis is introduced by the expression *šumma* (the equivalent of the conjunction "if") and has the verb in the present or past tense. This is the "omen", that is, the ominous sign which is to be interpreted. The apodosis usually has the verb in the future tense and forms the "oracle", that which is indicated or revealed by the interpretation of the sign. It may be useful to look at some examples which, although referring to various techniques of divination, all show the same structure:[4]

Astrology
If on the day of its disappearance the moon lingers in the sky (instead of disappearing all at once)—there will be drought and famine in the country.

Physiognomy
If a man has curly hair on his shoulders—women will love him.

Interpretation of dreams
If a man dreams that someone gives him a seal—he will have a son.

Extispicy
If the lung is bright red on the right and on the left—there will be fire.

Oil interpretation
If, from the center of the oil (thrown onto the water), two "bridges" form, one larger than the other—the wife of the enquirer will bear a male child. If the enquirer is ill, he will recover.

Interpretation of aromatic smoke
If when you pour (the aromatic substance) on the coals, smoke rises up (only) on the right, and not on the left—you will have the better of your enemy. If it rises up (only) on the left and not on the right—your enemy will have the better of you.

These examples enable us to make two immediate observations on the semiotic mechanism which they contain.

First of all, the structure of the sign is expressed in terms of the relationship between propositions and not between individual lexical units or between a signifier and a signified in the Saussurian sense. This results in the fact that non-verbal signs and events immediately take on predominant importance in that they can be best expressed in the proposition.

In addition, the relationship between the protasis and apodosis within each sign is an implicative relationship, where I use "implicative" to mean a still fairly generic inference. Within the Stoic school, as we shall see later, interest will be centered on the attempt to define the implicative link which characterizes the sign, and divergencies of thought will fuel a long and complex debate.

1.4 THE PASSAGE FROM PROTASIS TO APODOSIS

The first impression one receives when faced with the enormous quantity of divinatory propositions recorded in the Mesopotamian treatises is that the passage from omen-protasis to oracle-apodosis is entirely random and governed by pure chance. On a closer analysis, however, it becomes possible to distinguish certain general lines of organization in an otherwise amorphous mass and thereby to extract certain organizing principles.

Three theoretical cases of non-random passage from protasis to apodosis can be identified:

1. The first type of passage is linked to what is known as *divinatory empiricism*: the protasis and the apodosis record events which really occurred in conjunction in the past. This type of mechanism is found in what are known as "historical oracles", which always have the apodosis in the past tense rather than in the future tense. In all probability, this type reproduces the original form of divination.
2. The second type of passage is formed by the possibility of a *chain of association between elements of the protasis and elements of the apodosis*: this association can be of two kinds, a phonetic association between the signifiers or a tropic association between the signifieds.
3. The third type of passage is linked to *the presence of codes which cover a finite series of completely identifiable cases*.

In the later phases of the history of Mesopotamian divination, the treatises undergo an evolution towards exhaustive classification and abstraction. What begins to predominate is an abstract system which is, in a certain sense, totally deductive, even with respect to the likelihood of occurrence of the omens themselves. The Mesopotamian zeal for classification was directed more towards the inclusion of all cases abstractly possible than towards the concrete possibility of their occurrence. The result is that the matching of an apodosis to a certain protasis depends upon an abstract scheme and thus becomes foreseeable.

1.4.1 "HISTORICAL ORACLES" AND DIVINATORY EMPIRICISM

A small but by no means insignificant number of "historical" oracles remain buried if not almost fossilized under the mass of the thousands of other oracles contained in the Mesopotamian treatises. On the basis of internal analysis, these may be attributed to the epoch of the origins of divination, even though they actually appear in later treatises.

These historical oracles have four characteristic features: (i) they all have the apodosis in the past tense; (ii) the topics they treat refer to historical events which can be confirmed from other sources; (iii) the facts and people they mention belong, in most cases, to the epoch of Accad (c.2340–2160 B.C.); (iv) in almost all of them, the apodosis begins with a formula which is rarely found elsewhere in divinatory oracles, *amût* "(it is) the omen of".

Here are some examples:

> If (in the liver) the Palace Door is double, if there are three kidneys and if to the right of the bile bladder are to be found *dug* (*palšu*) two neat perforations (*pilšu*)—(it is) the omen of the inhabitants of Apišal, whom Naram-Sîn (c.2260–23) made prisoners by means of diggings (*pilšu*).

> If, on the right of the liver, two digits are to be found—(it is) the omen of the Epoch of the Competitors.

In both of the cases above, the apodosis refers to real events and historical figures of the epoch of Accad. It seems reasonable to believe that oracles formulated in this way were not greatly posterior to the epoch of the events to which the apodoses refer.

The fundamental point seems to be that this kind of oracle records "significant" coincidences, *a posteriori*, between a certain state of things which was considered ominous and a historical event. The coincidences later took on the value of paradigms.

Persuasive evidence for this hypothesis, which reflects the principle of *divinatory empiricism* (cf. Bouché-Leclercq, 1879–82, vol.1, p.298; Bottero, 1974), is provided by the "Mari livers", many of which contain a formula suggesting how the chain of coincidence came to be established:

> When my country rebelled against Ibbî-Sin (2027–2003), this (i.e., the liver) was found *in this state*.

The Mari model reproduces the form of an actual liver examined during an extispicy rite. It records the coincidence between this form, assumed to be ominous, and a decisively important historical event, that is, the rebellion against the last king of the neo-Sumerian period, Ibbî-Sîn.

The "divinatory empiricism" hypothesis can be taken further to hazard that the discovery of divination was founded on the discovery of coincidences between a series of omens and a series of oracles. This hypothesis seems even more convincing when we consider that all the "historical oracles" can be chronologically assigned to the very earliest period of Mesopotamian divination.

At the very heart of the practice of divination we would be close to a form of the *post hoc ergo propter hoc* principle by which any event which falls outside the bounds of the normal in any manner and which is followed by another event also considered extraordinary is placed with this latter event in a fixed pair. Once established, the connection between the two events becomes absolute; the second event, if not directly caused by the first event, is considered to be at least pre-announced by it.

What is being set out here is in fact the semiotic method of inference of causes from effects which is typical of abduction. It cannot be denied that in this case the method leads to absurd conclusions due to a fundamental error in its application. For what is taken as the *result* (or effect) (a certain clearly defined state of the liver) and which is taken to be an *example* of a certain *rule* (the rebellion against Ibbî-Sîn) is clearly in reality not that at all. However, the truth of the proposition is not important here, formally we are dealing with an abduction.

This principle is applied constantly. Divination is not usually concerned with the past, and if the apodoses of the historical oracles refer to past events it is only because the philosophy which lies behind this type of oracle is that history can repeat itself. In abduction, once the rule which explains a certain result has been inferred, it is possible to use this rule for further deductive applications.

1.4.2 ORACLES USING A CHAIN OF ASSOCIATION BETWEEN THE PROTASIS AND THE APODOSIS

The second possibility of a non-random link between the protasis and the apodosis is brought about by the presence of associative relationships between elements contained in the first proposition and elements contained in the second proposition.

In this class of oracles, the influence of the cuneiform model of writing is clearly discernible. As has already been seen, cuneiform writing tends to create or suggest a network of relationships between things which have no direct connection with one another. We have seen how the interpretation of a cuneiform writing sign gives rise to the possibility of a chain of interpretants. For example, the ideogram for the ear can mean not only "to hear", but also "to obey", "to learn", "knowledge" and "intelligence". In the same way, two homographic ideograms or two ideograms which have very slight graphic differences can set up semantic short circuits and cause utter confusion. We therefore have two types of associative link: (i) a link between the signifieds; (ii) a link between the signifiers.

1.4.2.1 *The associative link created through the signifieds*
The relationship set up between protasis and apodosis in the case of an associative link between the signifieds is one between a rhetorical expression and the corresponding degree-zero expression, usually based on analogy. Let us look at some examples:

If on the 29th of the month of Aiiar (April–May) there is an eclipse of the sun—
the king will die, harshly punished by Šamaš; general mortality.

If an anomalous animal birth is double, with two heads, one fused to the
other, and eight feet, but a single spine—the country will be torn apart by confusion caused by intestinal strife.

If a horse tries to copulate with an ox—there will be a reduction in the increase
of herd animals.

The eclipse of the sun in the first example can be seen as a metaphor in
relation to the death of the king; the metaphor of an eclipse as a sign of the
death of a monarch became standardized and formed part of the mantic
tradition in ancient Greece and Rome. There is a complex metaphor at
work in the second example. Here the protasis refers to the body of a single
animal ("a single spine"), which nonetheless has double *organs* ("two
heads" "eight feet"); a parallel is then set up with the organization of the
state ("the country"), which is single but weakened and made double by
"intestinal strife". The third example gives the case of attempted copula-
tion between two animals belonging to different species and therefore destined to infertility. This is considered to represent "a reduction in the increase of herd animals". Here the protasis functions (from the point of
view of sign production) as an *example* (cf. Eco, 1975, p.296; 1984) which is
valid for the whole class.

In general, these examples demonstrate how the logic governing the relationship between protasis and apodosis is based on the rhetorical level of
language and tends towards the symbolic. Obviously, the relationship between the rhetorical expression and the degree-zero expression is not at all
obvious in many cases, as the figurative language it uses is dependent on
the cultural context. In many cases, some of the relationships at play are no
longer discernible to modern analysis due to the great intervening distance
of time and place.

1.4.2.2 The associative link created through the signifiers

Let us now look at some examples in which a key word in the protasis differs only in very few aspects from a key word in the apodosis:

If it rains (*zunnu iznun*) on the day (of the feast) of the god of the city—the god
will be (angry) (*zêni*) with the city.

If the bile bladder is inverted (*naḫsat*)—it is worrying (*naḫdat*).

If the bile bladder is encompassed (*kussâ*) by the fat—it will be cold (*kuṣṣu*).

If the diaphragm is tight (*emid*)—divine aid (*imid*).

The similarity between the signifiers allows a certain fact, indicated by a
word with a certain sound, to be considered the sign of another fact, indicated by a word with a very similar sound.

1.4.3 SYSTEMATIC CODES

The third type of non-random linking between protasis and apodosis is achieved through the exploitation of systematic codes. As we noted before, Mesopotamian divination can be seen to have a diachronic evolution in the development of the relationship between the protasis and the apodosis which through the course of the period tends ever more towards the abstract. This process of abstraction culminates in the creation of codes which cover a vast, all-encompassing range of possible cases. The principle of divinatory empiricism gives way to an almost deductive logic by which the inference of the individual example depends on the general configuration of the code itself.

From the second quarter of the second millennium, in fact, historical records no longer reveal single oracles but rather hundreds of "treatises" or systematic collections of often very detailed divinatory signs.[5]

The new development of second millennium divination in the form of systematic treatises is characterized by its functional feature of grouping together different oracular signs in relation to a single object which was considered to be ominous. This object was broken down into the whole array of its component parts or variations, each of which became the subject of an individual protasis. This method results in a highly detailed operation of making real objects have pertinent meanings. If an object could be extended and divided, an omen-oracle pair was constructed for each of its individual identifiable aspects. For example, the portion of the liver known as the "Door of the Palace" undergoes the following treatment in an extispicy treatise:

> If, on the Threshold of the Door of the Palace, on the right there is a slit — . . .
>
> If, on the Threshold of the Door of the Palace, on the right, there is a lengthwise slit — . . .
>
> If, on the Threshold of the Door of the Palace, on the left, there is a slit — . . .
>
> If, on the Threshold of the Door of the Palace, on the left, there is a lengthwise slit — . . .
>
> If, in the middle of the Door of the Palace, there is a slit — . . .

As may be seen, all the protases are constructed according to a structural principle of binary opposition between the |Threshold| and |the middle| of the Door of the Palace, between |right| and |left|, between |slit| and |lengthwise slit|. It is thus the system itself, understood in an *ante litteram* structural sense, which has prime importance. The cases which have been observed in the past are no longer the only ones registered, but rather all possible, conceivable cases are laid out according to a system based on oppositions and abstract rules.

A striking example of this system and the potentially absurd limits to which it extends is given by a treatise which includes protases for the reading of as many as seven separate bile bladders for a single liver. The logic of the system (here based on the rule n → n + 1) takes precedence not merely over reality but also over probability. A further example may be seen in the treatise of teratology *Šumma izbu*, which envisages almost forty possible monstrous features for a human baby: the baby looks like a horse, a lion, a dog, a pig, an ox, an ass or like a hand, a foot, or even a goat horn or a brick!

Under the impetus of becoming systematic, divination changes radically. No longer is the impulse towards seeking out ominous events but rather towards the construction of s-codes (cf. Eco, 1976; 1984a, pp. 169-72) of the protasis sequences. It is from these sequences that the real *code* of linking to the series of apodoses will be constructed. In this way, even if they are not formally stated, general rules are constructed of the type: "whenever the number *x* is found in the protasis, assign the characteristic *y* to the apodosis"; in this way, for example, if the soothsayer finds the number seven (which the system always links, we can hypothesize, to the characteristic "perfection" or "totality") in the protasis, he can give "an empire will be established" as the oracle.

Many codifying rules may be found which are constant even if never formally expressed. For example, according to an unwritten rule, everything found on the *right* is linked to a favorable event, whereas everything found on the *left* indicates an unfavorable outcome. A rule of "canceling out" and "changing the sign", as in algebra, also seems to exist, whereby an omen which is in itself unfavorable, if found on the left becomes favorable and *vice versa*.

In this sense, the apodosis is deducible from the protasis in that the apodosis can be inferred simply by systematic observation of the characteristics of the protasis. It is the treatise which provides the *rule* (even without expressing it): it is easy for the soothsayer when faced with a new *example* to discover the *result* simply by applying the rule.

1.5 THE RENDERING EXPLICIT OF THE ENCODING RULES

Even though the second millennium treatises show the ceding of the empirical phase in favor of the remodeling of divination on a systematic and deductive basis, the rules of deduction, even though widely used, nonetheless remain strictly implicit.

It is not until the treatises dating from the first millennium that the next step in the evolution of divination is accomplished whereby the encoding rules are made quite explicit.

Evidence for this development is shown in a massive first millennium haruspicy treatise which contains a chapter listing the essential values of certain features expressed in protases. Here the text is set out, not in two columns as previously, but in three. The first column deals with the omen, or rather the apparently ominous feature of the object which is being taken as a sign. This is usually a quality expressed either by an adjective ("large") or by an abstract noun ("length") or possibly by a verb in the infinitive ("to be folded downwards"). The second column records the essential value of the oracle, for example, "glory", "power", "victory". The third column then offers an example of a complete oracle in which the protasis shows the quality stated in the first column and the apodosis shows the value given for such a quality in the second column. The following will demonstrate the relationship clearly:

Length   *Success*   If the station is *long* enough to reach the road, the prince will be successful in the campaign he is to undertake.

Here we can see quite clearly the increasing progress made towards abstraction, for what we have here amounts to the presentation of a key for de-coding the signs.

The exegetical rules are now quite clear. Presenting the treatise in three columns has the effect of spotlighting the encoding rules. The arbitrary nature of the linking of protasis to apodosis is stated clearly by providing the two terms of correspondence.

The process of abstraction does not stop here, however. Later it reaches the complete reduction of the values to the simple favorable/unfavorable dichotomy. In this way the extreme complexity and highly detailed nature of the oracles from the early period of divination contrasts very sharply with the extreme simplicity of the final period oracles, which offer a simple yes-no, binary logic.

TWO

Greek Divination

2.0 DIVINATION AND KNOWLEDGE

Divination forms the first homogeneous area of ancient Greek culture in which it is possible to talk about the use of signs. The term *sēmeîon*, which we encounter for the first time in this field, is a generic term which indicates a divinatory sign of any kind, including an oracular response, which is usually a verbal text.[1]

In addition to *sēmeîon*, various other terms are used to designate specific areas of divination (or, we might say, they serve as specific material manifestations of the expression). Among these, *oiōnós* seems to be etymologically linked to the signs given by the flight of birds; *phásma* is used at first to denote omens perceived in weather phenomena but later comes to mean vision in general; *téras* is the equivalent of the Latin *prodigium* and indicates any unusual and in some way monstrous phenomenon which can be taken as the basis for a divinatory interpretation (cf. Bloch, 1963; Benveniste, 1969). In all these cases something stands for something else, or, to put it more precisely, something is taken as the basis for a process of inference.

Even though the practice of divination was of relatively marginal importance in ancient Greece,[2] the divinatory sign gave rise to a literary and philosophical tradition which places it at the mythic origins of the process of knowledge.

The soothsayer (*mántis*), a person who is able to interpret a sign sent by the gods, is first and foremost someone endowed with wisdom. The wisdom which the soothsayer possesses cannot be identified with any restricted use of the term, such as technical knowledge, but is instead general and far superior to any type of human knowledge, as the very etymology of the term *mántis* implies, linked as it is to the root **men*, which was used to indicate a movement of growth or increase of the soul (cf. Crahay, 1974).

It is in Homer that we meet for the first time the expression which identifies divination as the knowledge "of things that are, of things that will be and of things which have been in the past":

> Kalchas, Nestor's son, far the best of the bird interpreters,
> who knew all things that were, the things to come and the things past,
> (*hòs éidē tá t'eónta tá t'essómena pró t'eónta*)

who guided into the land of Ilion the ships of the Achaians
through the seercraft of his own that Phoibos Apollo gave him.

(Iliad, I, 69-72)[3]

This passage illustrates the general, total nature of the knowledge represented by divination. It is a type of knowledge which can be matched in scope, though very much later, only by philosophical knowledge. The phrase *tà eónta* ("the things that are"), used by Homer to indicate the object of the soothsayer Kalchas' knowledge, appears later in the philosophical tradition, in Heraclitus, Empedocles, Plato and Aristotle, as a technical term used to indicate the object of philosophical knowledge in general.

The sign (which is the instrument through which this knowledge is activated) comes not from the human sphere but from the higher, more numinous, sphere of the divine. The sign is the instrument of mediation between the total knowledge of the gods and the more limited knowledge of humankind. It is also, as Colli (1977, p.379; 1975, p.40) has pointed out, the area in which divine knowledge erupts into the human sphere.

However, the gods do not speak the same language as mortals. The words contained in the oracular response, for example, are human only insofar as they are human sounds, for they fail to produce meaning when the code of human verbal language is applied to them. This lack of equivalence in the expression of knowledge content separates humanity from the gods; however, there is also a more radical difference in the very modality of the knowledge. Gods rule time by means of a simultaneous "sight" of past, present and future; divine omniscience stems precisely from the possession of panoptic vision. Apollo, according to Pindar's expression, has "the glance that knows all things" (*Pyth.,* III, 29).

Mortals, in contrast, can see only the present, while the other dimensions of time remain inaccessible to them, except through the mediation of the gods. Access may be achieved through visions which must then be translated into words, for mortals gain knowledge only through hearing. For example, poets record the memory of the past in their tales, translating the panoptic vision of the Muses (cf. Homer, *Iliad,* II, 484-86). In the same way, soothsayers reveal the future to their fellow mortals by translating into words the "visions" communicated by the god. Nonetheless, the message of the vision becomes blurred in the very process of translation (cf. Lanza, 1979, pp.99-100; Detienne, 1967).

This is why the divinatory sign is enigmatic, obscure and practically incomprehensible. In order to decipher it, an interpreter is needed, someone other than the person within whom the process of communication and transformation of knowledge takes place.

Plato identifies two distinct figures in this divine-human communication: the "mantic individual" (the person who receives the vision) and the "prophet" (the person who interprets the words spoken by the "mantic individual" during divine ecstasy). This distinction is made in a famous passage of *Timaeus*, which may stand as a short theoretical treatise on divination as it was understood by the Greeks and presents with notable perspicuity the tradition of the divinatory sign as a sign that could not be decoded directly:

> A sufficient token that God gave unto humanity's foolishness the gift of divination is that no one achieves true and inspired divination when in their rational mind, but only when the power of their intelligence is fettered in sleep or when it is overcome by disease or by reason of some divine inspiration. But it belongs to an individual when in their right mind to recollect and ponder both the things said (*tà rhēthénta*) in dream or waking vision by the divine and inspired nature, and all the visions (*tà phásmata*) that were seen, and by the means of reasoning to discern about them all how they are significant and for whom they indicate (*sēmaínei*) evil or good in the future, the past, or the present. But it is not the task of the person who has been in a state of frenzy, and still continues so, to judge the apparitions and voices which they saw or uttered; for it was well said of old that to do and to know one's own and oneself belongs only to those who are sound of mind. It is therefore customary to set up the tribe of prophets to pass judgement upon these inspired divinations; and indeed, these are sometimes named "diviners" by those who are wholly ignorant of the truth, that they are but interpreters of the mysterious words pronounced by means of enigmas and of those visions, but by no means diviners. The most just thing is to call them prophets, that is interpreters of what has been divined.
>
> (Plato, *Timaeus*, 71e-72a)

At the conceptual heart of this passage we find the verb *sēmaínō*, which indicates the revelation of the god. It is the god who is seen as the true producer, through the inspired human individual, of the divinatory text. The subject of *sēmaínō* is formed by two terms which stand for the two types of divinatory sign, that is, "the things said" and "the visions seen"; but the force responsible for the production of these signs is "divine and inspired nature", that is, the god who erupts into the human individual by possession (as indicated by the etymology of the second term, which is linked to *theós*). The human individual here is merely a channel of transmission or a mouthpiece. In order for the meaning to reach its intended receiver, a complex procedure of interpretation is required. Thus, if we take the verb *sēmaínō* as a predicate associated with a certain number of roles (or logical cases) and we relate it to a process of communication and to a process of interpretation, we can read the passage from Plato according to Figure 2.1 (a gross simplification in some parts).

The verb *sēmaínō* thus does not have the simple meaning of "to mean", in the sense of the establishment of a relationship between a plane of expression and a plane of content within the sign. Instead, it seems rather to refer to the very process of communication which the god activates with respect to humanity. In the passage from *Timaeus*, the verb seems to refer

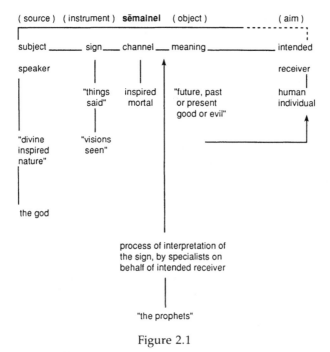

Figure 2.1

to the situation through which the god "indicates by means of (enigmatic) signs" something, as yet unknown, to a human individual.

There is a long tradition going back at least to Heraclitus, in the well-known fragment 93 of the Diels-Kranz edition, which confirms the use of the verb *sēmaínō* in this sense in divinatory contexts. L. Romeo (1976) in particular has drawn attention to this meaning of the verb in his clear yet complex analysis of the fragment. His interpretation is reflected in the following translation:

> The lord, who has the oracle in Delphi/neither discloses nor hides his thought,/but *indicates it through signs (sēmaínei)*[4]

This translation challenges a long tradition of interpreting the verbal form *sēmaínei* as "means" or using other expressions which had the effect of rendering the whole fragment contradictory, at best, or, at worst, incomprehensible.

What we have here is an opposition between two antithetical types of language. On one side we have human language, which is characterized by transparency and immediate decipherability (we can hypothesize that this type of language is circumscribed by both the terms of the oppositional pair "disclose [*légō*]"/"hide [*krýptō*]": human individuals reveal their thoughts completely by using language or hide them completely by not expressing them externally in words). On the other side there is the kind of language attributed directly to the gods in the Heraclitan fragment (and indirectly in the passage from Plato), which is indicated by the verb *sēmaínō* and which has the opposite characteristics: obscurity and the impossibility of immediate decipherment. The gods do not grant humanity a complete revelation, but neither do they completely deny humanity knowledge; rather, by means of the oracular sign, the gods provide a base for inference on which humanity must work to reach a conclusion. However, this is done without giving any kind of indication as to which path to follow in reasoning out the meaning.

The fact that ancient Greek literary and philosophical culture understood the divinatory sign as being obscure and ambiguous can be explained in two ways. The first explanation derives from Colli's notion of knowledge, according to which the divinatory sign may be seen as the "print" of the divine on a human individual, the indication of a point of contact (by which divine knowledge is communicated to humanity) and at the same time as *a vanishing point.*[5]

The second explanation has been proposed by Vernant (1974) and concerns the particular type of rationality which divination calls into play, both as effective practice and as theory. There is a connection with the differing roles of Fate in the divine and the mortal sphere. For humanity, Fate is conceived of as a linear succession of events (metaphorically embodied by the threads of the Moirai or the Parcae) which are connected to one another yet have no immediately apparent overall, integral meaning. The succession of events acquires meaning only when its end is reached, that is, when Fate is accomplished. It is only at this point that Fate becomes intelligible, and only then is it possible to understand, in the light of ulterior developments, the significance of previous, initially inexplicable, events. Up until this moment of illumination, humanity lives in basic ignorance, and this very ignorance may be taken as a defining characteristic of human existence.

For the gods, however, the Fate of each human is continually perceptible in its totality, for an individual's Fate has been irrevocably set and registered in eternity even before his or her birth. Divination thus comes into being in the gap separating the knowledge of humanity from that of the gods. For oracles (and in fact all other kinds of divinatory sign) were understood to reveal to a human individual, while still alive, the secret meaning of his or her Fate, which otherwise would be available to human perception only after death.

However, if divination were to carry out this prophetic function completely and thereby eliminate the gap separating human knowledge from divine, the result would also be the effective elimination of what distinguished human individuals from gods. This is why the gods do not so much reveal as blur Fate, as Heraclitus describes it. Oracles show a glimpse of Fate, but at the same time they disguise it, for they leave it to be guessed at by showing an obscure and enigmatic sign which is no more comprehensible to the enquirers than were the events which led them to consult the oracle in the first place. Divinatory logic therefore allows for the re-introduction at the human level of the "obscurity" of Fate (reduced, if not entirely eliminated, by the very nature of divine omniscience) by means of the ambiguity of the sign.

2.1 TWO TYPES OF DIVINATION

2.1.1 NATURAL DIVINATION

The passage from *Timaeus* and the fragment from Heraclitus both refer to a type of divination which is usually defined as "intuitive" or "in-spired". This type of divination forms part of the category of *mantikè átech-nos*, that is, divination which operates without the use of any kind of tech-nical device; it is therefore often called "natural divination" (cf. Cicero, *De Divinatione*).

The special feature of this type of divination is that the god's knowledge passes through nothing outside the human individual. Divine inspiration reaches the human individual directly through dreams (which are iconic texts) or is communicated through a prophet-mouthpiece who supplies a response (usually a verbal text). To use Romeo's phrase (1976, p.84), it is an endosemiotic type of divination.

The oracle at Delphi, undoubtedly the most famous and most presti-gious of the Greek oracles, worked according to the intuitive or natural model.[6] Here, the Pythia, the priestess of Apollo, supplied a response in the form of a verbal text. However, as we have seen, even inasmuch as this response was formulated in terms belonging to natural language, its meaning was by no means decipherable according to the simple applica-tion of the rules of the linguistic code at the denotative level. Later in this chapter we shall examine some instances of responses being misunder-stood precisely because of the blind application of this code without taking into consideration more complex rules (such as rhetorical or tropic rules, for example).

2.1.2 ARTIFICIAL DIVINATION

The second type of divination is that known as *mantikè technikè*, which com-mentators define as "conjectural", "inductive", "deductive" or "artificial". This type of divination was based on the analysis of signs (usually visual or acoustic, but in some way perceptible through the senses) which were pro-duced in the environment external to the human individual; these could be either spontaneous, such as lightning or eclipses, or provoked, such as the throwing of dice or extispicy (the analysis of entrails).[7]

This type of divination was based on a particular type of logic which springs from the hypothesis that there are homologous relations and cor-respondences between the microcosm, represented by the phenomenon considered to be a sign, and the macrocosm, or the general order of the universe (cf. J. Vernant, 1948; J.-P. Vernant, 1974).

In this respect, certain properties of space—for example, parts of the sky for astrology or the surface of the liver of a sacrificial animal for hepatoscopy—were apportioned to represent symbolically and mirror the organization of the cosmic order. In these special carefully delimited spaces, it was possible to read the configurations of future events free from the aleatory elements to which real events are subject and which the enquirer hoped to overcome through divination in the first place.

Two series are thus created, the series of structural configurations within the sign-text and the series of events to which these configurations refer. A code of correspondence is established between the two, allowing immediate passage from the sign to its meaning. The following extract from Homer illustrates this passage with a very simple example:

> For, I say to you, the son of all-powerful Kronos
> promised, on that day when we went in our fast-running vessels,
> we of Argos, carrying blood and death to the Trojans.
> He flashed lightning on our right, showing signs of favour.
>
> (*Iliad*, II, 350-53)

In this example, the sky becomes the signifying space, a microcosm in which it is possible to read the signs of Fate. The space is organized into a binary structure of two opposing regions, left and right. Each of these regions is linked to a semantic value (|left| → "bad omen", |right| → "good omen"). A more highly organized configuration of meaning can be derived from the circumstances of the appearance of the sign, that is, from its relation to the explicit (or, as in this case, implicit) question which the enquirer is asking the god. In this passage, the circumstances of the appearance of the sign is the setting out of the expedition to Troy, and the implicit question concerns the outcome of the undertaking. Thus the lightning which comes from the right side of the sky is seen to mean "successful outcome of the Greek expedition against Troy". In order to identify the final meaning of a sign, all divinatory systems are based on a more or less stable balance between the formal structures of the code (which allows for a thorough codification of the unusual or momentous event) and the multiplicity of the concrete situations to which the event-sign can refer in specific contexts.

In the present example from Homer, the code is so simple that it has become part of common knowledge and thus no indication is given of the need to refer to a soothsayer to decode the sign. This is not usually the case with artificial divination, the "technical" nature of which stemmed from the fact that in order to interpret a sign it was necessary to consult specialists endowed with the precise knowledge necessary for deciphering the various types of sign.

A soothsayer becomes essential in the only more slightly complex divinatory case which Plutarch records in his *Life of Dion* (24). The example relates to the expedition Dion made against Dionysius of Syracuse in 357 A.D., during which there was an eclipse of the moon. The soothsayer Miltas was called to interpret this sign and declared that it foretold that something which had been resplendent until then would be obscured. This could only mean that the tyrannical rule of Dionysius was destined to be overthrown by Dion's attack.

The two phases in this example are quite clear. The first determines a meaning through the code's matching system, and the second determines the meaning which derives from its application to the actual situation. Miltas also uses another, more sophisticated technique which exploits rhetorical transformations. The relationship between the macrocosm of the moon "obscured" by the eclipse and the microcosm of Dionysius' empire which is destined to be overthrown is established by means of the common element |resplendent|, which indicates literally a quality of the moon and metaphorically a quality of Dionysius' rule.

Some codes were already extremely elaborate at the basic level of matching. A case in point is the extispicy code. In this form of divination, the entrails of animals were observed, and particularly the liver (the technique then became known as haruspicy) in which special attention was given to the appearance and position of the lobe, the bladders and the doors.[8] We do not know precisely how the ancient Greeks established matches between signifying elements and the events to which they referred. However, Luc Brisson (1974), in a very interesting and thorough study of divination in Plato, has drawn attention to a passage in *Timaeus* (71 a–d) which, although not dealing directly with extispicy, describes a phenomenon which has many points in common with it. The passage describes the processes occurring when the rational soul, which resides in the brain, leaves its mark ("as in a mirror") on the liver, where the irrational soul resides: this allows us to see in the liver (in its different and differing aspects) the impressions left by the rational soul.

The "mirroring", however, is only metaphorical: what really happens is a highly developed process of encoding which almost recalls the mechanisms of "biochemical communication". The liver is seen in Plato's text as a sign text from which the irrational soul reads intelligible contents which have become perceptible through a process of codification. It is also a microcosm which reflects, even if in a rather odd way, the ordering of the macrocosm of the rational soul.

We can presume that extispicy codes functioned in a way similar to that recorded for the "intra-psychic" communication processes illustrated in *Timaeus*.

Nonetheless, it is Plato himself who provides one of the most scathing condemnations of artificial divination to be found in classical Greek culture. His anathema is contained in two texts: *Timaeus* (72b) and *Phaedrus*

(244 c-d). The former in particular contains a condemnation of hepato-scopy. Plato accepts the possibility of reading signs in the liver when this is still part of a living organism but states firmly that the liver cannot possibly reveal anything of significance when it is no longer living and is no longer under the illuminating effect of the rational soul.

Phaedrus contains both a more general and a more radical condemnation of artificial divination. In this text, Plato is praising madness, of which he considers divination to be a type, and distinguishes inspired, enthusiastic "mantica" from all other forms of investigation of the future. In this text, the "mantic art" is contrasted with the "oionistic art", or divination through observation of signs given in the flight of birds.

The motive for such a discrimination is clear: in artificial or technical divination, human reason dares to substitute for divine inspiration. In or-der to show that only a very weak, uncertain level of knowledge may be obtained in this way, Plato invents an etymological link between "oionis-tica" and *oíēsis* ("opinion"): "So also when they gave a name to the inves-tigation of the future . . . through the observation of birds . . . they called it the oionistic (*oiōnoistike*) art, which in modern times we call oiōnistic, making it more high-sounding by introducing the long O" (*Phaedrus*, 244 c). In inspired divination, in contrast, knowledge comes to the human in-dividual by means of divine possession, which is thus a guarantee of truth.

What we have here are the beginnings of an opposition between *sē-maínein* and *tekmaíresthai*, the former indicating, as in the *Timaeus* passage and in Heraclitus, the gift of the expanded knowledge of the god, while the latter indicates specifically human conjecture. This opposition calls to mind Alcmaeon's motto:

> Of things invisible, as of mortal things, only the gods have certain knowledge, but for us as mortals, only inference from evidence is possible.

> (Diels-Kranz, 24 b 1)

We shall have occasion to return to this motto later.

These passages from *Timaeus* and *Phaedrus* reveal not only Plato's opin-ions of divination but may be viewed as representative of the general con-sideration of ancient Greek culture with regard to natural divination. Even though artificial forms of divination were practiced in ancient Greece, nat-ural divination was always given prime importance and esteem, artificial divination being considered of only secondary importance beside oracular divination, which found expression through words rather than things.

This situation must be considered in relation to the fact that ancient Greek civilization was an essentially oral civilization. Writing was not only a fairly late phenomenon but it moreover depended entirely on speech, which it tended to reproduce phonetically. In other civilizations, such as those of Mesopotamia or China, writing was much older and functioned as an autonomous system with respect to spoken language, presenting in its own way, by means of graphic signs, the situations and events that speech represented in a different way. These writing-based civilizations gave preference to the type of divination diametrically opposed to that which operated in ancient Greece.

2.2 TWO MODELS OF ORACULAR DIVINATION

There are, however, notable differences between the image of oracular divination which is to be found in literary texts and the way in which it was actually practiced in the oracular sanctuaries. J.-P. Vernant (1974) refers to two distinct models.

In classical Greece, divination in practice had only a marginal role to play in the running of the *pólis*. The oracles were used not so much to obtain a prediction of future events but rather to consult them with respect to an already decided upon course of events. This would be proposed in the form of alternatives, and the oracle would be asked whether the way was clear for such a course of action.[9]

In this way, what amounts to a dialogue is set up between the enquirer and the oracle (cf. Crahay, 1974): the oracle replies to the question which has been put in closed form, predicting to the enquirer that she or he will or will not do a certain thing. The enquirer then puts a second question to the oracle, this time in open form, but limited to a ritual condition of success. Basically, the enquirer asks the oracle what obstacles must be removed in order for the undertaking to succeed. It is particularly interesting to note here that the formula normally used by the oracle when giving ritual advice reflects that which was used to record decisions of democratic assemblies. The oracle states "*lôion kaì ámeinon éstai*" (it will be convenient and preferable), just as decrees of the Assembly use formulas which place the emphasis on "preference" between opinions rather than on the imposition of a decision. We may see here that in ancient Greek culture the model of civic administration (in this case democratic discussion) is projected onto divination and not *vice versa*, as happened in Mesopotamia.

It is even more interesting to note that in this model of divination there is no trace whatsoever of ambiguous or obscure replies.

Ambiguity and obscurity belong rather to the realm of the other model of oracular divination—the "theoretical" model—which is to be found in the entire range of literature from Herodotus through the tragic playwrights to the philosophers. This model represents how the city culture sees divination. According to this model, the oracle is consulted not in order to receive advice but in order to know Fate directly. This leads to the assumption that the oracle is omniscient in that it has knowledge both of future developments of events and of the past, where the distant origins of present and future destinies of an individual or a group are to be found.

This model is no longer using a binary model, for it must reduce the infinite range of possible outcomes to a single, specific option.

An ambiguous or obscure response also reintroduces the uncertainty which characterizes the human condition and which the oracle is intended to dispel. Thus, in the oracle episodes of literary texts, the oracle does not seem to have any positive effect with respect to the course of events. The sign remains obscure until the accomplishment of Fate throws light on the matter and unravels—unfortunately by now too late to be of any use—the polysemy of the prophetic text.

2.3 THE PROBLEM OF INTERPRETATION IN LITERARY USES OF ORACLES

There is no doubt that in order to understand how the concept of *sēmeîon* was established in ancient Greek culture, reference to the use of *sēmeîon* in literary texts is of equal importance to the study of its meaning in practical divination. In this way, we can identify the semantic nucleus of the term which was passed on to the philosophical tradition as meaning "sign."

The problem of interpretation which the oracular sign presents may be seen as a frequent theme in the works of Herodotus and the tragic playwrights. The obscurity of the sign is primarily linked to the difficulty, which then inevitably becomes the impossibility, of solving this problem of interpretation. It must be said, however, that first of all the human individual is blinded by *hýbris* and clearly demonstrates a lack of sensitivity to the words of the prophecy in various ways: by forgetting the prophecy, by not following the directives of the prophecy, by not carrying out the consultation correctly. However, in the final analysis the fundamental error is always that of choosing the wrong term of the alternative interpretations presented by the ambiguous sign.

If the essential failing of humanity is a sin of pride, the resulting human error is in the area of knowledge and has a strictly semiotic nature.

Once again we come up against the opposition of "human language" vs. "divine language". The human individual interprets the prophecy according to the human code and fails even to attempt to understand the words of the revelation as being encoded in another language, the language of the god.

In semiotic terms, in all literary episodes of oracular divination, the human individual invariably interprets the text in a *literal mode* when it should have been read in what we may term an *enigmatic mode*.[10]

The basic idea presented by literary oracle episodes is that the prophecy always has a secondary meaning and, although this is hidden, it forms the only true meaning of the sign. It is the discovery of this second meaning and the rejection of the first, literal interpretation that we may call interpretation according to the enigmatic mode. What usually happens, however, is that the individual involved in the interpretation, given the human incapacity for attaining divine knowledge, invariably performs the opposite action, that is, rejects the possibility of a non-literal meaning for the prophecy.

There are, however, different types of interpretation error. The first type proceeds from an inability to find a meaning for the text, or rather to relate it to known, real circumstances. Objects to which the words of the prophecy could refer cannot be discovered, and the text seems wholly absurd. The second type of error consists in taking the words of the prophecy to refer to real, but mistakenly identified, objects. This type of error has two sub-types, depending on whether the error is due to a homonym or to ambiguity created through a play on words. This can be shown in a diagram (Figure 2.2).

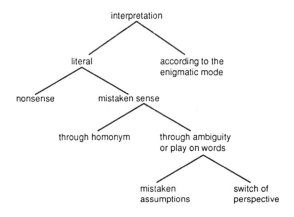

Figure 2.2

Let us now look at some oracle episodes which demonstrate the various types of interpretation error.

The inability to find a meaning for the prophetic text appears in several episodes in which rhetorical devices, some of them metaphorical, are featured. It is obvious that when the metaphoric vehicle is interpreted "literally", an absurdity on the level of meaning is produced, unless of course a possible world is imagined, one different from ours, one in which mules can become king of the Medes and heralds are painted red. The enquirer, who naturally takes into consideration only the real world, has difficulty in finding a meaning and a code of reference for these texts. Let us see what happens in the first of these episodes.

Herodotus tells the story of the inhabitants of the island of Siphnus, who had become extremely prosperous as a result of their gold and silver

mines and who decided to consult the oracle at Delphi to see if their pros-
perity was destined to continue. The Pythia replied:

> "Siphnus, beware of the day when white is thy high prytaneum
> White-browed thy mart likewise; right prudent then be thy counsel
> Cometh an ambush of wood and a herald red to assail thee."
> (Herodotus, *Historiae*, III, 57)

The story goes on to tell of the arrival of a Samian ship and of the embassy
to ask for money and of the sacking of the island of Siphnus.

Herodotus underlines the inability of the inhabitants of Siphnus to find
a meaning for the text ("They could not understand the oracle"); they
found the text, and in particular, it may be assumed, the expressions "ambush of wood" and "red herald", devoid of sense because they remained at
a literal level of interpretation. The god is in fact playing with various rhetorical devices: above all with a double enallage.[11] *Wood* (= ship) in the ancient world is *red*, as Herodotus explains, and the *herald* (= the ambassadors) organizes the *ambush*; this language is then further complicated
through use of metonymy (*wood* for *ship*, the singular *herald* for the plural
ambassadors).

A second example of lack of understanding of an oracle can be found in
an episode of the long, complex "oracular romance" which Herodotus
writes about Croesus. When Croesus asks the Delphic oracle if his reign
will be long-lasting, the Pythia replies:

> "Lydian, beware of the day when a mule is lord of the Medes:
> Then with thy delicate feet by the stone-strewn channel of Hermus
> Flee for thy life, nor abide, nor blush for the name of a craven."
> (Herodotus, *Historiae*, I, 55)

Once again a literal meaning is given to the prophetic text in the interpretation, and Croesus consequently believes that, since the situation referred
to in the text cannot occur (i.e., that "a mule is lord of the Medes"), it is
equally impossible that his reign will be interrupted.

Apollo himself finally explains the metaphorical trick to Croesus once
the events which the prophecy predicted have come to pass and Croesus
has fallen under the domination of the Persians. The "mule" is Cyrus, and
the connection is made by means of the "mixed blood" element which is
shared by both terms in the metaphor (Croesus and the mule) (cf. Figure
2.3). Croesus' blindness seems even greater in light of the fact that this

Figure 2.3

common element is doubly exemplified in Cyrus, for Cyrus is both "child of a noble mother and an obscure father" and of "Median mother and Persian father", as the text later unkindly points out.

In all fairness to the unfortunate enquirers of oracles, it is worth noting that the interpretation of the figurative meaning of a prophecy is in reality much more difficult than it may seem *a posteriori*. It depends upon encyclopedic knowledge of local matters as well as knowledge of the rhetorical devices which may be applied to such knowledge. This may be seen even more clearly when we consider the fact that even for the modern reader it is impossible to uncover the interpretation of the prophetic text when the literary text gives us no information on the appropriate sections of the encyclopedia. This occurs, for example, in the oracular episode with Arcesilaus (Herodotus, *Historiae*, IV, 163-64), in which we find, along with the metaphorical switches between "clay pots" and "men" and between "towers" and "ovens", which are explained as the story unfolds, the expression "the bull that is the finest of the herd". This is never explained and thus remains incomprehensible to us, too.

Let us look now at the case in which the text appears to be susceptible to literal interpretation, that is, in which a course of events may be identified as seeming to correspond to the text of the prophecy but which in fact turns out to be not the precise course of events it intends. We shall look first at errors of interpretation due to *homonymy*.

This particular device, accompanied by continual misunderstandings, characterizes the whole oracular romance of Cambyses. It is a story in which all the signs are linked to one another in a chain of internal associations. The story begins with a dream:

> Smerdis having gone to Persia, Cambyses saw in a dream a vision, whereby it seemed to him that a messenger came from Persia and told him that Smerdis had sat on the royal throne with his head reaching heaven. Fearing therefore for himself, lest his brother might slay him and so be king, he sent to Persia Prexaspes, the trustiest of his Persians, to kill Smerdis.
>
> (Herodotus, *Historiae*, III, 30)

After several chapters which relate the extravagance and cruelties of Cambyses, we come to learn of the rebellion of the two Magian brothers in Persia, one of whom, also called Smerdis, has assumed the throne. When Cambyses hears this, he understands the true sense of his dream. However, the story does not end here:

> Having wept his fill, in great grief for all his mishap, he (Cambyses) leapt upon his horse, with intent to advance forthwith on Susa against the Magian. As he mounted, the cap slipped off the scabbard of his sword, and the naked blade struck his thigh, wounding him in the same part where he himself had once smitten the Egyptian god Apis; and believing the blow to be mortal, Cambyses

asked the name of the town where he was. They told him it was Agbatana. Now a prophecy had ere this come to him from Buto, that he would end his life at Agbatana; Cambyses supposed this to signify that he would die in old age at the Median Agbatana, his capital city; but as the event proved, the oracle prophesied his death at Agbatana of Syria. So when he now enquired and learnt the name of the town, the shock of his wound, and of the misfortune that came to him from the Magian, brought him to his senses; he understood the prophecy and said: "Here Cambyses son of Cyrus is doomed to die."

(Herodotus, *Historiae*, III, 64)

Rather than events, the Magians' revolt and Cambyses' wound are signs which enable Cambyses to attain knowledge and to understand the oracle at last, free from ambiguities, and to break free from the bonds of word-play. The rebellion allows him to understand the difference between Smerdis his brother and Smerdis Mago; the mortal wound shows him the difference between Agbatana in Media and Agbatana in Syria.

Errors in interpretation can also be caused by *riddles*, which are not necessarily language based and can take various forms.

Perhaps the most famous riddle in oracular literature is that which ensnares Oedipus. Oedipus' suspicions are aroused by the insinuations of a banquet guest as to his paternity, and he therefore decides to consult the god of knowledge (Apollo), who predicts that he will kill his father and marry his mother (Sophocles, *Oedipus Tyrannus*, 787–98). Here the riddle concerns *assumptions of belief*: Oedipus is ignorant of the fact that his real parents are Laius, King of Thebes, and Iocasta, and he believes himself to be the son of Polybus, King of Corinth, and Merope. Because of this (mistaken) belief, and hoping to avoid the events predicted by the oracle, he leaves Corinth and goes to Thebes, where he unwittingly fulfills the very destiny which was predicted for him.

In other cases, the riddle concerns a *switch of perspective*. An emblematic case is provided by Croesus, who consults both the oracle of Delphi and the oracle of Amphiaraus to know whether he should make war on the Persians. Both oracles provide the same response, predicting that "if he should send an army against the Persians he would destroy a great empire" (Herodotus, *Historiae*, I, 53). Croesus interprets this response to mean that the Persian empire will be destroyed while, as he discovers having undertaken the war, the empire referred to is actually his own. Croesus is deflected from the correct interpretation of the oracle by an implied semiotic device: the assumption that, as it is Croesus who is consulting the oracle, the god will assume Croesus' perspective in the response. Obviously, from Croesus' perspective, the empire which will be destroyed can only be the Persian empire.

In this example, more than in the case of Oedipus, we can begin to see a typical aspect of the riddle: when the god gives the enquirer an interpretative problem to solve, the problem carries a strong aggressive charge which is potentially destructive to the human.

A confirmation of this aggression can be found in the analogous episode which recounts how the Delphic oracles predicted that the Spartans would measure the ground of Tegea with ropes (Herodotus, *Historiae*, I, 66). The Spartans interpret the reference to ropes as indicating the act of measuring the ground in order to distribute it to the conquerors (i.e., themselves) and therefore undertake an expedition against Tegea. However, the ropes are, in fact, operating in another *frame* or *script* (cf. Eco, 1984) and will serve the Spartans, reduced to slavery after their defeat, to measure the ground in Tegea which they must work as slaves.

The term given to this kind of response is *kíbdēlos*, which in its metaphorical sense means "ambiguous", "false", "deceitful" but which in its original sense refers to the extraneous element which adulterates precious metals. The result is, as with the examples we have just seen, the mixture of two metals, one good and one not, which makes glitter like gold what is not gold at all.

A similar device can be seen at work in the anecdotes recorded by Diodorus Siculus (*Biblioteca*, XVI, 91-92; XX, 29), where it is announced to a general that he will dine and sleep in the city he is besieging. These things do indeed occur, but the perspective is not that which the general assumed (i.e., that he would overcome the city); he in fact performs these activities as a prisoner.

2.4 THE SIGN AS CHALLENGE: DIVINATION AND RIDDLES

We have looked briefly at the aggressive charge which lies behind the obscure sign. This aspect links the divinatory sign to the true riddle, which is also obscure and unsolvable and which is mythologically the expression of the challenge which the gods make to humans.

Colli (1975, p.18) has demonstrated the relationship between divination, riddle and the other—threatening and destructive—side of Apollo.[12] For Apollo is not only the benevolent god who gave the art of divination and medicine to mortals, he is also the god of the bow and arrow. These attributes take on a directly semiotic value when we see that Apollo's arrow and the obscure sign are not at all two different things but two expressions of the same power of this god and that they can have the same function too, as may be inferred from a passage in Pindar (*Olymp*, II, 83-85).

The true target of Apollo's arrows is the human individual as interpreter. Leaving figurative language aside, the human-interpreter takes up a challenge which the god makes with hostile intentions; as we have seen in the examples taken into consideration above, failure to interpret the obscure sign leads to destruction.

There seems no longer to be any room for doubt about the close relationship between the divinatory sign and the riddle. This can be confirmed by a diachronic analysis of the riddle "genre", which originates precisely within the religious sphere of divination with the two self-same characteristics of divine hostility towards mortals and the idea of a challenge to a contest. Gradually the riddle becomes separated from the sacred context and takes up its own evolutionary history, during which it weakens its original characteristics even though it always retains some trace of them. The history of the riddle is the history of interpretation understood as contest until we come to the idea of interpretation as a dialectic confrontation between two opposing opinions.

For our investigation of the divinatory sign as an interpretation-provoking mechanism, it may be useful to look at some of the most important stages in the evolution of the riddle.

The first and most famous example of the appearance of the riddle in a sacred context is the myth of the Sphinx. The monstrous creature sent by Apollo proposed the riddle of the three ages of humankind to the Thebans. The prize in this contest was life itself, for whoever failed to solve the riddle was eaten by the Sphinx; whoever managed to solve the riddle—and only Oedipus was able to do so—caused the Sphinx to plunge into the abyss.

However, in the early evolution of the riddle, still in the archaic period, the contest between a god and a human becomes a contest between two humans. A link with the sacred sphere is maintained in that the two humans are two soothsayers. Strabo's anecdote relating the contest between Calchas and Mopsus illustrates this phase. Calchas asks Mopsus to "guess" how many figs are on a wild fig tree which they encounter along their path. Mopsus gives a highly detailed reply ("They are ten thousand in number, their measure is one medimmus; but there is one over, which you cannot put in the measure." [*Geography*, VI, 232-35]). Struck by such precision, Calchas is overcome by a "sleep of death".

When compared with the divinely inspired knowledge of the two contestants, the content of the riddle itself seems of minor importance, as shown by the banality of the object which is to be discovered. This kind of content irrelevance was also present in the riddle of the Sphinx, which seemed so disproportionate to the risks of life and death which it involved.

However, in the next stage of its evolution, when the riddle becomes entirely human, the text itself takes on a carefully worked out formal structure which is based on the formulation of a contradiction which, rather than designating nothing (as is usually the case in such situations), designates something real. This form is to be found in the legend of Homer's death:

> Homer asked the god who his parents were and where his homeland was; and the god replied: "The Island of Io is the homeland of your mother and there death will take you; but beware of riddles of young men . . . ". He came to Io. Here, sitting on the rocks, he saw some fishermen approaching the shore and

he asked them if they had anything. And they, because they had not caught anything, but had been delousing one another for lack of other employment, replied to him in this way: "What we have caught we have thrown in, what we have not caught we are still carrying" alluding in this way by a riddle to the fact that the lice which they had caught they had killed and thrown into the sea, and those that they had not caught they were still carrying in their clothes. Homer was not able to resolve the riddle and died from remorse.

(Aristotle, *On the Poets*, 8)

The elements of the riddle which we have already encountered are still present in this fragment: the challenge with respect to an element of knowledge and the risk of death for the contestant who is not able to solve the riddle; but this fragment also features the form of a contradiction which from now on becomes typical of the genre. More precisely, there are two sets of contradictory pairs here: "we have caught—we have not caught" and "we have thrown back—we are carrying", which can be set out in a square of opposition (Figure 2.4).

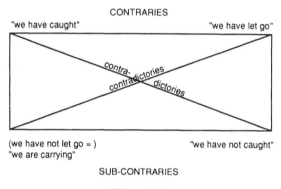

Figure 2.4

Each individual term of the first pair of contradictions ("we have caught"/"we have not caught") is in a linked relationship with a term of the second pair ("we have thrown back"/"we are carrying"), but not in the way we would expect intuitively (i.e., "what we have caught, we are carrying" and "what we have not caught, we have thrown back"). The riddle links the terms which are logically in opposition: "what we have caught, we have thrown back" and "what we have not caught, we are carrying". Nonetheless, as we know, the riddle is not absurd. A contestant in full command of sound reason should be able to unravel this problem.

When the riddle becomes entirely human, it emphasizes the competitive aspect as a contest of knowledge or as a test of intelligence and settles on the form of an apparently unsolvable contradiction.

The next and final stage in the riddle's evolution leads, in Colli's hypothesis (1975), to the birth of dialectic.

2.5 COMPETITION, DIALECTIC, RHETORIC

Dialectic, in the ancient Greek sense of the term, comes into being within the context of competition. It was a discussion between two people on some type of cognitive argument and thereby a contest designed to discover a victor.

The general course of the discussion followed this scheme (Aristotle, *Topics*): the challenger first asks a question in an alternative form, presenting two elements of a contradiction. The adversary chooses one of these and proves its truth. The challenger then has to prove the truth of the other element and thereby confute the adversary's affirmation. The procedure can involve a lengthy and complicated series of successive questions and responses all intended to prove directly, or more often indirectly, one or other of the alternatives.

In its early form, the language of dialectic was limited to a fairly restricted and, to a certain extent, élite environment. Significant changes occurred, however, with cultural developments at Athens and with the definitive adoption of democratic government; the forms of dialectic now entered the public sphere and became firmly linked to the political world. The discussion thus became ever more extended, and dialectic—in a somewhat adulterated form—developed into rhetoric.

Both dialectic and rhetoric are based on a strong spirit of competition. What distinguishes them, however, is that in the former there is no need of a judge to assign the victory to one of the two contenders, for the victory is evident in the discussion itself at the point when one of the contestants is led through the very development of the discussion into contradicting his or her original thesis. In the case of rhetoric, in contrast, the competition is more fiercely direct in that it is the listeners who judge who has made the best speech. Since there is no intrinsic punishment for failure in rhetoric (as there is in dialectic), it has to add a persuasive emotional element.

2.6 DIVINATION AND PERSUASIVE INTERPRETATION

The evolutionary process which we have examined so far began with the divinatory sign as a god's cognitive challenge to a human individual and ended with the cognitive competition of dialectic and rhetoric. But at this point the circle seems to close on itself with the introduction within divination itself of dialectic and rhetorical methods of debate.

A passage from Herodotus is very revealing in this respect. The passage recounts a sort of conciliation between *divination*, with its characteristic deterministic conception of the world, and *political eloquence*, with its vision of life as leaving everything open to constant discussion and argument. Herodotus tells how the Athenians, threatened by a Persian invasion, sent ambassadors to consult the oracle at Delphi. At first the Pythia presented them with the announcement of tremendous disaster. Worried, but not prepared to submit docilely to this Fate unless absolutely necessary, the Athenians asked for a second consultation and implored the god to give a more favorable response, reinforcing their plea by swearing not to leave the sanctuary until they had received such a response. The Pythia agreed to deliver a second response:

> Yet shall a wood-built wall by Zeus all-seeing be granted
> Unto the Trito-born (Athena), a stronghold for thee and thy children.
> Bide not still in thy place for the host that cometh from landward,
> Cometh with horsemen and foot; but rather withdraw at his coming,
> Turning thy back to the foe; thou yet shalt meet him in battle.
> Salamis, isle divine! 'tis writ that children of women
> Thou shalt destroy one day, in the season of seed-time or harvest.
>
> (Herodotus, *Historiae*, VII, 141)

This example shows clearly that the divinatory sign, in the case of the oracular response, is not received fatalistically. The messengers are not satisfied with the first response and in their turn challenge the god, threatening not to leave the sanctuary until they succeed in persuading the god to attenuate his hostile attitude to the city. What is even more interesting in this example is its demonstration that the oracular sign is open to discussion. For once they have obtained the response, the messengers record it and set off again for Athens, where they present it to the Assembly.

The discussion which takes place before the Assembly is in the typical form of dialectic discussion. The obscure sign sets off an interpretative process which offers various possibilities of development. However, dialectically it is basically a dichotomy between two opposing, mutually exclusive solutions: retreat to the Acropolis, which had in earlier times been fortified with a palisade, which the god thus intended by the expression "a wood-built wall" or prepare a fleet of ships, because what the god intended (*sēmaínein*) by the enigmatic expression "a wood-built wall" was a barrier of ships.

Each side of the contradiction is upheld by a different group: (i) "some of the elders" (backed by the readers of oracles) support the first solution; (ii) "others" (among whom Themistocles) support the second. Here we are only at the presentation of the problem, the next stage is to develop a proof which will contradict one of the two hypotheses.

The discussion follows the second horn of the dilemma almost as though saying "If we think that the right interpretation is that which suggests we prepare a fleet, what contradiction does this interpretation imply?"

The readers of oracles here point out that accepting the second horn of the dilemma leads to a contradiction with the portion of the text which predicts that Salamis will be the cause of death to many people. Accepting the validity of the sub-problem posed by the readers of oracles would mean the automatic confutation of the main hypothesis.

However, the thematic level of the discussion has undergone a shift, and now, in order to refute the hypothesis of the readers of oracles, it is sufficient simply to prove that the objection they raise is unfounded.

This is what Themistocles then proceeds to do by denying that the objection from the readers of oracles poses a real contradiction. Here too the argument seems to proceed by absurdities and hinges on a question of perspective. If indeed the readers of oracles were right in saying that Salamis (metonymy for a "battle by sea") would cause the death of many Athenians and if this second part of the prophecy had been directed, like the first, to the Athenians, then the god would not have used the epithet "divine" for the island, but rather "cruel". That is to say, there is a contradiction between the epithet "divine" used for the island of Salamis and the death of Athenians. It therefore follows that this second part of the response, which contains a prediction of death, must be understood to be directed towards the enemy.

It is quite clear here that in this second phase of the discussion the dialectic method is gradually giving way to a more properly rhetorical method.

Themistocles then puts forward as his final argument an interpretation which tends more to the positive proof of his own reasoning than the demonstration of the falsity of the basic premiss of his opponents. The judgement of the listening public is then made and grants victory to one side, using one of the basic elements of rhetorical discourse. The passage states that the Athenians "judged Themistocles to be a better counsellor (*hairetôtera*)" than the readers of oracles. The *discrete* binary logic of the dialectic alternative gives way to the *continuum* of the gradated logic of the preferable.

It could well be that the discussion so far has caused us to lose sight for a moment of the fact that the object in debate is a prophecy of Apollo. This is significant, for the logic applied to the interpretation of the divinatory response is precisely the same as that which governs political assemblies.

It is also extremely significant that in this case the opponents of Themistocles are readers of oracles (that is, specialized interpreters of divine responses) and that they are defeated. This may be seen as the paradigmatic confirmation of the fact that, in the Greece of the *pólis*, divination is subject to the methods of political rationality and not *vice versa*.

The obscure nature attributed to the divinatory sign fitted in very well with the basically oral Greek culture, which tended towards dialectic: it confirmed the sign itself as a mechanism which provokes interpretations, interpretations which must be tested by means of a confrontation between opposing speeches.

The sign refers to a reality beyond itself, a hidden and ambiguous reality which is nonetheless accessible through the confrontation of opposing interpretations. One might think that such a confrontation would be paralyzing, but surprisingly it proves to be both stimulating and productive.

The divinatory sign has thus moved away from two of its basic characteristics, the supremacy of vision and the conception of truth as a revelation—that is, truth as *a-létheia,* understood as the drawing aside of the veils under which it was hidden (*lanthánō*).[13]

In the passage from Herodotus examined above, it is not the soothsayers with their panoptic vision who reveal the hidden meaning of the sign. Here it is more *conjecture* (which in Herodotus is always expressed by the verb *symbállō* and its derivatives, an equivalent of the more widely used *tekmaíromai*) which allows the hidden meaning to be revealed.

The adoption of conjecture and the moving away from vision allow the sign to evolve from the field of divination into that of true science.

THREE

Signs and Semiosic Processes in Greek Medicine

3.0 INTRODUCTION

So far we have been looking at the vast, mysterious field of divination, where we have seen the earliest semiosic practices emerge, connected in ancient Greek culture to the beginnings of cognitive thought. It is now time to look at that other major area of operation of semiotically oriented thought which predates and is independent of strictly philosophical research: Greek medicine.

In this field may be seen not only the integral presence of semiosic processes but also the first real theoretical constructs around the sign and inference (cf. Vegetti, 1976, p.49 ff.). Later, when semiotic theorizing passed directly into the field of philosophy and rhetoric, many traces of its medical origins remained. These may be seen first of all in the examples used to illustrate the sign both by philosophers and writers of treatises of rhetoric (examples which were often taken from medicine and sometimes from physiognomy). More significant traces remained in the choice of a formal logical model of the sign in the form "if p, then q", which was, as we have seen, the model used in divination and which was taken over into medicine with different contents but the same form.

Whereas divination has sent down to us only somewhat indirect and isolated records, early Greek medicine produced an extremely rich documentation, the chief source of which is the *Corpus Hippocraticum*,[1] a large collection of very varied texts (approximately one hundred) which illustrate medical theory and practice during the fifth and fourth centuries B.C. These texts were not in fact written by a single author (as tradition had it, Hippocrates),[2] nor do they in fact all date from a period which could reflect the life span of a single individual. The collection contains works written for differing purposes and expressing various tendencies of thought within the field of early medical knowledge.[3]

Despite the heterogeneity of the material which forms the *CH*, fifth and fourth century medicine stands as one of the most important fields of research in Greek thought and may be compared in importance with the philosophy and historiography of the same period, disciplines with which it maintained extremely fertile relations of mutual exchange and influence. Werner Jaeger has said that Socratic thought would not have been possible without the *Corpus Hippocraticum*,[4] and the debt which serious historiography, inaugurated by Thucydides at the end of the fifth century B.C., owes to Hippocratic *téchnē* has also been pointed out.[5]

What medicine had to offer both philosophy and historiography was a specifically semiotic model of knowledge which worked both on the level of a solid formal structure (*logismós*, that is, inferential reasoning in both the abductive and deductive modes) and with a basically empirical orientation.[6]

As will be shown below, the medical sign is the product of inferential reasoning applied to recurrent phenomena which acquire meaning, and thus become signs, in the fact that they can be traced back to the *logismós*.

3.1 AMBIGUITY OF THE PROGNOSIS

In contrast with doctors of today, who read signs in connection with the diagnosis of illness, early Greek doctors used signs in connection with the prognosis. There is an entire treatise of the *CH*, the *Prognostic*, which is dedicated to precisely this function. The opening paragraph sets out its mode of use:

> I hold that it is an excellent thing for a doctor to practise forecasting. For indeed, if he discover and declare unaided by the side of his patients their present, past and future circumstances, and fill in the gaps in the account given by the sick, he will be able to inspire greater confidence that he knows about illness, and thus people will decide to put themselves into his care.
>
> (Chapt. 1)[7]

As may be seen from this passage, prognosis not only is understood as prediction of future events but also involves elements of knowledge pertaining to both the present and the past.[8] For the doctor must be able to describe also those symptoms and general facts which the patients omit to mention. The procedure outlined by the *Prognostic* contains certain clearly manipulative elements, for, by stating things that the patient had not mentioned or thought worthy of notice, the doctor can gain credit and trust so that the patient will feel ready to undertake the treatment prescribed. It is interesting to see here how a procedure which is intended to appear scientific and objective is concerned principally not so much with reflecting reality (symptomatic, in this case) as with manipulating reality. The doctor's discourse here uses also *"efficacious signs"* like those used in the incantatory rhetoric of Gorgias or in magic.[9]

This formula, with its three-fold reference to past, present and future is found elsewhere in the *CH*, for example in *Epidemics I* (and it is also found as a phrase which defines medicine in Plato's *Laches*, 198 d) and prompts us to set up a parallel with the similar formula used to identify the process of divination (cf. Brătescu, 1975, p.46).[10]

Nonetheless, even if on the one hand we can find common elements between medicine and divination, on the other, many of the treatises in the *CH* are fiercely emphatic in stressing the distance and differences between these two areas. The author of the treatise *On Regimen in Acute Diseases* (Chapt.8), for example, rails against the practices of incompetent doctors, comparing them to the practices of divinatory interpretation.

The attack is made upon divination from a semiotic point of view. For the divinatory sign is ambiguous and can have two diametrically opposed meanings, and it is therefore far from the realm of objectivity to which medical science aspires. The author of *Prorrhetic II* is harsh in his criticism of bad doctors, stating that their miraculous predictions place them on a level with soothsayers, and he proudly offers his own method in contrast, a method based on human signs and on conjecture:

> As for me, I shall certainly not make any divinations of that kind (*ou manteú-somai*), but I shall write of the signs (*sēmeîa*) through which it can be conjectured (*tekmaíresthai*), from among the patients, those who will get well and those who will die, those who will get well and those who will die quickly or more slowly.
>
> (*Prorrhetic II*, Chapt.1)

Divinatory inference (*manteúein*) is directly contrasted with conjecture (*tekmaíresthai*). The energy with which the doctors rail against divination and their efforts to distance themselves from it is clear evidence of the fact that they were trying to establish a new, autonomous epistemological paradigm, a "secular semiotics". It is also evidence, however, that the risk of confusion or of misunderstanding between the two areas was only too present.

In some respects, Hippocratic medicine does indeed seem to be the continuation of a previous, ancient, popular medicine which was based on principles of magic (cf. Parker, 1983, p.213 ff.). Certain areas of its terminology point clearly to such antecedents. For example, the central importance given throughout the *CH* to *kátharsis* ("purification") suggests the magical purifications of the *iatrómantis* or "doctor-seer" and of the mystic purifiers, such as Epimenides or the Bacides. In addition, the term used to indicate a medicine, *phármakon*, was originally used to indicate each of the two Athenian citizens who were, annually on the Thargelia or in times of pestilence, subjected to ritual observances, whipped and at least banished from the city, if not slaughtered, in a purification ceremony (cf. Lanata, 1967, p.45). This is why the attempts made by the Hippocratic doctors to differentiate themselves from the magical paradigm were so energetic, as may be seen in one of the most interesting treatises in the *Corpus: The Sacred Disease*.

Since magical medicine is just as interesting to the history of semiotics as is scientific medicine, we shall dedicate the next section to looking at the magical medicine paradigm and then examine the criticism of magical medicine presented in *The Sacred Disease*.

3.2 MAGICAL MEDICINE
AND MAGICAL SEMIOTICS

Many literary sources suggest the idea of a common mythical origin for divination and medicine. Both practices in fact were considered to be gifts of Apollo and were linked to him in various ways. Plato, for example, writes in the *Symposium* "Apollo discovered the art of archery, medicine and divination" (*Symposium*, 197 a). It is very striking from the semiotic point of view that the two earliest practices which begin sign-based knowledge should have been seen in their own time as having been originally connected. A strict connection between the two may be found in the ancient figure of the *iatrómantis*, the "doctor-seer" who combined the skills of a fortune-teller with an ability to cure disease. The term *iatrómantis* was originally applied to Apollo himself but was later used to refer to a series of figures linked in some way to him, all of whom combined their visionary and medical gifts with the ability to perform purifications.

One of the fundamental elements which characterized the figure of the *iatrómantis* was the ability to use a diagnostic procedure. As a visionary, the *iatrómantis* was capable of identifying the hidden cause of an illness, a cause which was always linked in some way to a supernatural intervention. In ancient times, illness was seen as *míasma*, that is, contamination, caused by contact with a divine or demonic entity.[11] It was for this reason that a doctor-priest was needed who would be able to read the signs which gave access to the world of the dark supernatural forms considered to have caused the state of contamination. Once the diagnosis had been made, the *iatrómantis* could indicate the magic instruments necessary to purge the *míasma*.

This conception of illness and magic is clearly illustrated by a writer of the neo-Pythagorean school, Alexander Polyhistor:

> (According to the Pythagoreans) the whole air is full of souls which are genii or heroes; these are they who send men dreams and signs of future disease and health, and not to men alone, but to sheep also and cattle as well; and it is to them that purifications and lustrations, all divination, omens and the like, have reference.[12]

This passage contains all the elements of a scared semiology linked to magical medicine. Demons are the source of diseases which afflict humanity; however, they are at the same time the source of information about the invisible world, as they send signs (including that special type of sign, dreams) to human individuals, signs in which they allow the origins of the disease to be identified. The circle of communication is then completed by means of special signs which the human individuals are required to produce, that is, cathartic and apotropaeic rites. Apotropaeic rites involved the recital of *epōidaí* or incantatory verbal formulas which were considered effective in exorcising evils which caused illness. We are dealing here with linguistic signs which both completed the communicative circle with the supernatural and were themselves "efficacious signs" in the sense that they were intended to affect the world and not merely reflect it.

3.3 CRITICISM OF MAGIC
AND SACRED SEMIOTICS

Let us now turn our attention to the criticisms of magic made on the specifically semiotic and epistemological levels. The author of the treatise *The Sacred Disease* makes two lines of attack: (1) he offers in opposition to the notion of "sacred" the notion of natural structure (*phýsis*) and rational cause (*próphasis*); (2) he shows the logical inconsistency of the reasoning on which the procedure of magical medicine is based and offers in opposition an inferential type of reasoning based on *tekmērion* (which appears here already with the sense of "proof" or "reliable sign").

The author of this treatise is trying to overcome the idea of a divine origin for illnesses, not only for the "sacred disease", or epilepsy, but also for all other types of disease. He is attacking the notion of "sacred" as something which is caused by divine intervention. In fact, the term *hierós* in Greek, even though it was quickly adopted for religious use, originally referred not to the Olympian gods and goddesses but to an animistic conception. *Hierós* was everything which reveals aspects of marvellous or supernatural life, and an illness was sacred in the sense that it was sent by a supernatural force. The term *iásthai*, "to cure" (from which *iatrós*, "doctor", is derived), originally meant "restore, give back strength through appropriate magico-medical operations" (cf. Ramat, 1962, p.20).

The idea of illness being caused by a direct intervention "from the vertical transcendental plane on certain points of the horizontal plane of natural causality" (cf. Vegetti [ed.], 1976, p.291) seems to exclude any idea of the regularity of phenomena and at the same time to deny any possibility of controlling such phenomena or of predicting them. However, the notion of "nature" which the author of the treatise opposes to "sacred" brings into play once again the regularity of cause and effect and thereby makes the imposition of medicine on a scientific basis possible. In addition, while the notion of *phýsis* identifies the objective, homogeneous repeating structure of cause and effect, the related idea of *próphasis* (elsewhere called *aítion* or *aitíē*) introduces the possibility of explaining the various phenomena.

3.4 THE FORMS OF LOGICAL ARGUMENTATION AND "TEKMÉRION"

The argument of *The Sacred Disease* is more convincing than that of the opponents thanks to the type of logical argumentation the author adopts. He points out the internal contradictions of the magical medicine system and confutes them by means of a *tekmérion* ("proof", "reliable sign"). Here is an example:

> And there is another great proof (*méga tekmérion*) that this is no more divine than other illnesses; it attacks those who are phlegmatic by nature, but it does not attack those who are bilious: now if it were indeed more divine than the other illnesses, this disease would occur equally to all types of people, without making any distinction between bilious and phlegmatic.
>
> (CH, *The Sacred Disease*, Chapt.2)[13]

The argumentation here follows the strict form of what will later be called *modus tollens*, that is, "If *p*, then *q*; but if not-*q*, consequently not-*p*". We can explore the formula with the details from the author's example: "If this illness were more divine than other illnesses (*p*), it would affect everyone indiscriminately (*q*); but this does not happen (because it affects phlegmatic types but not bilious types) (not-*q*)"; it consequently follows that it is no more divine than other illnesses (not-*p*). It should be noted that the author uses the falsity of the consequent in the *modus tollens* ("the illness does not affect everyone indiscriminately") as a sign (*tekmérion*, "reliable sign", "proof") of the falsity of the antecedent ("epilepsy is no more divine than other illnesses").

Of course, it is not until Artistole that the *modus tollens* as a reasoning scheme is theorized and a strict definition is given of *tekmérion*. It is then the Stoic philosophers who provide a formal analysis of the argumentative scheme and declare that all argumentative schemes should be considered signs. It is nonetheless interesting to note that the Hippocratic author is already linking the expression *tekmérion* (which from Aristotle onwards takes on the definite meaning of "irrefutable sign") with the inferential scheme of the *modus tollens*. Logic and semiotics may thus be seen here to have found a point of convergence and fusion. Their fusion will later be made complete by the Stoic philosophers.

3.5 SIGHT AND THE OTHER SENSES

However, the ability to use a strict formal reasoning and signs which can be fitted into a logico-inferential scheme is not the only characteristic which distinguishes the secular semiology of medicine from the sacred semiology of divination. As Lanza (1979, p.103) has demonstrated, another important point of divergence between the divinatory paradigm and that of Hippocratic medicine lies in the very different roles which sight plays in the process of knowledge in each field.

Sight has a fundamental role in divination and magical medicine as the primary, and in certain respects unique, source of cognitive activity. It is significant that Apollo, the god of divination, was considered, in the words of Pindar, to be he who has "the glance that knows all things" (*Pyth.*, III, 29). Nothing can escape his sight in the past, present or future; he has "power over time". Human individuals, on the other hand, can know only what they happen, by chance, to see. Only the soothsayer and poet have a second sight which enables them to see beyond the limits imposed on the vision of ordinary mortals. This is why soothsayers are often blind, so that they might be more receptive to this second sight. A similar limitation on the faculties of perception occurs during dreaming, when the awareness of external stimuli is weakened almost to the point of totally disappearing.[14] In both the poet and the soothsayer, vision is transmuted into words which thus become signs and compensate for the lack of presence. Such a conception involves a dependence of the sign on the god and a dichotomy between what is accessible to sight and what is not. We can find the beginnings of an overcoming of the dependence on the god for knowledge of the invisible in the well-known motto of Anaxagoras, "Things that are apparent are the vision of things that are unclear" (*ópsis adélōn tà phainómena*) (D-K, 59, B 21a). Here the phenomenon takes the place of the god. Sight however remains central. Characteristically, one of the older treatises, *On the Diseases of Women*, states that the doctor "will see" the presentation of the neck of the womb by means of his finger (Chapt.60).

The works which make up the *CH* certainly continue along the path opened by Anaxagoras, but at the same time they give decreasing importance to the role of sight in the process of knowledge. There are certain reasons inherent in the Hippocratic *téchnē* which lead to the devaluation or at least the redimensioning of the role of sight. The treatise entitled *On the Art* states plainly that "some, but only a few, diseases have their seat where they can be seen; others, and they are many, have a seat where they cannot be perceived" (Chapt.9). In order to gain knowledge about these latter illnesses, a doctor has to draw conjectures from tactile, auditory and sometimes even taste-related signs. The doctor's prediction is worked out by using the whole range of sign typology, moving through time into a hidden past and future. In addition to this, when signs do not appear spontaneously, a doctor may "force nature" to produce evidence (Chapt.13).

It is now possible to view a panorama of the range of the *visible/invisible* opposition at the point when it passes from the realms of divination, where it was invented, to other areas of knowledge. It appears in the legal context in the antithesis between "apparent" and "non-apparent goods", which according to Gernet's analysis (cf. Gernet, 1968) can be expressed as the opposition between material goods (above all, funds and inherited goods) which can be perceived and credit in general, which is "invisible" (for example, credit held with a banker with whom one has deposited money). In the strictly philosophical field, this opposition takes on a purely ontological character and gives rise to a duplication of levels of reality. In Heraclitus, for example, the "hidden" constitutes true reality in opposition to the "apparent", a dichotomy which reveals its influence in the two fragments "An unapparent connexion is stronger than an apparent one" (D-K, 22, B 54) and "the real constitution of things is accustomed to hide itself" (D-K, 22, B 123). Thus it may be seen that, while in divination the "visible" referred clearly to the completely physiological function of the organs of sight, once the transposition occurs into other fields of knowledge, this link becomes much more tenuous. Indeed, it disappears altogether in science, where visible and invisible are conceived of as two separate worlds, the communication between which is made possible not by sight, but by conjecture.

3.6 ANALOGY AND CONJECTURE

Vegetti (ed., 1976) has demonstrated the semiotic nature of the revolution effected by Hippocratic thought. By relating these medical writings to the scientific and philosophical culture of the time of their composition, he has shown how the Hippocratic texts were involved in a struggle to establish a "semiotic method" in opposition to the so-called "analogical procedure", which was typical of Ionian philosophy and of those doctors and intellectuals who subscribed to its principles. The Ionian philosophy was, rather than a true philosophy, more *physiología*, that is, an investigation of nature (*phýsis*), or the search for a principle of nature (*archē*).

For the Ionian philosophers, nature was in substance the world as the observer saw it, but a world which had a double aspect. It was simultaneously multiple, because made up of an infinity of phenomena, yet unified, since each single phenomenon showed the same principle, which could be traced in every other fragment of the real.

The only cognitive procedure possible in this context is that of *analogy*. When faced with any single phenomenon, one need only re-trace the path of *phýsis*, which will lead, analogically, from the single phenomenon to the *archē*. From the semiotic point of view, Ionian philosophy reasons as though any type of sign-production modality can be reduced to the sole method of *recognition of samples*: all fragments stand for a totality which is totally homogeneous to each and all of them (cf. Eco, 1975, p.296; 1984b, p.48).[15]

A different paradigm is imposed from Alcmaeon of Croton onwards, whereby the semiotic principle of conjecture is proposed:

> The gods have immediate knowledge of invisible and mortal things, but men must conjecture (*tekmaíresthai*).[16]

For the Ionian philosophers and for the medicine of their followers, there was a continuity between the principles of nature, its phenomena and the observers of those phenomena. With Alcmaeon there originates a deep fracture between humankind and reality. Knowledge of the world of experience cannot be gained spontaneously, for the world of experience is no longer transparent. The semiotic method hinges on this fracture inaugurated by Alcmaeon, for this fracture imposes the necessity of replacing the procedure of analogy with a procedure based on evidence. From now on, human knowledge has to adopt the principle of *tekmaíresthai*, of proceeding by evidence and conjecture. What is missing in Alcmaeon at this stage, however, Hippocratic medicine develops: the setting of the conjectural method in a formal logical structure.

3.7 ANALOGICAL METHOD AND SEMIOTIC METHOD

At this point we may ask what form the methodology of conjectural research takes in the Hippocratic treatises. A first answer can be supplied by an analysis of the debate which raged between Regenbogen (1930) and Diller (1932) on precisely this question. Their polemic was based on the opposition of "semiotic method" and "analogical method". However, what was considered was an analogical method significantly different from that which we have considered so far, for they were using "analogical" in a very loose sense, with the result that it comes very close to the semiotic notion of "homomateriality".[17]

In this particular sense, the idea of "analogical" is understood in a strictly technical sense, as the institution of a parallelism between a phenomenon which was to explained and a known phenomenon, with a consequent possibility of inferring the latter from the former. According to Regenbogen, this particular type of research methodology is used by the author of the group of treatises made up of *On Generation*, *On the Nature of the Child* and *Diseases IV*. These texts often compare non-observable processes with observable processes; the former are explained by use of analogy with the latter, as, for example, when a parallel is set up between the development of the fetus and that of plants (Littré, 1839, VII, 528, 22 ff.) or that of a bird (*ibid.*, VII, 530, 14 ff.). The author of the treatise follows the principle of Anaxagoras (according to which the visible allows us to see the invisible) and systematically applies it throughout the treatise. The comparison with the visible object—a comparison which forms the basis for the analogy—is consistently seen as proof of the object being hypothesized.

The analogical procedure is not exclusive to the field of medicine and biology. For example, when Herodotus speaks of the Nile (the course, the source and the length of which he is ignorant), he states, "and I guess, conjecturing (*tekmairómenos*) as to things unknown from visible things, it takes its rise from the same measure of distance as the Ister (Danube)." (*Historiae*, II, 33) The reasoning is as follows: the course of the Danube is known from its source to its mouth, and on the same line of longitude, according to Herodotus' conception, flows in the opposite direction to that of the Nile, that is, from north to south towards the Black Sea, just as the Nile flows from south to north towards the Mediterranean; in addition, the Danube is the longest river in Europe just as the Nile is the longest river in Africa. Given these elements, the course of the Nile can be imagined in analogy to that of the Danube.

However, according to Diller (1932, p.17), analogy cannot cover all cases of inference from the visible to the invisible, and he quotes several examples to prove this, among them an example of experimental inference contained in Chapter 8 of the treatise *On Airs, Waters, Places*. This experiment attempts to prove that water which comes from snow and ice loses the qualities of lightness, clarity and freshness, while it keeps the qualities of heaviness and murkiness. In order to demonstrate this, the author suggests pouring water into a receptacle in winter and, having measured it, exposing it to the outside air so that it freezes. The next day, the water should be taken into the warm again and melted. When it is measured again it will be noted that the quantity has diminished significantly. This is proof (*tekmérion*) of the fact that, when it froze, the water let its lightest and most delicate part go, and this simultaneously proves that water which comes from snow and ice is of poor quality. This experiment is defined as *tekmérion* and is based on the setting up of a parallelism between two series of real data.

However, Diller quite rightly questions whether this experiment is really a case of analogical procedure. In fact, the only analogy which can be set up here is that the same rules apply for a small quantity of a material (e.g., water or ice) as for that material in its entirety. What happens in the experiment can be expressed in the formula "part:part = whole:whole"; true inference consists in drawing conclusions about the whole from the parts. It is Diller's opinion that here we have a type of inference which is not analogical in the same sense that the inference we saw in Herodotus is analogical, since "everything takes place within the process which is to be explained, without any analogous process being brought to bear" (p.19).

The author of the treatise uses the same reasoning, according to Diller, when he claims that the finest and purest part of water drunk by an individual is expelled from the organism and the densest and murkiest part remains as sediment within the organism. The proof (*tekmḗrion*) of this is to be found in the observation of patients suffering from bladder stones who expel an extremely clear urine as the dense, murky part of the water they drink condenses to form the bladder stones.

The point these examples have in common is that something not perceptible is explained by recourse to perceptible phenomena. However, these phenomena are not *análoga* of what is to be explained but rather signs. They establish, with respect to the process which is to be explained, the same relationship which exists between effect and cause. Thus, for Diller, semiotic inference (he uses the term *semeiotisch*, which he links strictly to the medical procedure, p.20), should be understood in the precise sense (as it is later used by Aristotle) of inference from the consequent. Furthermore, for Diller, while analogical inference explains the "*Sosein*" of an unknown process or state, semiotic inference indicates its "*Dasein*".

More recently, this problematical area has been investigated by Lonie (1981, p.79 ff.),[18] who has underlined that in the treatises taken into consideration by Regenbogen—and also in other texts in the *CH* in general (for example, *On Airs, Waters, Places*)—may be seen examples of complex explicative processes which use both semiotic inference (inference of causes from observable phenomena) and analogical induction.

Chapter 12 of the treatise *On the Nature of the Child* (= Littré, 1839, VII, 486, 3 ff.) is particularly interesting in this respect. The author of this treatise establishes the theory (a non-observable element) by which the spermatozoon, when it reaches the warm, moist environment of the womb, acquires an ability to breathe (*pneûma*) whereby it opens a fissure to the outside environment. It blows out and, in a second phase, breathes in fresh air through this hole. In order to prove this theory, the author uses an analogy with three different classes of object where the same phenomenon occurs: wood, leaves and edible substances. The behavior of wood when burning is described, wood expels hot air from the points where it has been cut and at the same time draws into itself another cold breath. The action of the two counterbalanced movements causes smoke and steam to gather around the wood. This is described as an observable phenomenon ("we see this happening") from which an inference (*eklogismós*) can be drawn about the cause of the phenomenon itself. The inference is expressed in the form of a *modus tollens* ("If not-*p*, then not-*q*; but *q*; therefore *p*"): "If this double counterbalanced movement did not exist, then the breath (smoke and steam) would not gather around the wood, as it came out" (Littré, 1839, VII, 486, 20-21).

The author of the treatise goes on to illustrate the same kind of behavior in the other examples of *análoga* and then formulates a general rule by induction: "Everything that is heated releases breath (*pneûma*) and draws in cold breath to replace it." Finally the author states that the phenomena which he has described are to be considered "necessary proofs" of his theoretical affirmation about the spermatozoon.

Three distinct elements in the cognitive procedure are illustrated in the example we have just examined. First of all there is the institution of an analogy between a non-observable fact (the behavior of the spermatozoon in the womb) and some observable phenomena.

Second, there is a semiotic inference (which Diller described, calling it "semeiotic inference", and which Lonie terms "causal inference") which consists in tracing the observable phenomenon (for example, the emission of smoke and steam during the burning of wood) to its cause or to the nature of the process. It is interesting to note that this type of inference is very common in the treatises considered and that the term used to describe the phenomenon from which the inference is drawn is *sēmeîon*.

Third, there is the formulation, by induction, of a general rule which is considered to be valid also for the first term (the term to be demonstrated) of the analogy. In consideration of these points, we can say that the overwhelming value of the analogy consists in the way that it enables an initial proposition (relative to non-observable events) to be validated by recourse to propositions concerning analogous, observable events which can be considered examples of a generally valid rule. Lonie (1981, p.85) illustrates the relationship between analogy, general principle and initial statement by means of a diagram (Figure 3.1).

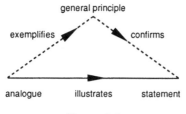

Figure 3.1

3.8 SEMIOTIC METHOD IN THE METHODOLOGICAL TREATISES

In the group of more theoretical treatises of the *CH* (*On Ancient Medicine, On Airs, Waters, Places, Prognostic, On Regimen in Acute Diseases, The Sacred Disease, Epidemics* (I and II) and the principal surgical works), it is possible to see quite clearly the formulation of the semiotic methodology which Diller refers to (1932) and which Lonie (1981) identifies as a procedure of "causal inference". In this section we shall try to examine in depth the elements of this methodology without going into the other procedures with which it could be associated (which seemed more appropriate in the discussion of analogy).

Each of the works cited above has to deal with the problem of the meaning of the observed data.[19] As the individual phenomenon (*hékaston*) is no longer linked (or traceable) to a presumed unity of nature, as was the case with the *physiología*, it needs to be interpreted, that is, reconnected to a system of reference.

It is at this point that the inferential procedure (or *logismós*) begins, and this is, to begin with, essentially abductive.[20] The individual phenomenon which the doctor observes is hypothesized as a case of some general rule. In other words, the *hékaston*, which is by itself insignificant, is thought of as a *sēmeîon*, a sign which refers to a system from which it receives meaning.

The first, ascending movement of the construction of a system of reference is followed by a second, descending movement of verification. If the hypothesized system is valid and works, it can be proved by applying it to other cases. The sign is thus transformed into a *tekmērion* and the method becomes deductive. Using Eco's scheme for abduction (Eco, 1984a, p.40), the process can be illustrated as shown in Figure 3.2.

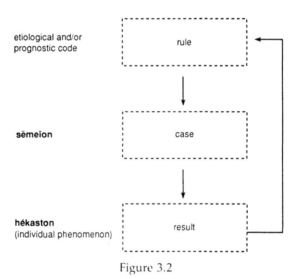

Figure 3.2

Vegetti (ed., 1976), p.49) demonstrates this double abductive-deductive movement of the Hippocratic *téchnē* very well:

This also gave the *hékaston*, devoid of "metaphysical" privileges, a new dignity. The *hékaston* was on the one hand required to be a sign, *sēmeîon*, of something other than itself, of a system to which it was supposed, by inference, to belong; on the other hand it was assigned the role of "proof", *tekmērion*, of the validity of the inference itself, which was measured by the possibility of finding confirmation in the *hékasta*. The semeiotic method of the

Hippocratic *téchnē* functioned as follows: as a "dialectical" movement which began with the *hékaston* which was observed (but we could also say of the scientific experiment), transformed it into a *sēmeîon* by means of a logical-conceptual inference (*logismós*) and then into a proof or *tekmérion* to end, should the circle reach its close, with the ability to understand and operate on other, different *hékasta*.[21]

The scheme which the doctor has to construct is certainly a code, but a very special type of code, for it is a code based on probability. As Di Benedetto has shown (1966; 1986, p.132), the texts which make up the *CH* are strewn with expressions indicating tendency or probability such as "the majority", "most", "above all", "often", etc. This does not mean that the doctors who wrote the Hippocratic texts were not involved in the construction of systems of reference which were of general application. It simply means that the logic of *hoi pleîstoi* ("the majority") was being substituted for the logic of *pántes* ("all"). It is precisely this nature of probability which abductive or hypothetical inference has which distinguishes it from strictly deductive inference.

3.9 THE FORMAL STRUCTURE OF THE SIGN

The concept of *sēmeîon* ("sign", "symptom") is one of the central concepts in the *CH* texts. The formal structure which is used to introduce the sign is relatively constant in that it implies its use in an implicative scheme of the type:

$$p \supset q$$

In linguistic terms, p and q are often represented by a proposition (or a sequence of propositions), the linking of which forms a hypothetical period, as may be seen in the following passage from *Prognostic*:

> But the other symptoms must also be attended to. For if the patient should show himself bearing up against the illness, or manifest, in addition to the signs mentioned before, some other symptoms indicating recovery, the illness may be expected to turn to an abscession, with the result that the patient loses the blackened members but recovers.

(Chapter 9)

In this example, the first part of the implication consists of a sequence of two conditional propositions introduced by *én* ("if") which refer to observational data (protasis), while the second part has a complex period (apodosis) which contains a medical prediction. The semantic content of the protasis is usually observational data such as lists of symptoms, and the apodosis may even contain a diagnostic statement, although this is very rare because of the central importance of prognosis in early medicine. The apodosis might in addition also contain (and sometimes be replaced by) indications for treatment.

3. 10 ANCIENT EXPRESSIVE MODULES

The "if p, then q" model—which is used very often (for example in the treatises which deal more with techniques of treatment) to introduce the illness itself—is extremely old and can be linked to the analogous illness-presentation modules used in Assyrian-Babylonian and Egyptian medical treatises.[22] The Assyrian-Babylonian implicative model implies the presence of a protasis, introduced by *šumma* ("if", "in the case that") and containing the indication of the symptoms, which is then followed by an apodosis which contains indications for treatment. This structure is revealed in the following example:

> If a man's cranium has an inflammation, his temples are afflicted by SA.ZI (?) with disturbances to the eyes, his eyes being affected by darkening, misting, disturbances, reddening (?), with the veins inflamed (?), and much watering of the eyes, you must cut up in a grinder 1/3 of *ka* of *lolium* (and) having soaked it, strain it as much as you can, and then take 1/3 of *ka*, mix it with rose water, shave (the patient's head), apply it, binding it on, and don't take it off for three days.[23]

The implicative structure of the Assyrian-Babylonian module can be considered a sign structure (even if it does not specifically mention signs), with the special feature that the semantic level is directly replaced by the "praxeological" level.[24] Here, the sign (that is, the antecedent of the conditional) indicates, without any further mediation, a certain behavior.

This extremely ancient module is occasionally to be found also in some of the treatment-technique treatises which form the earliest material of the *CH*, such as *On Diseases II* and in the ancient portion (A) of the gynaecological treatise *On the Diseases of Women*. However, these are only sporadic appearances, alongside modules which are based rather on the relation between symptoms and illness.

The treatise *On Internal Affections* is a special case, for here the expressive module of the presentation of the illness has a very particular form. It is made up of three structural elements: (A) an initial proposition (or series of propositions) introduced by "if" in which an internal, invisible phenomenon is presented as the "cause" of the illness; (B) a second series of propositions, introduced by the expression *táde páschei* ("the patient suffers such things"), which present the symptomatology (i.e., the phenomena visible to external observation) of the illness; (C) a third series of propositions concerning treatment indications. Very often part A is sub-divided into two to give: A_1 (the direct causes of the symptoms) and A_2 (the causes of the illness itself).

These structural elements can be seen in the following example, taken from Chapter 8 of the treatise:

> (A₁) If (*én*) there is a break in the chest and the shoulders, (A₂) a fact which often occurs due to excessive strain, (B) these are the symptoms (*táde . . . páschei*): hacking cough, often bloody expectoration; usually shivering and fever; acute pain in the chest and the shoulders. The patient feels as though a stone is pressing against his/her side; pain goes through him/her like a needle. (C) These things being so, fatten up the patient with milk and then immediately cauterize the chest and shoulders.[25]

What is interesting from the semiotic point of view in this module is that the inference between the first two elements ("If A, then B") is not abductive (that is, from causes to effects) but rather deductive. This means that importance is given to the system, which has already been reconstructed, of the causes which can produce particular symptoms. This is the point of view of the writer of the treatise, however; in practice a doctor would work backwards from the symptoms to their causes. *On Internal Affections* also includes a prognostic section (D), which is placed either between (B) and (C) or after (C). The example quoted above continues, "In this way the patient will soon be cured".

Another interesting comparison for the ancient Greek modules may be seen in those of ancient Egyptian medicine. The Egyptian models differ from the Assyrian-Babylonian modules in including a section dedicated to diagnosis. As Vincenzo Di Benedetto (1986, p.91) has shown, the Egyptian modules can be divided into three structural elements. The first section (A) is introduced by the conjunction "if" and presents the symptomatology which may be seen by a doctor when examining a patient; a second section (B) gives the cause of the illness, presenting it (as in section A) in the words of the doctor who examines the patient; a third section (C) then gives the treatment which the doctor is to prescribe or carry out. An example taken from the Ebers papyrus (written c.1550 B.C.) will show these structural elements:

> (A) If you examine a man who is suffering with his stomach, all the parts of his body are heavy as though tiredness were overcoming him: you must then put your hand on his stomach and find it like a drum in that it comes and goes under your hand. (B) Then you must say "It is an inertia in eating which will not permit him to eat anything else." (C) Then you must prepare a remedy which will empty him (there then follows the list of ingredients for the remedy).[26]

In this example we may see an abductive procedure, for the symptomatology provides the starting point for reconstructing the etiological situation, that is, a hidden reality which must be interpreted by means of the available external data.

All these modules for the presentation of medical symptomatology later provide a basis for reflection—sometimes distinguishable only as unconscious forms but more often surfacing as examples—when philosophy attempts to define the formal structure of the sign.

FOUR

Plato

4.0 INTRODUCTION

Plato may be considered the first true heir of the great cultural tradition which precedes him. This tradition gave rise in his works to a vast and fully worked out theory of language even though this did not produce a separate theory of the sign, as it did with Aristotle and the later schools of philosophy.

Two important facts, however, may be observed: first, the analysis of the contexts in which Plato used semiotic terms enables us to reconstruct a fairly homogeneously based theoretical field, the borders of which define the sign; second, certain aspects of Plato's theory of language had an intrinsically semiotic character, a situation which was not repeated in the linguistic theories of later philosophers. These two areas will be examined separately.

4.1 SIGNS

4.1.1 DIVINE COMMUNICATION

In accordance with the divinatory tradition, Plato talks of "signs" in all contexts that set up communication between gods and humankind (*The Republic*, 382; *Timaeus*, 71 a–72 b; *Phaedrus*, 244 b-c). In these contexts he uses the verb *sēmaínō*, which in the sphere of divination, as we have already seen, has the sense not so much of "to mean" as "to send a sign", which is thus the means of divine communication. The sign can be a verbal text, as with the response of the Pythia at Delphi, or a visual text, as with the images in a dream (cf. *Timaeus*, 71 e) or images imprinted on the liver, which functions like a mirror (*Timaeus*, 70 b).

A sign can also be a natural event, such as a flight of birds; but in this case (the classic case of technical divination), the communication is mediated and not direct enough to have true value, thus it produces opinion rather than knowledge (cf. *Phaedrus*, 244 c). The most efficient communication with the supernatural is that effected by means of what Socrates calls the "demonic sign", which manifests itself as an inner "voice" (cf. *Phae-*

drus, 242 b-c; *Apology*, 31 d) speaking directly to the intended receiver of the communication.

4.1.2 THE SIGN AS IMPRINT ON THE MIND

In another series of contexts, the sign appears as an imprint (*týpos*) precisely in the sense that an imprint left by a seal is a sign. This conception of the sign appears in *Theaetetus* (191 a–195 b), where in order to solve epistemological problems Plato develops the metaphor of the mind as a waxen tablet on which signs produced by the sensations (*tôn aisthéseōn sēmeîa*) are imprinted. When these signs are deeply imprinted on the mind, they form the basis for the workings of the memory and the formation of true opinion.

False opinion is created, according to Plato, whenever an individual is incapable of assigning each thing to its own sign (195 a), that is, of matching the sign printed on the mind with the new sensation, such that the relationship established in the process of renewed perception is identical to the relationship between copy and original (*apotypṓmata kaì týpous*) (194 b).

4.1.3 THE SIGNS OF WRITING

The subject of memory—which was touched upon in connection with signs imprinted on the mind in *Theaetetus*—forms an important part of Plato's argument in *Phaedrus* (247 c–276 a), where he is focusing on the signs of writing. The myth which Socrates relates here tells how the signs of the alphabet were a gift of the Egyptian god Thoth to Thamus, the king of Thebes. The god invited the king to make the signs known throughout Egypt since, he said, they were a medicine for knowledge and memory (*Phaedrus*, 274 e). Thamus, however, does not accept the gift very enthusiastically, for he is convinced that the signs of writing would have an effect opposite to that claimed by the god, that is, that they would weaken the memory. The king fears that, trusting writing, people would no longer recall things from within themselves, but from outside, through external signs (*týpoi*) (*Phaedrus*, 275 a).

Socrates then develops this concept and establishes an opposition between "written words" and "the speech written on the mind". The latter is "living and animate"; it is written with knowledge and is able to select suitable receivers of its message. Written words, however, have only the appearance of life, and in reality are able to say only one, and always the same, thing, just like pictorial images which when interrogated "maintain an immense silence", and, moreover, are addressed indiscriminately to everyone.

Even though prime importance is given to the discourse written on the mind, it is nonetheless possible to set up a semiotic relationship between the two terms. Phaedrus suggests that written words may be considered "an image (*eídōlon*)" of the discourse written on the mind (*Phaedrus*, 276 a); however, they remain extrinsic signs, able only "to refresh the memory of those who know already" (277 e). These semiotic relationships can be represented in a triangle (Figure 4.1). The broken line indicates the fact that for Plato written words in themselves are inadequate for the attainment of true

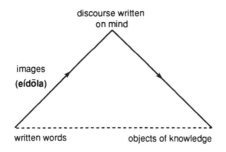

Figure 4.1

knowledge, for this must be mediated by the internal discourse; they can thus produce only opinion (275 b).

4.1.4 THE SIGN AS INFERENCE

There is finally a series of contexts in which the term "sign" (*sēmeîon*, alternating with *tekmḗrion*) is used for something indicating a fact, an event or a state from which another fact, event or state can be inferred, according to the model which we have already encountered in our exploration of Mesopotamian divination and early Greek medicine ($p \supset q$).

In *Theaetetus* (153 a), for example, it is said that the fact that motion and friction produce heat and fire, which in turn produce all other things, is a sufficient sign (*hikanòn sēmeîon*) to argue that motion produces being and generation, while rest produces non-being and destruction. The *Seventh Letter* (332 e) uses the same terms to talk of the sign; here the fact of having or not having friends is given as the greatest sign of someone having a virtuous or wicked character. In *Gorgias* (520 d–e) it is said that an excellent sign (*kalòn sēmeîon*) of success achieved is that those who render a service receive adequate recompense. In each case, the sign is expressed by one proposition linked to another by a relation of implication.

This concept of the sign serves as the basis for the development of the idea of *sēmeîon* as a sign distinguishing one particular thing from all other things. A passage in *Theaetetus* (208 c–209 c) states that the distinctive sign of the sun which is sufficient (*hikanón*) to know or recognize the sun lies in the fact that the sun is the brightest of all the heavenly bodies which move around the earth. The underlying logical form of this superficial formulation is of course the implicative form ("If a heavenly body moving around the earth is the brightest of all such bodies, then it is the sun").

However, at this point Plato begins to question the epistemological value of knowledge by means of signs, and asks if grasping the distinctive sign of a given object ("the sign in which the object one is investigating is different from all other objects" [208 c]) means grasping also the reason (*lógos*) of this object. This question is of no small importance, and it may be noted that it appears again in Aristotle in the form of the search for the relationship between the "sign" and the "cause" of a phenomenon. Plato—and indeed Aristotle later follows suit in this respect—here makes a distinction between the sign and the cause of knowledge (*lógos epistḗmēs*), stating that the sign contributes to forming right opinion but not knowledge.

4.2 THEORY OF LANGUAGE

4.2.1 THE SEMIOTIC NATURE OF PLATO'S CONCEPTION OF LANGUAGE

In philosophy subsequent to Plato, the theory of signs and the theory of language represent two completely separate areas. The objects of their respective analyses are considered to be different, and different terms are used in discussing them (Aristotle, for instance, terms the linguistic sign *sýmbolon*, not *sēmeîon*). In Plato's philosophy, however, such a diversification is not present, and in contrast it may be observed that his theory of language has a distinctly semiotic character.

In Greek culture the sign was in general conceived of as being a perceptible element which referred to (or enabled the attainment of knowledge of) a non-manifest object (*ádēlon*, *aphanés*, etc.). As we have already seen in the case of medicine, and before that in divination, signs constituted the mediation between the level of things accessible to the senses and the level of non-accessible things.

The linguistic sign is seen in precisely these terms in the Platonic dialogues (especially in *Cratylus* and *The Sophist*); it is the *dēlōma* ("revelation") of a non-perceptible object (this can be either the "meaning" or the "essence" of the object in question). The verb *sēmaínō* ("I signify", "I manifest by signs") is constantly alternated with the verb *dēlóō* ("I reveal", "I manifest") when speaking of an expressive form whose content cannot be apprehended by the senses. This occurs, for example, in a passage in *Cratylus* (422 e) where Socrates is investigating the capacity of *prôta onómata* (the primary, minimal elements of language) to make evident (*phanerá*) all entities. In this respect he compares them to the gesticulative signs used by mutes who are able to indicate (*sēmaínein*) things with their hands, heads or other parts of the body, even though they are not able to manifest them (*dēloûn*) with verbal language.

Cratylus frequently mentions the task of revelation (*dēlōma*) which belongs to language. However, Plato makes a distinction between the revelation accomplished by names from that accomplished by utterances in general (cf. Lorenz and Mittelstrass, 1967, p.8). The latter reveal something about objects (*The Sophist*, 262 d), while only "correct" names reveal objects as they are (cf. *Cratylus*, 422 d). The criterion of correctness for a name rests in fact on its nature of revelation.

In *The Sophist* (262 a), the name is expressly defined as a "vocal sign" (*sēmeîon tês phōnês*), an expression which is used as an equivalent to *dēlōma* and has the function of manifesting the "essence" of the thing it names: "I would say in fact that there is a double type of our phonic signs (*têi phōnêi . . . dēlō-mátōn*) which indicate the being of something" (*The Sophist*, 261 e).

Special combinations of these "vocal signs" give rise to utterances (*lógoi*) which bring a higher level into play. *The Sophist* takes into consideration the problem which Aristotle later terms the opposition between "semantic" and "apophantic"; in Plato, this is seen as an opposition between the *onomázein* ("to name") level and the *légein* ("to utter") level (262 d). The individual vocal signs, both *onómata* ("names or nouns") and *rhémata* ("verbs"), manifest a content at the precise moment that they name something. The correct combinations of these vocal signs are situated on a different level, since, as well as manifesting a content, they present it as "being the case" or "not being the case" of a given event, state or process, that is, they constitute an assertion (cf. De Rijk, 1986, pp.199-200).

4.2.2 THEORY OF LANGUAGE IN *CRATYLUS*

The fundamental problem dealt with in *Cratylus* is the "correctness of names". This problem is present from the beginning of the dialogue in the form of a debate between Cratylus and Hermogenes, who choose Socrates as judge. Basically, Cratylus adopts what we might term a "naturalist" position, while Hermogenes defends a "conventionalist" position. However, these two positions reveal certain inner stratifications and distinctions which merit further attention.

First of all, both sides consider the act of naming at what might be called the dawn of language. For Hermogenes, this act is the result of convention and stems from an agreement between people who already possess a preliminary knowledge of things. In contrast, Cratylus holds that the act of naming occurs completely naturally and does not presuppose any kind of agreement between individuals.

The debate turns to the analysis of the act of naming and, ignoring the diachronic instance of language formation, focuses on correctness in the relationship between the name and the object to which it is synchronically applied. Both Hermogenes and Cratylus offer the same solution for this case, for they both state that names always refer correctly to their objects. The only difference in their positions here is that for Cratylus the correctness of names follows a natural law, while for Hermogenes the rules governing correctness are of a conventional nature. As proof of this, he offers the fact that names can be changed without disturbing their relationship with their objects.

The third part of the debate follows naturally from the previous part and regards the extension of the validity of the relationship of correctness. For Cratylus, the correctness of a name is "universal", it is the same for Greeks as for the barbarians, whereas for Hermogenes, it must be limited to the particular linguistic community which has adopted the convention.

The positions adopted for the parts of the debate can be shown in a ma-

	original act of naming	correctness	validity of correctness
Hermogenes	result of agreement	always / based on laws of convention	limited to particular linguistic community
Cratylus	natural	always / based on natural laws	universal

Figure 4.2

trix (Figure 4.2). As we have seen, both parties take for granted the correctness of names with respect to their objects. However, they each give a different explanation as to who or what guarantees the correctness. Natural law, which Cratylus proposes for this role, focuses on the relationship between the name and *the name-bearing objects*, but it attaches no importance to what the *users* of the name may think about it. In complete contrast, Hermogenes' candidate for the guarantor of correctness is a rule which concerns the *users* of a name without taking into consideration the nature of *the name-bearing object* (cf. Kretzmann, 1971, p.127).

4.2.3 LANGUAGE AND DIALECTIC

In addition to the notions of Hermogenes and Cratylus, a third theory is put forward in the dialogue: Socrates' confutation of the positions of both contenders. As usual, Socrates is the mouthpiece for Plato's opinions, and the motives for his negation of both the other positions in the debate can be traced back to the general conception of philosophical method which Plato advocates.

Indeed, if either Cratylus or Hermogenes were right, dialectic as a method for attaining knowledge would be impossible (cf. Weingartner, 1969, p.6). Plato sees language as a necessary means for philosophical research, but sees truth as lying rather in things than in words, as the conclusion of the dialogue indicates. Both Hermogenes' and Cratylus' theories threaten this principle.

Hermogenes' theory at first sight seems to be a "classic conventionalist" theory by which the principle of the criterion for correctness of names rests on convention and agreement (384 c–d). However, he also puts forward another position, and this is what Socrates attacks and demolishes. He states that "whatever name you give to a thing is its correct name" and explains that "if one replaces that name with another name and no longer uses the previous name, the later name is by no means less correct than the earlier one" (384 d). At this point Socrates forces Hermogenes to change his point of focus and to state that anyone can effect this change of names, not only a community, but even a single individual.

The result of this, of course, is a doctrine of autonomous idiolects, each so itemized as to represent the speech of a single individiual. This explodes Hermogenes' conventionalism into total subjectivism, and Socrates drives the point home by comparing it to Protagoras' relativism (386 a). Such a "Humpty-Dumpty position", as Weingartner calls it (cf. Weingartner, 1969, p.7), deprives language of its communicative function and makes dialectic impossible, for it is no longer possible to distinguish true statements from false statements.

However, Cratylus' position also leads to an utter impossibility of dialectic. His theory reveals traits of "total iconism", for, according to it, the name reveals the nature of the thing it names by imitating it. But the imitation must be total to be convincing. The arrangement of sounds which failed to attain perfect imitation even by the merest hairsbreadth would therefore be nothing more than "the noise which someone makes by beating a bronze pot" (430 a).

Since for Cratylus linguistic production seems to give rise in some cases to correct imitations and in others to nonsense, dialectic would, in both cases, be nothing but a meaningless tool. Let us take, for example, a dialectic analysis which begins by asking "What is justice?" with the hope of attaining, through debate, knowledge of the entity in question. There would be two possible outcomes. In the first case, if the expression |justice| naturally reveals the object which it names, the research would be over before it began; in the second case, if the expression |justice| was analogous to the "noise produced by beating a bronze pot", the question itself would have no meaning. As dialectic must reach true judgements, there must be the possibility of uttering false judgements which will be corrected during the course of the debate. It is precisely this possibility which Cratylus' theory eliminates.

4.2.4 THE NAME AS TOOL

One of the fundamental points of *Cratylus* is the search for an objective criterion which enables a truth value to be given both to utterances and to names. In order to achieve this aim, Socrates temporarily shifts the discourse from the linguistic to the ontological plane, stating that things (*prágmata*) contain within themselves a stable essence and do not depend on subjective judgements (386 e).

The same feature of objectivity is attributed by Socrates also to actions (*práxeis*), which, like things (*prágmata*), are a kind of entity (*ónta*). Once we expect actions to have certain effects, they can no longer be carried out arbitrarily. However, for Socrates, speech (*légein*) and naming (*onomázein*, which is a part of speech) are both forms of action and consequently must be carried out in a non-arbitrary manner. Figure 4.3 illustrates this series of divisions.

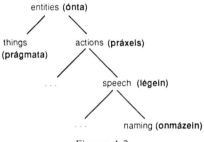

Figure 4.3

The intuition that speech and naming are types of actions is not further developed in the dialogue but nonetheless remains as an important indication of a possible pragmatic development which Greek theory of language might have had.

In order to demonstrate that language has an objective link with reality (in that it attempts to achieve effective communication), a comparison is made between the name and a tool or instrument (*órganon*). Just as the shuttle separates the threads of a fabric, so a name is "an instrument of teaching and of separating reality" (388 c). In other words, names first of all make a taxonomy of reality, separating the objects which make up reality according to their natures (cf. Kretzmann, 1971, p.128); second, names make it possible to communicate this taxonomy.

4.2.5 THE FORM ("*EÎDOS*") AND THE MATERIAL OF NAMES

If the aim of names is to permit the acquisition of knowledge about things and the communication of such knowledge to others, then whoever has "denominated" reality (the namer, that is, the personification of an accepted linguistic authority), by categorizing it in a certain way, must already have a preliminary knowledge of these things.

In order to guarantee the correctness of names, the "namer" behaves just like the maker of shuttles. Just as the maker of shuttles looks at the *eîdos* ("form", "idea") of the shuttle, so the namer looks at the "name in itself", that is, the ideal form of the name (389 b, 390 a), in order to make the name.

In the same way, not all materials are suitable for use in making a particular tool, and the material most suited to the particular form of a specific tool must be used to make it for best results (for example, iron for drills and wood for shuttles). Thus, names are made with sounds and syllables rather than other types of material so as to perform their function efficiently.

It is not necessary, however, that the phonic form (or, the surface form) of names be the same in all languages, for each language subdivides the sound continuum in different ways (in the same way that each smith makes his own particular use of different pieces of metal in the construction of tools intended for the same purpose) (389 e). This is how Plato explains the diversity of languages which are all, however, organized in such a manner as to follow the same models. What varies from one language to another is the *material*, the surface configuration of names and syllables which each name adopts.

What remains constant through all languages is the *form* (*eîdos*, *idéa*) of the name which fits each individual object (390 a). The form can be understood according to Kretzmann's interpretation (1971, pp.129-30) as the essential function and aim which each name has to separate objects in such a way as to respect their natural joints. In this way, for example, the Greek name |hippos| and the barbarian names |cheval|, |horse|, |cavallo|, |Pferd|, etc., are all correct if they accomplish the cutting of reality according to its "natural joints". It would seem that with Plato there is an assumption that these joints are the same for all cultures.

Plato here is dealing with what we might term a "Hjelmslevian" question,[1] and thus, rather than speak of function (as Kretzmann puts it), we can discuss form and substance, expression and content (as Hjelmslev does). The expressive form (Plato's *material*) can vary from language to language, but in order for the name to be correct, the form of the content (Plato's *eîdos* or *idéa*) has to cut the material of the content according to the same articulations. Thus |hippos|, |cheval|, |horse|, |cavallo| and |Pferd| are all correct names if they cut the content material continuum ("the horsehood" within the range relative to animals) according to precisely the same joints.

The application of names has to correspond to a correct taxonomy of the reality continuum, accomplished by the method of division (*diaíresis*) of reality. The proof of this may be seen in the fact that the task of judging whether the various "namers" have performed the job well falls to the dialectician, the personification of scientific and philosophical authority (390 d).

4.2.6 A FIRST SEMANTIC THEORY

Donatella Di Cesare (1981) identifies two different semantic theories expressed within *Cratylus*. The first of these refers to an ideal language situation and the second to a historically real language situation. This section will deal briefly with the first of these theories.

At a certain point of the dialogue (393 d), Socrates states that what is really important for a name is to signify (*sēmaínein*) the essence of a thing (*ousía toû prágmatos*), which is then clearly expressed (*dēlouménē*) by the name. Once the name expresses the essence of a thing, letters may be added or taken away without any significant effect.

Socrates gives the example of the name of the letter *bêta*. This names the letter |b|, but adds to this *êta* (|e|), *taû* (|t|) and *álpha* (|a|). In spite of these additions, *bêta* correctly names |b|, as it shows the "value" of the letter which it is supposed to name. The same reasoning applies to all other names: they are correct if they name the essence of the thing they are the name of. Meaning is therefore identified with this essence of the thing.

A little later on in the dialogue (394 b-c), Socrates introduces another concept, *dýnamis* ("force"), which also seems to be identified with meaning. He claims that those who are skilled in names look at their force (*dýnamis*) and do not let themselves be distracted by additions or transpositions of letters. Thus the names *Astyánax* ("Astyanax" = "lord of the city") and *Héktor* ("Hector" = "he who holds firm"), even though they have only the letter |t| in common, mean the same thing (*tautòn sēmaínei*).

Thus the meaning of the name is given by these two elements: the essence of the thing named and the *dýnamis* of the name. In fact these coincide in that the name, through its meaning, must express the thing it is naming. The relationship between name, meaning and thing can be represented by a triangle (Figure 4.4).

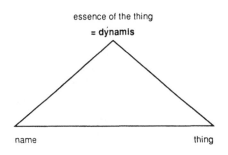

Figure 4.4

As Donatella Di Cesare (1981, p.103) points out, the name for Plato does not "reflect" the thing, but only its essence, and it is for this reason that there can be different names for the same object. In order to reflect the essence of the thing, the name must "associate the individual thing to the genus to which it belongs" (ibid.). This affirmation corresponds to what Lorenz and Mittelstrass (1967, pp.6-8) stated with their attribution of a predicative function to the name. The specific meaning of a name, or its *dýnamis*, therefore consists in assigning objects to their appropriate concepts or to the genus to which they belong. It is with respect to this operation that the correctness or incorrectness of names can be judged objectively.

If we pause for a moment to consider the results of the theory of meaning set out in the first part of the dialogue, we can see that Socrates' entire demonstration is directed towards showing the coincidence of the linguistic structure with the logical-ontological structure. By means of names, language cuts reality according to the same joints naturally present in reality itself. Thus, by imitating and representing the structure of reality, language provides a mediation between the world of ideas and the sensible world, for the name represents the very genus which can be predicated for an object and which, although ephemeral in nature, can be made concrete in phonic material.

However, as we said earlier, Plato by no means considers the identity described in the first part of the dialogue to be a concrete reality, but more an ideal objective. In the final part of the dialogue, following this etymological digression, a second and very different semantic theory is set out.

4.2.7 A SECOND SEMANTIC THEORY

Socrates' etymological theory expounded in the central part of the dialogue along with the related reflection on the origins of language were ostensibly being used to demonstrate the substantial identity between linguistic and ontological structures in general and between the essence of the object and the *dýnamis* in particular. However, the conclusion they reached turns out to be exactly the opposite. Language does not reflect the objective structure of the real world, but it is instead the expression of the idea of the real world which the name-giver holds.

Meaning is therefore identified with the representation of reality which is formed within the subject (cf. Di Cesare, 1981, p.131), and this representation is the result of opinions, sensations and impressions made upon the subject by objects which make up the real world. Pagliaro (1956a, p.73) characterized this movement from a first to a second semantic theory as an analysis of two different aspects of language: (i) the relationship between the signifier and the object, in the first part of the dialogue; (ii) the relationship between the signifier and the signified, in the second part of the dialogue.

According to this second theory, the triangle representing the relationships between name, meaning and thing takes on a different structure (Figure 4.5).

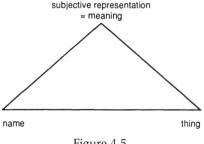

subjective representation
= meaning

name   thing

Figure 4.5

Language thus does not reflect the world of ideas or the essence of things, but rather the empirical world. It forms a historical reality which contains the vision of the world which was held by the first name-givers when they were trying to impose an order on the real world by classifying and categorizing it, using names as "separating tools". This however does not mean that a faithful reflection of reality can never be achieved by means of language; it simply implies that such a reflection is possible only when a complete knowledge of things has been reached.

In this theory, the mediating function of the soul is of particular interest, as it brings Plato's theory very close to modern theories of language which see language as a psychic element. In this, Plato is showing the influence of the Sophists, the only earlier philosophers to emphasize the psychic dimension of language (in contrast to those who held that reality could be reflected directly in language with no further mediation required).

4.2.8 MIMESIS

The first part of the dialogue is dedicated to the confutation of the conventionalist theory. The last part is dedicated to the confutation of the theory of reflection propounded by Cratylus. In fact, the central part of the dialogue, that dealing with etymology, already leads to the conclusion that language is a subjective representation, and this conclusion itself contradicts Cratylus' theory. Nonetheless, Socrates takes the debate further to demonstrate the absurdity of Cratylus' thesis by bringing up the problem of mimesis, and he proposes a provisional definition of the name as "an imitation with the voice of the thing which is being imitated; and the person who imitates is naming with the voice what is being imitated" (423 b-c).

What is interesting here is that imitation also seems to have, in general terms, a semiotic nature, for the imitation "reveals" (*dēloî*) the essence of the thing.

However, mimesis is by no means a simple concept, and Socrates looks at it under three aspects: (i) portraits, (ii) doubles and (iii) "metaphysical" reflection. Let us look at each of these aspects in order.

A portrait, like a name, can be compared with the object it imitates. According to Socrates, it is thus possible to observe the phenomenon whereby certain elements present in the original are absent in the imitation or elements not present in the original are added to the imitation. The copy is therefore iconic but presents variations within a continuum. According to Socrates, this is what happens with names too, which is virtually the same as saying that names have a *signic* nature. Cratylus, however, is not of the same opinion, for he thinks that names have the nature of absolute resemblance without which they cannot be considered to be names at all. The two opinions can be schematized as shown in Figure 4.6.

Socrates next introduces the concept of the double. If all the characteristics of the original were reproduced in the mimesis, then the result would be not an imitation but an identical occurrence of the same object. We would no longer have a situation of representation but would be faced in-

	"name/object" relationship	nature of mimesis
Socrates	iconic	continuous
Cratylus	iconic	discrete

Figure 4.6

stead with a complete duplicate, and there would be no way of telling which was the represented and which the represented. In other words, a name has a *signic* nature precisely because of its difference from the object to which it refers.

Socrates' third case, which we have defined as "metaphysical reflection", focuses on how individual sounds imitate fragments of the real world. Contrary to what we might expect if sounds really did completely reflect things in their essences, the word *sklērótēs* ("hardness") contains within it a *lámbda* (lll), which expresses "softness", "slipperiness". Thus the word imitates "hardness" only in part, and in part it has nothing to do with "hardness". With the use of other examples, Socrates then goes on to negate another, more fundamentally philosophical hypothesis whereby language reflects the Heraclitan view of reality as eternal flux and movement (411 c, 436 e). Socrates states that this is far from being the case, since many words in language present reality as perfectly unmoving.

4.2.9 USE AND CONVENTION

Socrates' criticisms of Cratylus' thesis nonetheless result in a positive proposal. Having observed that the name *sklērótēs* ("hardness") is not entirely correct (since it contains within its signifier elements which do not correspond to the actual qualities of the thing designated), he notes that the word nonetheless carries out its communicative function perfectly, for the Greeks understand one another when they use this name.

Socrates attributes the responsibility for such understanding to the factors of use (*éthos*) and convention (*xynthḗkē*). These factors not only *describe* a relationship between users of a name, but also *bear witness* to the denotative relationship between the name and its object (cf. Kretzmann, 1971, p.138). The idea that the name is a "revelation" (*dḗlōma*) of the object it designates is not rejected, but the responsibility for this revelation is shifted from the relationship of resemblance between the two terms to the convention which associates them (435 a–b).

However, Plato does not simply substitute a conception whereby semiosis occurs through resemblance with a conventionalist conception. The ideal situation for him remains that in which names are images which reproduce the essence of the objects they name. It is rather the limits of natural language which make recourse to agreement and subsequent convention necessary (435 b–c). This is the point at which some commentators have identified a compromise between the conventionalism of Hermogenes and the naturalism of Cratylus.

The final lines of the dialogue also reveal a shifting of the function assigned to the linguistic sign, whereby there is an accentuation of the communicative function over the cognitive function. Language is not a sufficiently valid tool for the attainment of knowledge of reality. Such knowledge requires a much more direct path, such as the recourse to things themselves (439 b). However, language can be seen as an excellent tool for the effective accomplishment of human communication.

4.3 THEORY OF LANGUAGE IN *LETTER VII*

An interesting treatment of the elements involved in a theory of meaning may be found in *Letter VII*, a text attributed to Plato but whose authenticity has often been questioned (cf. Edelstein, 1966). Many scholars agree that the text contains nothing assuredly non-Platonic, and it contains sufficient material of interest in its own right to merit a careful analysis in this context.

The central part of the letter contains a theoretical passage (342 a–344 d) dealing with the elements that make attainment and transmission of knowledge possible. These elements also come into play in the process of semiosis. These are the name (*ónoma*), the definition (*lógos*), the image (*eídōlon*), knowledge (*epistémē*) and finally the knowable object (*gnōstón*) which is truly real (*alēthôs ón*) (342 a–b).

According to Morrow's interpretation (cf. Morrow, 1935, p.68), these elements are organized according to an internal order. On one side may be placed the factors which represent the tools of knowledge, that is, names, definitions, images or diagrams, and on the other, in diametric opposition, are placed the real, knowable objects. It is *epistémē* (which Morrow translates as "subjective apprehension"), which mediates between the tools and the object of knowledge. *Epistémē* is further subdivided, Plato states later in the letter (342 c), into right opinion (*alēthḕs dóxa*), knowledge (*epistémē*) (curiously, the name of the genus also appears here as the name of the type) and reason or intuition (*noûs*), which Plato states is closest to the real, knowable object.

The letter says that these three elements, which jointly make up *epistémē* and which must be considered as one step, reside "neither in vocal utterance nor in bodily forms, but in souls (*en psychaîs*)", a fact which distinguishes them, Plato points out, both from the real object and from the tools of knowledge. This reference to the soul, which suggests a parallel with the role assigned to the soul in the second semantic theory in *Cratylus*, prompts a linking of the concept of *epistémē* to the concept of meaning. This interpretation is supported by a reading of the passage in the light of later traditions, such as the Aristotelian tradition which locates meaning in the soul (*tà en têi psychêi*) (cf. *De Interpretatione*, 16 a). The five elements can be arranged on the semiotic triangle (Figure 4.7).

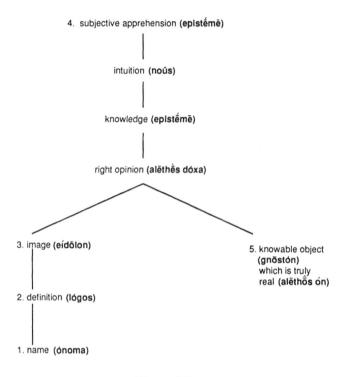

4. subjective apprehension (**epistémē**)

intuition (**noûs**)

knowledge (**epistémē**)

right opinion (**alēthḕs dóxa**)

3. image (**eídōlon**)

2. definition (**lógos**)

1. name (**ónoma**)

5. knowable object (**gnōstón**) which is truly real (**alēthôs ón**)

Figure 4.7

The intention of this passage of the letter is to demonstrate the defective nature of the tools of knowledge. As a means of overcoming this problem, Plato sets out a doctrine which comes very close to Peirce's theory of semiosis as a "fugue of interpretants". This can be appreciated if we look at the example which is used throughout the argument of the letter.

The example used is that of the "circle", an example of an intended mathematical nature. Plato easily demonstrates that the referent of the expression |circle| is not an object of the real world, subject to growth and decay, but an entity of a different type. Such an entity can be reached only by passing though the entire series of preliminary steps and especially by passing through a continual process of replacing one of these steps with another: it is this "passing in turn from one to another, up and down, which with difficulty implants knowledge" (343 e). Each individual element is incomplete in itself (as are Peirce's interpretants) and contributes to the attainment of knowledge when inserted into this never-ending process of substitution and confrontation. This process of continual substitution makes it possible to overcome the imperfection of tools of knowledge.

The imperfection of the name is, as we know from *Cratylus*, due to the fact that in language as we know it the name is not the image of the thing which it names but is only linked to this by convention. According to *Letter VII*, this de-stabilizes the name since we could use the expression lstraight linel to refer to circular things and the expression lcirclel to refer to a straight line without causing any changes in the things themselves (343 a–b).

It might be possible therefore to use the definition of the circle as "that figure which is everywhere equidistant from the extremities to the center" (342 b). However, even though this expression adds certain factors, it is nonetheless also made up of nouns and verbs and thus presents exactly the same difficulties as were present with respect to names. Incidentally, drawing attention to the fact that the definition is "formed by nouns and verbs" accentuates aspects of the signifier rather than aspects of the signified. The definition is simply another expression which in the cognitive or semiosic process can be substituted for the name. Plato had already touched upon the question of the substitution of names when he presupposed the interchangeability of lcirclel (*kýklos*), lcurved (line)l (*strongýlon*) and lcircular (line)l (*peripherés*) (242 b-c).

Something is added from the third level, that of the *eídōla* ("images"). Here the circle is known as "what is portrayed and obliterated, which is formed by the lathe and which decays" (242 c). This represents the substitution of an iconic interpretant for the previous verbal interpretants. In order to know what the true nature of the circle is, we need not only verbal explanations but illustrations and demonstrations too. But at this level knowledge still has an uncertain nature in that objects exist in which the essence (*tò ón*) is contaminated by the quality (*tò poîón ti*) or by properties which are incidental and sometimes contrary to the true nature of its metaphysical entity. For example, each point of the circle can be cut by a tangent so that when this extremely small part of the circumference is isolated it would be impossible to know if it formed part of a circle or a straight line (343 a; cf. also Taylor, 1912, p. 361).

The theoretical section of *Letter VII* concludes by taking up once again a concept which quite closely resembles that of unlimited semiosis, though here it is obviously expressed in purely Platonic terms: "It is while each of these objects is rubbed against the others, comparing one with another—names, definitions, visions and sense perceptions—proving them by kindly proofs and employing questionings and answerings that are void of envy—it is by such means . . . that there bursts out the light of intelligence and reason regarding each object in the mind of those who use every effort of which human individuals are capable." (344 b-c).

This metaphor of "rubbing" works both within the framework of the epistemological idea of the sudden flaring and flash of intuition and within the framework of the semiotic idea that final meaning is not obtained through the immediate and simplistic substitution of a signifier with a signified, but rather by means of a sequence of successive, repeated moves — such as those which form the process of unlimited semiosis.

FIVE

Language and Signs
in Aristotle

5.0 INTRODUCTION

With Aristotle certain major changes and developments occurred which
had a lasting influence on the history of the sign. The first of these was the
vast and far-reaching work of normalization which Aristotle operated on
the vocabulary of science and the professions where signs and conjectural
thought in general had been used. Aristotle took the vast semantic field in
which strong and weak uses of terms such as *sēmeîon, tekmḗrion, aitía,
próphasis* and *eikós* oscillated through the fifth century in medical, historical
and philosophical writings and reduced it to the terms of a strict system of
classification and definition, fixing precise uses of the terminology and setting the bounds of the different fields of knowledge.

As Lanza (1979, p.107) has shown, this operation had only a partial practical success, however, for Aristotle only really achieved a rigid division and
classification within the theoretical sphere. A passage in *Prior Analytics* and
another in *Rhetoric*[1] set out these theoretical distinctions. On the practical
level, however—even within the language of the *Rhetoric* itself, and generally
in others of Aristotle's scientific works, as Le Blond (1939/1973, p.241) has
pointed out—the use of the various terms which make up the semiotic-
gnoseological vocabulary remains loose, and the terms are often used without
any special distinctive shades of meaning. Nonetheless, the revision of terminology which Aristotle achieved on the theoretical level was profound and became the basis for a tradition which continued through later treatises up to the
Roman school of rhetoric in the first century A.D.

However, the effects of this theoretical distinction went beyond a mere
normalization of the vocabulary and inevitably entered into the dynamics
of the thought and conceptions formulated around the notion of conjectural thought.

We have already seen how the question of time was central both in
the non-scientific sphere of divination and in the proto-scientific sphere
of medicine. In both of these fields of knowledge, simultaneous awareness of the past, present and future, although treated in very different
ways, formed an essential element. Aristotle took up this question and

conceptualized it, forcing it to meet the requirements of theoretical classification.

In the classification of the types of speech set out in his *Rhetoric*, Aristotle
identified two categories of intended receiver of speech: the observer (*theōrós*)
and the decider (*krités*). The former operates within the present and is represented by the kind of audience which receives a celebratory or epideictic
speech. The latter, in contrast, operates in the other two dimensions of time,
which belong to the other two types of speech. The judge (*dikastés*), for example, decides on the past, and the member of the Assembly (*ekklēsiastés*) decides
on the future.[2] As Lanza (1979, p.102) notes, this classification is completely
extraneous to the object considered but clearly demonstrates Aristotle's attempt to link the traditional division of the types of speech to the three dimensions of time which had been associated, from the age of Homer, with the es-
oteric or technical realms of the manifestation of knowledge.

5.1 THEORY OF LANGUAGE AND
THEORY OF THE SIGN

5.1.1 THE SEMIOTIC TRIANGLE

The second important factor in Aristotle's consideration of the questions relating to signs was the separation, and consequent separate treatment, of the
theory of language from the theory of the sign. This may seem surprising to
modern scholars and merits careful attention precisely because modern semiological theories assume *a priori* that the terms which make up verbal language
are "signs". Indeed, according to one particular brand of structuralism, they
are the signs *par excellence*, and many scholars have actually gone so far as to
propose that the terms of verbal language can provide a model for all other
types of sign. However, Aristotle distinguished the elements which go to
make up a theory of language with the name *sýmbola*, while the other elements of a theory of signs he termed *sēmeîa* or *tekmḗria*.[3]

As will be seen below, the theory of signs in fact forms part of the theory of syllogism and has both logical and epistemological features of interest. The sign lies at the center of the problem of how knowledge is ac-
quired, whereas the linguistic symbol is principally connected to the
problem of relationships between linguistic expressions, conceptual ab-
stracts and states of the world.

Aristotle sets out his theory of the linguistic symbol in *De Interpretatione*,
expressing it in a model made up of three terms: *spoken sounds*, which are
"symbols" of the *affections of the soul*, which are themselves images of external *things*:

> Now spoken sounds (*tà en têi phōnêi*) are symbols (*sýmbola*) of affections in the
> soul (*tôn en têi psychêi pathēmátōn*), and written marks (*graphómena*) symbols of
> spoken sounds. And just as written marks are not the same for all peoples,

neither are spoken sounds. But what these are in the first place signs (*sēmeîa*) of—affections of the soul—are the same for all; and what these affections are likenesses (*homoiṓmata*) of—actual things (*prágmata*)—are also the same.

(16 a, 3-8)

It must be stated, first of all, that the appearance here of the term *sēmeîa* apparently as a synonym of *sýmbola* should not be taken to mean that the two expressions are interchangeable. In this passage, Aristotle is using the term *sēmeîon* in a weak meaning, which confirms the tendency we have already noticed toward a certain blurring of the edges of expressions belonging to the semiotic vocabulary whenever one is not talking of a strictly theoretical demarcation. Aristotle is also using *sēmeîa* here to show that the existence of sounds and letters can be considered the proof of the parallel existence of affections of the soul.

Nonetheless, leaving aside the graphological level, it is possible to construct a semiotic triangle of the type shown in Figure 5.1. As the figure

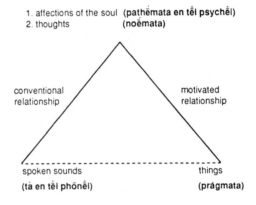

1. affections of the soul (pathḗmata en têi psychêi)
2. thoughts   (noḗmata)

conventional
relationship

motivated
relationship

spoken sounds
(tà en têi phōnêi)

things
(prágmata)

Figure 5.1

shows, there is a different relationship between the different pairs of terms which form the triad. Between sounds and affections of the soul, the relationship is unmotivated and conventional since, according to Aristotle, affections of the soul are the same for everyone but are expressed in different ways according to different languages and cultures, as also occurs for written forms.[4] However, between affections of the soul and things there is a motivated relationship which is practically iconic since the former are images of the latter. It would be a mistake, however, to equate the concept of conventionality of the elements of language which Aristotle propounds with the concept of the arbitrariness of the linguistic sign developed by Saussure. In Saussure's theory, in fact, there is an arbitrary relationship between two entities which belong exclusively to the realm of language; the signifier and the signified are the two sides of the sign as a linguistic unity.

In Aristotle, however, the conventional relationship exists between elements of language (nouns, verbs, *lógos*) and elements which do not belong strictly to language in that they are psychic entities. It should be remembered too that Aristotle's theory of language is not expressed solely in the context of works dealing mainly with logic, such as *De Interpretatione*, but appears and is developed also in works dealing with aesthetics. In these, where the poetic function of language is primarily being dealt with, the importance of the principle of conventionality is to a certain extent reduced (cf. Belardi, 1975, p.75 ff.).

5.1.2 "SPOKEN SOUNDS"

The terms at the corners of the triangle have interesting and problematical aspects. We can start by asking what precisely Aristotle meant by the expression *tà en têi phōnêi*. Different critics have suggested different answers to this question.

Donatella Di Cesare (1981, p.161), for example, claims that Aristotle gives the same value to this expression as Saussure gives to the term "signifier" in his explanation of the nature of the linguistic sign. Belardi (1975, p.198), on the other hand, states that *tà en têi phōnêi* must refer not to the signifiers but to "linguistic expressions" understood in their full form of *ónoma* (noun), *rhêma* (verb) and *lógos* (speech) and in the form of *katáphasis* (affirmation) and *apóphasis* (negation). He justifies this interpretation by the fact that these elements, which form part of Aristotle's analytical method, are defined as "symbols" of the affections of the soul (*Prior Analytics*, 16 a, 25; 24 b, 2).

There is no doubt whatsoever that Aristotle intended the expression "spoken sounds" to indicate something which emphasized clearly both the phonic nature and the nature of "signifier". However, it must not be forgotten that Aristotle's point of view when examining facts of language, at least in his *Organon*, is very different from that of Saussure.

In the *Organon*, Aristotle is interested in assaying the possibilities and trustworthiness of the use of language in the analysis of reality. There would appear to be a trustworthiness when there is a reciprocal relationship between the realms of the real and of language. For Aristotle, the symbolic nature of language with respect to the real world is a symbolism at two removes, since the name stands for an image which is itself an image of a thing; therefore (according to the rules of logical organization followed in *De Interpretatione*), the item at the left corner of the triangle must be *interchangeable* with what stands at the apex.

It is from this fact that Aristotle's use of the notion of *sýmbolon* stems, a use which he takes from a tradition which goes back to Democritus (D-K, 668, B 5, 1). This term became part of linguistic terminology to indicate conventional linguistic expressions thanks to its etymology. In Greek, the term *sýmbolon* indicates each of the two halves into which an object (such as a medal or a coin) is intentionally broken in order to serve later as a sign of identity or as proof of something (cf. Belardi, 1975, p.198; Eco, 1984a, p.130). When the two halves are later put together and seen to match perfectly, this is taken as indicating the existence of a previously established relationship (such as a relationship of hospitality, or friendship or paternity) the proof of which had been specifically entrusted to the perfect matching of the two *sýmbola*. The situation is thus set up that each of the two parts can be exchanged for the other without any resulting loss of the value as proof. Thus, since in this way each part presupposes the other, or has an absolute correspondence with the other, the expression *sýmbolon* could take on the meaning of "that which stands for something else". However, the fact that Aristotle prefers to use the word *sýmbolon* rather than the word *sēmeîon* (which can also indicate "stands for") in the context of his theory of language leads us to hypothesize that the reference set up by the symbol is of a very particular nature. In fact, in the case of the sign, the two terms in the reference (which, as we shall see later, is an implication) are not always reciprocal. The first term can refer to the second term without the second term necessarily referring to the first. In the case of the symbol, however, the two terms are completely reciprocal. It is no coincidence that the term *sýmbolon* was also used (from the third century B.C. to the third century A.D.) in the sense of a "receipt", often made out in two copies, the two parts of which thus have the same value.

It is this etymological sense which is important in Aristotle's special use of the expression *sýmbolon* in *De Interpretatione*. Names are symbols of affections of the soul in the precise sense that there occurs between them, in accordance with a previously established agreement (*synthḗkē*), a perfect matching and a complete interchangeability which guarantee the correctness of the name (cf. Belardi, 1975, p.199).

As *sýmbolon*, the name is no longer, as it was for Plato, *dḗlōma* ("revelation"). For Aristotle, the name is the "spoken sound significant by conventions" (*phōnḕ sēmantikḕ katà synthḗkēn*) (*De Interpretatione*, 16 a, 19). This can be taken as marking the passage from a linguistics with a certain semiotic nature, such as Plato's linguistics displayed, to a linguistics which no longer talks of signs and which is intrinsically non-semiotic. Whereas Plato thought of linguistic expressions as signs which "revealed" something that was not perceptible (the essence of the object, or the *dýnamis*), for Aristotle linguistic expressions are rather symbols which establish conventionally a pure relationship of *equivalence*[5] between two objects in relation, without any concern that one of the terms "reveals" the other.

5.1.3 ANIMAL LANGUAGE

The *conventional/natural* opposition[6] makes it possible to distinguish between human language and sounds made by animals,[7] which are also, after all, equally (i) vocal and (ii) interpretable.

The concept of "voice" (*phōnḗ*) has in itself several interesting features. *De Anima* states that a sound can be defined as a voice when (i) it is emitted by an animate being (II, 420 b, 5) and (ii) when it has meaning (*sēmantikós*) (II, 420 b,

29-33). Now, even though the noises made by animals are defined as *psóphoi* ("noises") they nonetheless have both of the above-mentioned characteristics. What distinguishes animal sounds from human voices is the fact that (i) they are not conventional (and consequently can be neither symbols nor names) but are rather "by nature" (cf. *De Interpretatione*, 16 a, 26-30) and that (ii) they are *agrámmatoi*, that is, they cannot be broken down into letters and they are "non-combinable" (ibid.; *Poetics*, 1456 b, 22-24).

The concept of "combinableness", as Morpurgo-Tagliabue demonstrate (1967, p.33 ff.), is central to the semantic nature of human language, the simple sounds of which (*adiaíretoi*, "invisible things") can be put together into larger units which then have meaning.[8] Animals, on the other hand, make only sounds which are indivisible and non-combinable (cf. *Poetics*, 1456 b, 22-24).

Table 5.1 illustrates the characteristics of human language in comparison with sounds made by animals. It is worth pointing out that the semantic nature of animal sounds is expressed in the verb *dēloûsi* ("reveal", *De Interpretatione*, 16 a, 28). This demonstrates once again that for Aristotle, when convention is not in question, as with animal language, the semiotic nature of an expression is emphasized. Animal sounds are symptoms which reveal their cause.

human language	*animal sounds*
— by convention	— by nature
— combinable indivisible elements and divisible elements	— non-combinable indivisible elements
— letters	— no letters
— elements which have meaning	— elements which reveal (*dēloûsi*) something
— symbols	— not symbols
— names	— not names

5.1.4 THE "AFFECTIONS OF THE SOUL"

Returning to Aristotle's triangle of signification, the next term which is worth analyzing more deeply is the expression *pathémata en têi psychêi*. It will be noted that where we might expect to find the idea of "meaning", what we actually find is a psychic entity, something located not within language but within the very minds of the language users. In addition, while Aristotle sees the "affections of the soul" as psychic events, he by no means sees them as being individual. As he says, they are elements which are identical for everyone, and this statement links theory of language with a sort of social psychology, or with a universal, rather than individual, psychology (cf. Todorov, 1977, p.16).

It should also be noted that there is a certain ambiguity to be seen in this term. Aristotle says that the *pathémata en têi psychêi* are likenesses or images (*homoiómata*) of external objects. In this way he seems to be saying that the same relationship exists between objects and psychic entities as between an original and a copy. However, he later uses the expression *nóēma* ("thought", "notion" [16 a, 10]) to indicate mental representation. Here, though, he stresses that under certain conditions thoughts can be true or false. It would thus follow that *noēmata* are conceived of as forms of judgement.

These two ideas seem to be completely different from one another, and the fact that they were both used in relation to the same linguistic expressions seemed to suggest that these were synonymous, a situation which was contradictory and confusing. However, as Belardi (1975, p.109) has pointed out, neither of these two ideas completely covers the area of psychic representation, and they in fact refer to two different faculties of the soul. The *pathḗmata* call into play the *passive* faculty of the soul to receive impressions from objects of the outside world, and the *noḗmata* reflect the *active* faculty of the soul in forming judgements. This relationship of the two ideas is confirmed by the reference Aristotle makes to *De Anima*, a treatise in which *pathḗmata* are discussed along with other faculties of the soul.

5.1.5 SEMANTIC AND APOPHANTIC

It is necessary at this point to turn our attention, albeit briefly, to a distinction in Aristotle's linguistic thought: the distinction between the categories of "semantic" and "apophantic". *De Interpretatione* (16 a, 9 ff.) introduces the problems relating to the difference between *phásis* ("what is said") and *katáphasis* (an "affirmation"). Names or nouns (but also verbs in this case) on their own constitute "something which is said", but they cannot alone constitute an affirmation or a negation. As a consequence, two types of mental representation (*noḗmata*) are distinguishable: (1) that "which is not concerned with true or false" and (2) that "which must be either true or false".

What is being set in opposition here is the notion of *meaning* and the notion of *truth conditions*. The first type of mental representation includes names (and verbs) taken on their own; these can have a meaning, but they cannot be true or false. Aristotle proves this by looking at the term "hirco-cervus" or goat-stag (*tragélaphos*). This term "certainly means something" (that is, a monstrous mixture of a goat and a stag), but it cannot be stated to be true or false. The "something" which Aristotle refers to here focuses on the purely semantic dimension, which is governed by rules which are very different from those of referentiality.

The second type of mental representation covers those linguistic entities which can be considered to be propositions. It is when we come to affirmative or negative statements that it becomes possible to speak of truth or falsehood. It is therefore only in this case that it becomes possible to speak of the qualities of being true or false ("apophantic") as a dimension which goes beyond (rather than being opposed to) the dimension of having meaning or not ("semantic").

The question remains, however, as to what specific means can be used to pass from the semantic dimension to the apophantic dimension. Here it is quite clear that Aristotle intends the use of the verb *as a predicate* to supply this means. Aristotle draws attention to the predicative function of the verb when, in talking about judgement, he reduces the verb to |copula + predicate|: "There is no difference", he says, "between saying that a man walks and saying that a man is 'walking' " (cf. *De Interpretatione*, 21 a, 38). Here the verb is seen as a noun taken in a predicative function (cf. Morpurgo-Tagliabue, 1967, p.62).

However, in order for the verb to carry out this function it must be attached to something else (that is, a noun); on its own, when its predicative function cannot be put into effect, it cannot affirm anything (*De Interpretatione*, 16 b, 19-25).

Aristotle demonstrates the impossibility for the verb on its own to affirm the existence of anything (that is, to make assertions) through the example of the verb "to be": not even the verb "to be", on its own, is able to state that something is. In this respect it is perhaps worth quoting Umberto Eco's comment on this situation:

> (Aristotle's) line of thought is the following: a) outside the sentence, no verb can state that something really exists or actually does something; b) verbs can perform this function only in a completely assertive sentence; c) not even *to be* and *not to be*, uttered in isolation, assert the existence of something; d) however, when they are inserted into a sentence, they are signs . . . that the existence of something is asserted.
>
> (Eco, 1984a, p.28)

5.2 THE THEORY OF THE SIGN

5.2.1 DEFINITION

For Aristotle, the theory of the sign is completely distinct from the theory of language and may be located rather at the point of intersection between logic and rhetoric. Signs are dealt with therefore both in *Prior Analytics* and *Rhetoric*.

The idea of the sign simultaneously has two fundamental aspects. First of all it has an epistemological and ontological interest in that it is an instrument of knowledge which serves to guide the attention of knowing subjects to operate the passage from one fact to another (cf. Todorov, 1977, p.19; Simone, 1969, p.91). Equally important, however, is the strictly logical nature of the sign, stemming from the fact that it has a formal mechanism which regulates its function.

The general definition of the sign (*sēmeîon*) is given in *Prior Analytics* (II, 70 a, 7-9). There are many translations of this passage, but it would seem to me that the one which best identifies both the meaning and significance of Aristotle's passage is that made by Preti in 1956 (here translated from the Italian):

When, a thing being, is another thing, or when a thing becoming, becomes another thing before or after, *these latter things* are signs of becoming or being.[9]

I have italicized to call attention to the feature of Preti's version of this passage which distinguishes it from other versions and faithfully reproduces the very problematical and complex nature of Aristotle's definition which later developments in the theory of signs made in various schools of philosophical thought emphasized even more.

First of all it is worth pointing out that all the interpretations of this passage concur in stating that the idea of the sign proposed by Aristotle involves the setting up of a relationship of implication. The sign is seen as reflecting the implicative relationshship "p implies q", an understanding of the sign which is, as we have seen, fairly common and which operated also in other fields apart from philosophy.

On closer examination, however, and even more so in this definition, the sign may be seen to coincide with one of the terms of implication. Preti's version suggests that the sign coincides with the *second* term of implication, and therefore Aristotle's definition should be read as saying that "q is the sign of p". If this is the case, the definition represents the sign relationship as "if q, then p", and leads, when applied to inferential arguments, to the inversion of "p implies q" to give "q implies p".

It is this aspect in particular which led to the problematic nature of the idea of the sign and which gave rise to a fierce and complex debate among the post-Aristotelian schools of philosophy, even though no later explicit reference was made to Aristotle.

This type of inversion also seems to be present at the basis of the requirement, in order for the sign to be valid, of a more rigid implication between p and q than that given by material implication, for example. It would seem that Aristotle's definition already requires the condition "if not-q, not-p" ("q, or not-p"), which is precisely the kind of rigid implication which the Stoics later considered necessary for the sign to be valid.

Apart from the difficulty outlined above, it cannot be denied that both in the definition of the sign and the entire treatment of the sign made by Aristotle, there is an underlying ambiguity in the way of conceiving the two terms of the implicative relationship. On the one hand, the two terms are *facts* (or *properties*) (it is by no means coincidental that one of the central words of the definition is *tò prâgma* — "fact"). Aristotle's examples indeed seem to be the expression of facts or properties, for example: "A woman may be shown to be pregnant by the fact that she has milk in her breasts", where the sign is "having milk".

On the other hand, the sign is conceived of as a proposition in that it can be the premiss on which a syllogism is developed: "A sign, however, means a demonstrative premiss which is necessary or based on opinion" (*Prior Analytics*, II, 70 a, 6-7). In fact, the definition of the sign as proposition, which can form the premiss in an inferential argument, is central in

Aristotle. The basic role which he attributes to the *sēmeîon* is that of being one of the elements which furnish premisses for the type of syllogism known as enthymeme.

5.2.2 ENTHYMEME AND SIGNS

There are two complementary aspects present in the concept of enthymeme, and indeed post-Aristotelian tradition has often developed each of these separately. First of all, the enthymeme can be considered to be a reduced syllogism, since one of its premisses is not stated because it is held to be well-known or obvious.[10] The second important aspect of the enthymeme is that it was considered to be a syllogism which tended towards persuasion rather than demonstration. As such, it was not necessary for its premisses to be true; it was sufficient for them to be merely probable (*hōs epì tò polý*). Aristotle explicitly develops the second aspect of the enthymeme in *Prior Analytics* (II, 70 a, 9-10) and in *Rhetoric* (I, 1357 a, 30-32).

The sign, therefore, has its principal application in the context of persuasive discourse, that is rhetoric, where, in the form of a proposition, it is involved in the mechanisms of the enthymeme in which it carries out the role of "protasis", or premiss. Here, however, we find a first distinction between the idea of *sēmeîon* and that of *eikós* ("likely" or "probable"); these two terms are linked by the fact that each can figure as a premiss in enthymemes. What distinguishes the idea of *eikós* is essentially its character of probability, which links it firmly to opinion, thereby removing it and isolating it to a particularly fragile area of knowledge, beyond the possibility of scientific proof.

5.2.3 INFERENCE FROM THE CONSEQUENT

The situation of the idea of *sēmeîon* is quite different and much more complicated, for *sēmeîon* is not a simple category but a composite class which covers types having very different characteristics one from another. Before looking at these internal differences, it is perhaps useful to point out that there is a unifying factor for the various types of sign in contrast to the idea of *eikós*. In the case of the sign, "following" rather than probability forms the center of interest. Inferential reasoning, when based on signs, typically proceeds *ek tôn hepoménōn*, "by what follows", that is, it tends to infer cause from effect. It is for this reason that both correct and misleading applications of this type of reasoning are possible.

Aristotle develops the theory of reasoning by what follows in the *Sophistici Elenchi* (167 b, 1-5). It can lead to misleading conclusions, as when someone, having observed once that the ground was wet after it had rained, concluded that in general, if the ground is wet, then it has rained. Another example involves properties rather than events, as in the rain example: if someone, having discovered that honey had the property of being yellow, concludes that you can know something is honey from its being yellow; in this case there would be the risk of mistaking gall for honey (*ibid.*, 167 b, 6-8). Aristotle here decisively identifies this type of inference with the specific type of inference by signs: "In rhetorical discourse, in the same way, demonstrations taken from signs are based on what follows" (*ibid.*, 167 b, 8-9).

We can now go back to *Prior Analytics* and be in a better position to understand why Aristotle first of all proceeds to make a basic distinction between two types of sign: the *tekmérion*, a "necessary" or "irrefutable" sign,[11] and the general *sēmeion*, which has the opposite characteristics.

This distinction (which, as we shall see later, involves not merely two but three types of entity, for there are two types of not-necessary signs) in fact functions as an attempt on Aristotle's part to establish a typology of signs in order to establish the forms of the possible developments of the syllogism. There are three different ways that the syllogism can use the premiss which a sign expresses, each way corresponding to the possible position of the middle term in the different figures. In this way it is possible to have inferences which start from a sign in the first, second or third figure.

5.3 THE LOGICAL MECHANISM

5.3.1 THE *TEKMÉRION* AS SIGN IN THE FIRST FIGURE OF THE SYLLOGISM

Before going into the technical details of this distinction, it is important to note that the epistemological value which Aristotle assigns to the sign appearing in the first figure of a syllogism (that is, the *tekmérion*) is very different from that assigned to signs in the second and third figures (that is, the generic *sēmeîon*).

What happens in the two latter cases is that the typical illusion reported in the *Sophistici Elenchi* (167 b, 1-5) occurs. One believes that a possibility of conversion exists between the reason and the consequent, without this in fact being justified. In such cases, then, inference from consequences to causes is extremely hypothetical and dangerous.

In the first case, that of *tekmérion*, there is also a type of inference which begins with the consequence, as shown in the example "If a woman has milk in her breasts, then she is pregnant". Here "having milk" is both a consequence of being pregnant and a sign that a woman is pregnant. However, the important distinction here, with respect to the other two cases, is that there does indeed seem to be the possibility of conversion between cause and effect. Or rather, as Preti observes (1956, p.6), it seems that Aristotle is taking into account, in this case, a stricter type of implication than material implication.

Let us now look at how Aristotle develops the technical aspects of the three types of sign, beginning with the sign in the *first figure*:

For example, the proof that a woman is pregnant, because she has milk in her breasts, is by the first figure; for the middle term is "having milk". A stands for "being pregnant", B for "having milk", and C for "woman".

(*Prior Analytics*, II, 70 a, 12-16)[12]

If we translate Aristotle's reasoning into the standard illustrative scheme of the syllogism, we find:

1.	**A** "being pregnant"	is predicated of	**B** "a woman who has milk"
2.	**B** "having milk"	is predicated of	**C** "a woman"
3.	**A** "being pregnant"	is predicated of	**C** "a woman"

In this example, the sign "having milk" is not only the middle term in the syllogism scheme as shown above, but it is also the intermediate term from the point of view of the extension of the syllogism. Thus the relationships between the terms of the syllogism can be expressed in a diagram (Figure 5.2).

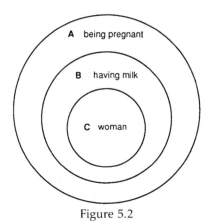

Figure 5.2

5.3.2 THE SECOND AND THIRD FIGURES OF THE SYLLOGISM AND *SĒMEÎON*

In the second and third figures, the middle term constitutes the link which enables the inference, but it does not occupy the central position either in the formula or in the extension. This means that, as Allan has said, the lable "major" or "minor" is arbitrary in the second or third figure since either of the two terms can be called major or minor (Allan, 1970, Chapt.10).

It is, however, quite certain that Aristotle adopts the point of view of extension in his treatment of premises. The secondary importance which he gives to the second and third figures is linked to this point of view.

Let us look now at the type of sign which appears in a syllogism based on the *second figure*: "If a woman is pale, then she is pregnant". Aristotle offers the following analysis:

> The proof that a woman is pregnant because she is pale is intended to be by the middle figure; for since pallor is a characteristic for women in pregnancy, and is associated with this particular woman, they suppose that she is proved to be pregnant. A stands for "pallor", B for "being pregnant" and C for "woman".
>
> (*Prior Analytics*, II, 70 a, 20-24)

We can form the following scheme in correspondence to this syllogism:

1.	**A**	is predicated of	**B**
	"being pale"		"someone who is pregnant"
2.	**A**	is predicated of	**C**
	"being pale"		"this woman"
3.	**B**	is predicated of	**C**
	"being pregnant"		"this woman"

In this case, the sign "being pale", which is also the middle term, has an extreme position and is shown simultaneously by the two terms "being pregnant" and "woman".

Aristotle condemns this inference as being invalid.[13]

As may be seen, this example represents the most typical case of inference drawn from consequences. The condemnation of such inference is found also in the corresponding passage in *Rhetoric* (I, 1357 b, 17-21): "If someone is panting, it is a sign that they have a fever". This kind of sign also produces a syllogism on the second figure in which the middle term, "panting", takes the major extreme position and is predicated of both the other terms, "have a fever" and "person".

The definition of this type of sign given in *Rhetoric* adds two interesting details which are not to be found in the definition given in *Prior Analytics*. The first of these is that the sign is refutable even if it turns out to be true (*kàn alēthès êi*): it thus becomes possible to build an inference which corresponds to the truth, even if only by chance. The accidental nature of the truth values comes about because the syllogism is *formally* incorrect, but nonetheless there are some cases in which it leads to *materially* true conclusions (cf. Plebe, 1966). The second interesting addition is that attention is drawn to the fact that this type of sign establishes a relationship "from the universal to the particular". This seems to occur because in such cases it is the extensionally major term which functions as middle term and because this is predicated first of a class and then of an individual.

Let us look now at a sign which appears in a syllogism based on the *third figure*. Aristotle gives the following example in *Prior Analytics*:

> The proof that the wise are good because Pittacus was good is by the third figure. A stands for "good", B for "the wise", and C for "Pittacus". Then it is true to predicate both A and C; only we do not state the latter, because we know it, whereas we formally state the former.

(Prior Analytics, II, 70 a, 16-20)

To put it more precisely, the sign is the protasis of the conditional phrase "If Pittacus is good, wise men are good". A syllogism can be constructed on this according to the following scheme:

1.	**A**	is predicated of	**C**
	"being good"		"Pittacus"
2.	**B**	is predicated of	**C**
	"being a wise man"		"Pittacus"
3.	**A**	is predicated of	**B**
	"being good"		"being a wise man"

In this example, the middle term is Pittacus, which takes the position of the minor term when extended.

Aristotle also condemns as refutable (*lýsimoi*) syllogisms constructed on this type of sign. He states that they remain refutable (like those constructed on the second figure) even if they should happen to lead to an accidentally true conclusion. The parallel passage in *Rhetoric* (I, 1357 b, 10-11) states that this type of syllogism establishes a "from the particular to the universal" relationship. In this case too, it is the position of the middle term, which when extended becomes the minor term, that suggests such a determination, for the reasoning here moves from the property of a particular individual to reach the conclusion that such a property is a characteristic of an entire class to which that individual belongs.

5.3.3 CLASSIFICATION

Having set out the distinction between the three types of sign according to the position of the middle term in each of the figures, Aristotle goes on to make a general recapitulation in which he consolidates the terminological distinction and restates the comparative cognitive strength of each type of sign. The name *tekmérion* ("sure indication" or "proof") is used only for the signs which actually have the position of middle term (that is, those which are the middle term even in an extensional sense and on which a syllogism is formed in the first figure). The generic term *sēmeîon* is kept for those signs which have the extreme position within the syllogism (on which, therefore, an inference is developed in the second or third figure) (cf. *Prior Analytics*, II, 70 b, 1-6).

With respect to what we have said above, we must make a small clarification of the idea of *éndoxon*, which is a particularly striking characteristic of syllogisms based on *tekmérion*. In *Topics*, Aristotle states that the most reliable dialectical syllogisms are those which derive from premises which are *éndoxa*. These propositions "are those which commend themselves to all, or to the majority, or to the wise—that is, to all of the wise or to the majority or to the most famous and distinguished of them" (*Topics*, I, 100 b, 21-23). These are in fact the conditions which permit the dialectical confirmation of a hypothesis (cf. Viano, 1958a).

The corresponding passage in the *Rhetoric* gives an analogous classification which distinguishes between the necessary sign (*anankaîon*), which corresponds to *tekmérion*, and the weak sign (*mē anankaion*), which corresponds to the generic *sēmeîon*.[14] This latter sign is further subdivided into "signs-which-appear-in-the-from-universal-to-particular" relationships (that is, signs in the second figure of the syllogism) and "signs-which-appear-in-from-particular-to-universal" relationships (that is, signs in the third figure of the syllogism). Aristotle's classification of signs could thus be set out as shown in Figure 5.3.

5.4 A SPECIAL TYPE OF
NON-LINGUISTIC SIGN: PHYSIOGNOMY

Aristotle's particular conception of the sign as a thing or fact which serves to draw the attention of a knowing subject to another thing or fact allows importance to be given to a type of knowledge which is obtained independently of verbal language. In this way, non-linguistic sign systems appear to be particularly important in Aristotle's theory of signs.

In *Prior Analytics*, after setting out the theory of the sign, Aristotle offers an interesting, yet curious, application of this theory to a very particular type of sign, the signs of physiognomy. The example he gives demonstrates how it is possible to tell a character trait from a visual sign, in this case the large extremities of the lion are taken as a sign of its courage.

Aristotle is concerned with two points in particular. First of all he is attempting to acquire knowledge of a psychological nature by taking as his point of departure a fact perceived through the senses. He is also trying to establish the closest possible link between two facts which experience shows him to be associated (in this case, large extremities and courage), as a guarantee of the reliability of such knowledge. In order to prove the validity of his physiognomy example, Aristotle has to make three assumptions:[15] (i) that "natural affections transform body and mind"; (ii) that there is a single sign for a single fact, that is, of the affection of the mind which is to be discovered; (iii) that every genus has its own affection and its own sign (*ídion . . . sēmeîon*).

It is clear that Aristotle is attempting to rationalize and invest with

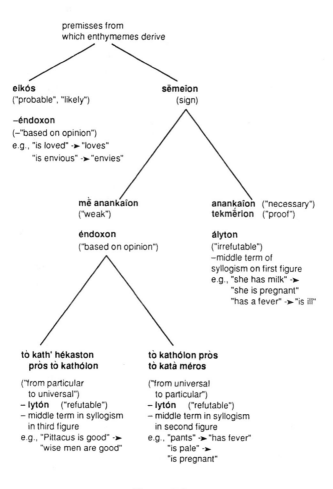

Figure 5.3

philosophical dignity a subject which more properly belonged to the field of augury and divination. However, here it is no longer the god who assures the correspondence between an element which can be perceived from physical appearance and something which belongs to the realm of the invisible (be it the character of a person or, more generally, the fate awaiting that person). In Aristotle's opinion, the correspondence between a physical element and the inner make-up of an individual is due to the fact that any type of affection transforms both body and mind, as happens, for example, when people learn music and thus transform not only their physical ability to play a musical instrument, but also their inner sensitivity.

As was the case with augury, this subject also carries the risk of falling into ambiguity. The second and third assumptions are introduced precisely to eliminate this possibility. Ambiguity could result in two different sets of circumstances: (i) if many signs refer to a single affection (a situation which we could compare closely to synonymy): the only epistemological solution here is to assume that signs are exclusive, that is, that a single fact is indicated by a single sign; (ii) if a genus has many affections so that it is not possible to be sure which affection the sign is referring to (a situation which we could closely compare to homonymy): here Aristotle proposes to resolve the problem by establishing the affection which belongs most appropriately to each genus and its sign so that the sign refers uniquely and exclusively to its appropriate affection.

By establishing the three assumptions dealt with above as a preliminary measure, Aristotle is able to make physiognomy into a science. Indeed, following these assumptions, it is possible to establish that in the case of the lion, large extremities are the sign of courage (*Prior Analytics*, II, 70 b, 16-17).

Up to this point, Aristotle's reasoning can be seen to be based on what might be termed a deductive level. It is possible, however, to detect here another scheme of argument which could be carried out before the rules of deductive argument had been formulated. We can imagine a moment when it is observed that a certain affection, courage, is associated with the genus of lions; at the same time, it is observed that the characteristic of having large extremities is associated with lions. At this point, the hypothesis can be formulated that the sign of courage is represented by the possession of large extremities.

The logical process involved in this type of reasoning can be represented as follows:

1. "being courageous"	is predicated of	"lions"
2. "having large extremities"	is predicated of	"lions"
3. "being courageous"	is predicated of	"those who have large extremities"

A third-figure syllogism—as this one is—according to Peirce constitutes an induction, even though of such a "timid" type that it practically loses the nature of genuine induction (cf. Peirce, 2, 730). Such a syllogism would have a pronounced hypothetical nature.

However, Aristotle does not in practice follow this line of reasoning because he cannot accept as valid from the logical point of view a procedure which is devoid of any guarantees of truth. He is therefore obliged to fix this (let it not be forgotten, fairly aleatory) sign of courage into a scheme which is once again deductive. To put it another way, the observation of the association between courage and large extremities must be transformed into a strict, invariant link. Aristotle thus aims the whole force of his argument to demonstrate that whenever courage is found, it is found in the presence of large extremities and *vice versa*. In technical terms, the ideal situation, the arrangement offering the greatest certainty, occurs when there is a condition of *conversion (antistréphein)* between what functions as a sign and what it refers to, or rather, when the extension of the first term is precisely equal to that of the second. We thus have the necessity (which is purely logical and by no means semiotic) that a single sign refer to a single affection, for it is only in this way that conversion between the two terms is possible.

At this point the problem of hypothesizing a sign of courage becomes instead that of finding between "courage" and the "genus of lions" some element of mediation which the latter invariantly possesses.

The element of mediation, which seems also to justify the association, is "having large extremities"; this thus becomes the sign on which the following scheme of deductive syllogism is constructed (*Prior Analytics*, II, 70 a, 32-38):

1.   **A**   is predicated of   **B**
      "being courageous"   "those who have large extremities"
2.   **B**   is predicated of   **C**
   "those who have large extremities"   "lions"
3.   **A**   is predicated of   **C**
      "being courageous"   "lions"

What Aristotle fails to point out, however, is that, as we have seen, the beginnings of the deduction itself are rooted in a previous inference of a hypothetical nature. This example is however extremely interesting in that previous to the presentation of the formal scheme, attention is concentrated on establishing the criteria which are necessary to say that something is a sign of something else. The statement that something is the sign of something else, in fact, is only possible by formulating a hypothesis which can only later be verified deductively.

5.5 THE UNDERMINING OF KNOWLEDGE GAINED THROUGH SIGNS

To be perfectly honest, Aristotle displays a pronounced lack of faith in the reliability of knowledge obtained from signs. In Aristotle's conception of the sign, even when there is a link of necessity between the two terms of the sign, knowledge of the unknown term seems to be gained from external sources, without the cause being understood.

In *Posterior Analytics* (I, 75 a, 28-36), Aristotle contrasts reasoning *based on essence* with reasoning *based on signs*. Here the latter is defined as reasoning which is based on accidental determinations. It therefore follows that only with the first type of reasoning is it possible to attain knowledge of causes. This does not, however, mean that knowledge based on signs is totally extraneous. For in certain cases, those which involve necessary signs, it is possible to trace the cause back from the sign. For example, the observation of the fact that a woman has milk in her breasts makes it possible to trace the cause of this fact, that is, that she is pregnant; in the same way, the noting of a high fever in someone allows us to trace the cause of this fever to an illness. However, this type of reasoning cannot produce a true fact-based knowledge, which can be obtained only by *starting from causes*. Reasoning based on signs starts not from causes but from effects, and it enables merely the affirmation of a fact—that is, the *hóti* ("that")—without leading to the understanding of the cause—that is, the *dióti* ("why").

In Chapter 13 of *Posterior Analytics*, Aristotle underlines the fact that truly scientific demonstration does not consist in the discovery or conclusion of causes, but rather *is* scientific precisely because it *begins from* causes. Here he makes the distinction between "knowledge that something is" and "knowledge why something is".

Aristotle does accord the *hóti* sciences a certain right to exist, but they are considered to be irretrievably inferior since they rest on facts without ever reaching knowledge of the necessary and hardly reaching even knowledge of the universal. But what exactly *are* these *hóti* sciences? From the examples Aristotle provides, it would seem that they are pre-eminently evidential sciences, which are based on signs and which have a strongly hypothetical nature (in contrast to sciences which have a deductive character). Among other examples, Aristotle mentions the case of astronomy (*astrología*), which is a term used both by a certain nautical science (*nautiké*) and by a science based on mathematical principles (*mathēmatiké*). According to Aristotle, only the latter is a science of causes. In the same way, medicine is contrasted to geometry. For circular wounds, for example, it is up to the doctor to know *that* they will heal more slowly, while it is the responsibility of the expert in geometry to know *why* this is so.

We thus have medicine and navigational science ranged against mathematics and geometry. Aristotle's feelings about the worth of signs and sign-based knowledge could hardly be clearer!

It may be interesting to observe how Aristotle manages to develop a *hóti* reasoning and a *dióti* reasoning within the same science. There is a two-fold difference which distinguishes these two types of reasoning. A *hóti* reasoning is made, first of all, when the syllogism is based not on immediate premisses (which, in Aristotelian epistemology, means assuming the first and the closest cause); *hóti* reasoning is used also when, even though based on immediate causes, the deduction comes not from the term which indicates the cause of a fact, but rather from the best-known of the two terms (both of which refer to the fact). In other words, the specific difference of the *dióti* syllogism is once again that it goes from the cause to the effect and not from the effect to the cause.

Aristotle's example for this is extremely interesting. Given that there is a certain relationship between the non-twinkling of planets and their closeness to the earth, Aristotle shows how it is possible by using these two terms to develop two different types of reasoning of different epistemological value.

On the one hand, it is possible to deduce the closeness of the planets from the fact that they do not twinkle ("If they do not twinkle, they are close"). In this case the reasoning is of the *hóti* type, and it is possible to observe that in this context the "non-twinkling" is typically a sign of the fact which becomes the conclusion, that is, the fact of their "closeness" to the earth.

The syllogism constructed on the sign does not begin from the cause of the non-twinkling of planets (which consists in their closeness), but begins rather from the effect, which is taken as a middle term, in order to reach the cause. It is even possible that the cause is never really known.

Aristotle then offers, in opposition to this type of reasoning, a type which deduces the non-twinkling of planets from their closeness. This then becomes a *dióti* reasoning which shows the reason why something occurs or is, since it takes the cause precisely as a cause of the effect. Formally this occurs when it is indeed the term which indicates the cause which is taken as the middle term.

Between syllogisms of the *dióti* and the *hóti* types there is therefore a relationship of inverse symmetry. One merely has to invert the terms of the latter to obtain the former. Nonetheless, this is not always possible, as the commentator Philoponus notes:

> It is often necessary that when the cause is given also the effect is given, whilst it is not necessary that when the effect is given the cause too is given: thus the fact of being pale is not necessarily the effect of being pregnant, but if a woman is pregnant, she is always pale: this same fact can have many different causes.

> (Philoponus, in *Posterior Analytics*, Wallies, 69)

The casual nature of the inferential procedure typical of the sign (from pallor to pregnancy) is here underlined by hypothesizing the case that an effect can have multiple causes. In such a situation, according to Philoponus, a true *hóti* syllogism could not be constructed, but only a *dióti* syllogism. However, Aristotle himself had foreseen the case whereby an effect could have different causes,[16] and had noted that this made the tracing of cause from effect difficult and in addition fraught with the risk of casual coincidences.

However, according to Philoponus, it would be possible to observe the opposite case, that is, the case whereby it is possible only to make a *hóti* reasoning. It is possible to trace back from the fact that a woman is pregnant (as effect and sign) to the fact that she has had sexual intercourse (as cause). However, the converse is not necessary, because being pregnant does not always necessarily, that is, inevitably, follow sexual intercourse (cf. Philoponus, in *Posterior Analytics*, Wallies, 169-71).

There is one last characteristic which distinguishes *hóti* reasoning from *dióti* reasoning. *Hóti* reasoning is typical of the simple, nonspecialist observer of phenomena, whereas *dióti* reasoning is the realm of the scientist (*Posterior Analytics*, II, 79 a, 2-3).

It can thus be seen that Aristotle gives little epistemological value to evidential sciences and signs in general, because in his theoretical conception of science there is room neither for research nor hypothesis, on which a semiotic conception of knowledge would, on the contrary, insist as a basis. Le Blond puts the case quite succinctly:

> [For Aristotle, science] is not primarily *research* but *possession*; the *Analytics* give hardly any guidance on research: they describe completed knowledge, which passes from causes down to effects and coincides perfectly with the dynamism of things—obviously a singularly confident notion, one which gives prime importance to the perfect knowledge of reality.
>
> (Le Blond, 1939, p.105; our translation)

5.6 DEDUCTION AND ABDUCTION

It would be a mistake to believe that Aristotle's theoretical position outlined above was followed religiously in the methods of research used, for example, in his scientific works. It would also be a mistake to accept categorically Aristotle's assertion of the absolutely deductive nature of the *dióti* sciences. As Umberto Eco has shown (1983, p.198), finding the *why* of a certain phenomenon for Aristotle meant finding a good middle term which would explain that phenomenon. However, this middle term, in some cases, could be rather daring and sophisticated and not correspond to any already ascertained knowledge. It could thus be what could be termed in Peirce's sense a "hypothesis".

The reasoning adopted by Aristotle in his treatise *De Partibus Animalium* is extremely revealing in this respect. When dealing with animals with horns, Aristotle finds several "surprising facts" which require explanation. For example, (i) all horned animals have only one row of teeth, that is they have no upper incisors (633 b–664 a), (ii) all horned animals have four stomachs (674 a-b), (iii) all four-stomached animals have no upper incisors (674 a), etc.

Aristotle is faced here with the problem of explaining why horned animals do not have upper incisors. As Eco emphasizes, Aristotle "must figure out a Rule so that, if the Result he wants to explain was a case of this Rule, the Result would no longer be surprising" (1983, p.201). In fact, according to Peirce, when an odd or strange circumstance is explained by supposing it to constitute a case of a certain general rule, we are dealing with hypothesis or abduction.

Aristotle's reasoning proceeds in precisely these terms. He supposes that, in the case in question, hard material was probably deflected from the upper incisors to the head in order to form horns. In turn, the lack of upper incisors causes the development of a fourth stomach and also serves as the middle term from which a further syllogism can be developed.

Given in terms of the syllogism (in the formalization made by Peirce, which is then adopted by Eco), the first line of reasoning can be traced as follows:

Rule = All deflecting animals (that is, animals which have deflected hard material from the mouth to the head) have no upper incisors.
Case = All horned animals have deflected hard material.
Result = All horned animals lack upper incisors.

The "deflection of hard material" is simultaneously the middle term of the syllogism and the explanation of the phenomenon. Eco draws attention to the very pertinent fact that the effort required to explain hypothetically *why* a phenomenon is as it is, by constructing a strictly *deductive* form, in reality differs not at all from what Peirce calls *abduction*. Both cases involve working on hypotheses which enable "surprising" phenomena to be explained.

What Eco suggests is that, below and prior to the deductive level which Aristotle takes into consideration, there lies an abductive level, which he refuses to recognize but which he nonetheless uses when he has to formulate scientific definitions. Defining the *why* of a surprising fact "means to figure out a hierarchy of causal links through a sort of hypothesis that can be validated only when it gives rise to a deductive syllogism which acts as a forecast for further tests." (*ibid.*, p.203).

In the final analysis, it is precisely this failure to recognize the preliminary inferential movement which prevents Aristotle from recognizing the hypothetical nature of science and, at the same time, the usefulness of sign-based knowledge.

SIX

Theory of Language and Semiotics in the Stoic Philosophers

6.0 INTRODUCTION

The Stoic school of philosophy was responsible for the most rigorous and profound reflection on semiotics which is to be found in ancient philosophy. However, like Aristotle, the Stoics focused their research on two very distinct areas of thought. First of all we can find elements of semiotic interest in their theory of language, which involved an analysis of the relationship between language, thought and reality (corresponding to the terms "signifier", "signified" and "external object"), and then also in their theory of the propositional "sign", which is related to their theory of inference.

These two aspects of Stoic philosophy come together, as we shall see below, in their common link with the *lektón*, an entity which held special status in Stoic thought. At the basis of the concept of *lektón* lies the particular dialectic between the entities which share the property of being "bodies" (*sốmata*) and those which are, in contrast, incorporeal (*asômata*). To be more precise, it can be said that Stoic ontology takes into consideration only those entities which have the characteristic of being three-dimensional objects and of possessing in addition some persistence through time. These alone are bodies, and only these are considered to be existent. However, both in the theory of language and in the theory of the propositional sign, incorporeal entities such as *lektá* are taken into consideration along with corporeal entities.

Before preceding any further, or going into greater depth on Stoic ontology, it is necessary to clear two possible misunderstandings from the floor. The first concerns the fate which awaits incorporeal entities; rather than simply being relegated to the sphere of non-existence, they are accorded instead a "derivative existence" (cf. Long, 1971a, pp. 89-90). The second possible misunderstanding concerns the very notion of body. Contrary to what we might expect because of modern ideas of body, "bodies" for the Stoics could also be qualities, inasmuch as they were considered to be matter in a certain state. The properties of a certain individual consist in states or modes of the being of such an individual, and their existence depends on the existence of this individual. If the individual exists, that individual's properties are existing dispositions of matter (cf. Rist, 1969, pp.52-55). What we have at this point is an ontology centered on the idea of "particular", which is seen as a material object with definite shape, defined as the sufficient and necessary condition for its existence. The shape is the characteristic element of an object, what makes it identifiable as such (cf. Long, 1971a, p.76).

The semiotico-linguistic theory of the Stoics has its roots and develops within the terms of these ontological assumptions. The need for a theory of meaning stems precisely from the problems involved in the identification of "particular" and is connected to a theory of perception. It must be remembered that the Stoics believed that images (*phantasíai*) produced on the mind by external objects gave rise to true perception if they reproduced the exact configurations of those objects.¹ Images play a very important role in the Stoic theory of meaning, as indeed they did in Aristotle's theory of meaning.

Another important element to keep in mind when dealing with this area of Stoic philosophy is that one of the ways of identifying a "particular" is by identifying it linguistically. Thus A's ability to communicate with B that he or she is talking about X, and B's ability to indicate to A that the reference has been understood, become fundamental.

6.1 THEORY OF LANGUAGE

6.1.1 THE SEMIOTIC TRIANGLE

The passage from Sextus Empiricus which contains the basic outline of the Stoic theory of language appears in the context of a conflict of opinions about truth. It is important to point out here that, for the Stoics, a theory of truth — that is, the search for a basis on which to construct the verification of propositions — cannot be developed independently from a conception of the structure of the world and of what can be said about it.

The passage from Sextus Empiricus is as follows:

> True and false have been variously located in what is signified (*tò sēmainómenon*), in speech (*phōnē*), and in the motion of thought. The Stoics opted for the first of these, claiming that three things are linked together: what is signified, that which signifies (*tò sēmaînon*) and the object of reference (*tò tynchánon*). That which signifies is speech (for example, the word "Dion"), what is signified is the specific state of affairs (*autò tò prâgma*) indicated by the spoken word and which we grasp as coexistent with (*paryphistámenon*) our thought but which the barbarians do not understand although they hear the sound; the object of reference is the external existent, that is, Dion himself. Of these, two are bodies, speech and the object of reference. But the state of affairs is not a body but a *lektón*, which is true or false.

> (*Adversus Mathematicos*, VIII, 11-12)²

Based on what Sextus Empiricus reports, it would seem that also for the Stoics the phenomenon of signification can be schematized in the form of a triangle (Figure 6.1). As the figure shows, the terms "signifier" and "signified" are used here (as they are in Saussure's theory), but not the term "sign".

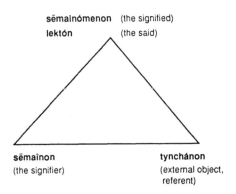

sēmainómenon (the signified)
lektón (the said)

sēmaînon (the signifier)

tynchánon (external object, referent)

Figure 6.1

As in Aristotle, the idea of *sēmeîon* belongs to a different, not strictly linguistic, sphere of the theory. It is worth noting here too that a very particular example is used, that of a proper noun or name.

However, even though the use of three terms to express signification (one of these terms being the external object, which strictly speaking is outside of language) recalls Aristotle, the correspondence between the two models is only partial. Only the first and the third term, that is, the signifier and the object, can be directly compared in the two triangles.

6.1.2 LEKTÓN AS "STATEMENT"

The term at the apex of the triangle, first called *sēmainómenon* and then *lektón*, represents a unique case. Especially in its second denomination, it represents a term which is peculiar to Stoic philosophy of language and refers to a complex yet extremely interesting concept. A first indication of its special nature can be seen by contrasting it with Aristotle's terminology. At the apex of the triangle of signification, Aristotle had placed psychological entities, which were considered to be identical for everyone. The Stoic *lektón*, as the passage from Sextus Empiricus implies, is completely different: barbarians, even when hearing the sounds and seeing the object, cannot understand it.

As Todorov (1977, pp. 17-18) demonstrates, the basic difference between the concepts lies in the fact that, while the entity taken into consideration by Aristotle is located at the level of the mind of the speakers, that considered by the Stoics is located directly at the level of language. Todorov interprets the *lektón* as the capacity of the first element to designate the third element. This interpretation depends heavily on the fact that the example used by Sextus Empiricus is a proper noun for which, though it has the same capacity of designation as other nouns, there is some doubt as to whether it actually has meaning; in fact the usual conclusion is that it does not.

Barbarians certainly hear the sound sequence |Dion| and see ||Dion||, but they are not capable of connecting the sound to its object of reference. Understanding, then (as happens for Greeks with respect to this example), consists precisely in the perception of the connection between the spoken word and the object to which it refers. Long (1971a, p.77) also identifies *lektón* with this connection, though in the sense that it operates as the statement which an utterance makes with respect to some object. In this case, the more appropriate translation of *lektón* would be "what is said", as such an expression covers both the notion of "judgement" and that of "the state of affairs signified by a word or set of words".[3]

The idea that *lektá* could operate as "affirmations about objects" may be seen in a passage from Seneca (*Epistulae Morales*, 117, 13), which sets out a triadic scheme of signification analogous to that given by Sextus Empiricus, but using a proposition (|Cato walks|) where he had used only a name (|Dion|). Seneca draws attention to the distinction between the object of reference, which is a material object—in this case, Cato—and the assertion about this object (|Cato walks|), which is an "incorporeal". This assertion is the *lektón*, and Seneca proposes three different Latin translations of the term: *enuntiatum* ("utterance"), *effatum* ("affirmation"), *dictum* ("assertion").

It is easier to see how the predicate "true" or "false" can be applied to Seneca's example, a proposition, than to that used by Sextus Empiricus.[4] Only *lektá* which make up a complete proposition (i.e., a clause) can be true or false.[5]

6.1.3 THE RELATIONSHIP BETWEEN *LEKTÁ* AND THOUGHT

In Aristotle's model of signification, linguistic expressions are symbols of psychological states (*pathēmata en têi psychêi*) and/or thoughts (*noēmata*). In this way there is no clear distinction between the notion of "meaning" and the notion of "thought". The same conception reappears in Ogden and Richards' well-known theory in the present century (cf. Ogden and Richards, 1936, p.37), which produces a semiotic triangle with the notion of "thought" at the apex.

The conception held by the Stoics is quite different. Passages from both Sextus Empiricus and Diogenes give evidence of the fact that the notion of meaning was quite distinct from the notion of thought, even though there was a certain type of relationship between them. The passage from Sextus Empiricus reads:

> The Stoics held as a common view that true and false are in the *lektón* and they

say that *lektón* is that which is (subsists, *hyphistamenon*) correspondent to a rational presentation (*logikē phantasía*), and a rational presentation is one in which what is presented (*phantasthén*) can be shown forth in speech.

(*Adversus Mathematicos*, VIII, 70)[6]

A passage in Diogenes (*Vitae*, VII, 63) expresses precisely the same idea and uses the same terms. From these two passages we can then see that the Stoics operated a clear distinction between *lektá*, which represent the level of "meaning", and "rational presentations" (*logikaì phantasíai*), which we could define as forms of intellectual activity, or thoughts. The latter entities are peculiar to the human species[7] and can, if necessary, be expressed in words (this is what the adjective *logikaí* refers to).

It is also possible to see from these two passages that the two terms, *lektón* and thought, are put in relationship one to the other. Long (1971a, p.82) makes the following comment on the passage from Sextus Empiricus: "I take this difficult passage to mean that *lektón* is defined as the objective content of acts of thinking (*nóēsis*), or, what comes to the same thing in Stoicism, the sense of significant discourse." Before looking more closely at this latter assertion, let us examine for a moment the former comment.

It would seem that the relationship established between *lektón* and the activity of thought is such that it functions as the content or result of such activity. However, this new relationship—indicated in these passages from Diogenes and Sextus Empiricus—introduces an extra element with respect to what Sextus Empiricus says elsewhere (*Adversus Mathematicos*, VIII, 11-12), when he relates *lektón* with the signifier expression (that is, with the *sēmaînon*). In fact, if *lektón* is now defined as something which exists in conformity with a rational presentation, it is clear that the accent has been shifted from the previous relationship with the activity of thought.

This shift of accent, apart from demonstrating an apparent contradiction or a false dilemma, has resulted in the difference of opinion and interpretation of ancient commentators and modern scholars of Stoicism alike. Mignucci (1965, pp.92-93) shows how *lektá*, because these are incorporeals, "cannot be split from something corporeal which in some way provides a support for them and allows them to have their expressibility". The problem remains of establishing whether what provides support for *lektá* are (i) sounds of the voice; or (ii) the activity of the mind which thinks them. The first of Sextus Empiricus' two definitions[8] would suggest solution (i), whereas the second,[9] and also the definition given by Diogenes,[10] would suggest solution (ii). In the same way, some modern scholars, such as Mates,[11] declare that it is words which provide support for *lektá*, while Zeller[12] and Bréhier[13] take the other point of view.

As indicated above, however, this is in fact a false dilemma and certainly cannot be resolved by means of philology, for the texts contain an equal quantity of "proofs" for each point of view. What we have to do here is to consider a double underlying assumption which seems to be at work in the Stoic theory.

On the one hand, the presence of significant discourse implies intellectual activity, in the absence of which it would not be possible to have meaning; on the other hand, any result of intellectual activity needs the significant sounds of the voice for objective expression. It is therefore possible to draw these consequences from the fact that *lektá* are defined both as the content of rational presentations and as meanings of words. This indicates the need to postulate a strict connection between the content of the representative activity of the mind and its having meaning by means of words. The two terms cannot, therefore, be considered separately from one another.[14] At this point, the full meaning of Long's second comment becomes clear, for we have in fact reached it here: the meaning of significant discourse and the objective content of acts of thinking must be considered to be the same thing.

Long supports this conclusion by reference to another passage from Diogenes Laertius (*Vitae*, VIII, 49-50) which states that the criterion for truth[15] is given by the "presentation" (*phantasía*). Diogenes explains that *phantasía* has a primary role in that it is not possible, without it, to apprehend some of the fundamental processes of knowledge, such as assent (*synkatáthesis*), apprehension (*katálēpsis*) and the act of thinking (*nóēsis*): "For presentation comes first, then thought (*diánoia*), which is able to speak (*eklalētikḗ*), expresses in speech (*lógōi*) what it experiences as a result of the presentation" (translated by Long, 1971a, p.83).

This passage from Diogenes is important because it revives the Platonic notion[16] of thought as "internal speech".[17] This serves to demonstrate that there exists for the Stoics a basic identity between the processes of thought and the processes of linguistic communication. The fact that the cognitive processes are based on *phantasía* highlights the role that mental images play in the linguistic theory of meaning.

6.2 THE THEORY OF THE SIGN

6.2.1 *LEKTÓN* AND THE THEORY OF THE SIGN

The *lektón* not only has a central importance in the Stoic theory of language but is equally fundamental to the Stoic theory of the sign and in a certain way serves as a mediating factor between the two theories. For the Stoics, signs (*sēmeîa*) are above all *lektá* in that they are made up of propositions.

This means that there is a "rightful" fusing of the doctrine of language and the doctrine of signs in Stoic semiotics, as Umberto Eco has pointed out (1984a, pp.31-32). As Eco says, "In order to have signs, propositions must be formulated, and the propositions must be organized according to a logical syntax which is reflected and made possible by the linguistic syntax." It must be remembered, however, that the Stoics do not reach the point of saying that words are signs (Augustine is the first to make such a statement), and there remains a lexical difference between the *sēmaînon/ sēmainómenon* pair and *sēmeîon*.

Nonetheless, the fact that signs are *lektá* is revealing, given the need which the Stoics felt to translate the non-verbal sign into linguistic terms and to link, even if only in an indirect and implicit manner, the two theories.

Sextus Empiricus gives the following definition of the sign:

> The Stoics, in attempting to establish the conception of the sign, state that a sign is a proposition (*axíōma*) that is the antecedent (*prokathēgoúmenon*) in a sound conditional (*en hygieî synēmménōi*), which serves to reveal the consequent (*ekkalyptikòn toû légontos*). And they define the proposition as a complete *lektón* that is assertoric (i.e., true or false) in itself; a sound conditional is one which does not begin with truth and end with a false consequent. . . . The antecedent, they say, is the precedent clause in a conditional which begins in truth and ends in truth. And it serves to reveal the consequent, since in the conditional "If this woman has milk in her breasts, she has conceived", the clause "If this woman has milk in her breasts" seems to be evidential (*dēlōtikón*) of the clause "she has conceived".
>
> (*Outlines of Pyrrhonism*, II, 104-106)[18]

Later on, we shall return to the various problems which this passage presents. For the moment it is sufficient to stress that the passage defines the sign as a complete *lektón*, that is, as a proposition which is placed in a relation of implication to another *lektón*, that is, to another proposition, according to the scheme $p \supset q$.

It should be noted that, as in Aristotle, the interest of the sign lies in the knowledge which it makes accessible, the point of view remains strictly epistemological and the sign belongs to a field which is quite distinct from both logic and semantics in the pure sense. The sign is not every proposition which appears as an antecedent in a true conditional, but only the kind of proposition which allows the consequent to be discovered (that is, it gives access to new knowledge). We shall return to this point later.

Another very important point to be noted is that, while the Stoics consider the sign from the same point of view as Aristotle, the logical setting in which they place it is totally different. It is generally agreed that Aristotle uses a logic of classes while the Stoics introduce propositional logic. The effect of their innovation is that attention is shifted (i) from the substance to events (cf. Todorov, 1977, p.21), with respect to the ontological point of view; (ii) from nouns/adjectives, which function as the predicate, to propositions, with respect to linguistic expression. It is in fact possible to notice a certain reluctance in Aristotle to deal with substance and properties as signs. What can be treated as signs are the facts and events expressed by propositions. Even though he does not note the difference, Aristotle does in fact give some examples of signs where events and not substance are considered (for example, the sign dealt with in *Rhetoric*, I, 1357 b, 16-18: "If she has milk in her breasts, she has given birth "). However, the theory of the sign has only a very marginal part in Aristotle's philosophy. The sign is relegated to the process of the syllogism (where it constitutes a premiss) and is limited to the field of rhetorical-dialectic procedures unless it is a *tekmérion*, or a necessary sign. There is no place for the *sēmeîon* in true science, which is founded on perfect syllogisms.

In post-Aristotelian schools of philosophy, the position of the sign changes radically. Inference from signs moves out from its beginnings in rhetoric and dialectic to science in general and even reaches the highest levels of philosophy. Both the Stoics and the Epicureans see the sign as representing the *standard* procedure for the passage from the known to the unknown.

According to Preti (1956, pp.7-8), an important link between Aristotle and the later schools with respect to the theory of the sign is provided by Nausiphanes, a follower of Democritus and one of the teachers of Epicurus. Although only fragments of his *Tripod*[19] survive, it is possible to reconstruct the essential points of his theory which link the two traditions. For Nausiphanes, philosophical discourse (which for Aristotle is based on syllogism) and rhetorical discourse (based on enthymeme) in fact have the same logical structure. In both cases it is necesssary to distinguish between the *"consequence"* (*akólouthon*), the "premiss" (*homologoúmenon*) and "what derives from the premiss" (*tínōn lēphthéntōn tì symbaínei*—the syllogism?). In both types of discourse the problem is to start from things present or manifest (*hypárchonta*) and to reach in a methodical way things which are invisible or obscure. The passage between these is achieved through the method of *akolouthía*, "the relation of consequentiality or following", of implication or entailment,[20] which is common to both philosophy and rhetoric.

As can be seen from what Sextus Empiricus says,[21] the possibility of passing from things evident (*apò tō̂n enargō̂n*) to the understanding of things obscure (*ádēla*) by means of the sign acting as a relationship of *akolouthía* represents the central point of Stoic doctrine (as it does of the doctrine of all those whom Sextus Empiricus terms "the Dogmatists"). But this is not all. A further demonstration of the centrality of semiotics is given by the fact that proof is considered to be a sign.[22] This last fact illustrates how philosophy of science has been condensed into semiotics and stands as confirmation of the tendency of the post-Aristotelian schools to reduce or transform the syllogism into implicative inference.

6.2.2.1 *Sign types: (A) "common" and "particular"*
The terminological distinction between *tekmérion* and *sēmeîon* disappears in Stoic semiotics. The former term is no longer used, and all signs are desig-

nated *sēmeîa*. A plausible explanation of this development would be the fact that the Stoics no longer talk about the syllogism or its division into terms (a division which undergirded the syllogism) when talking about signs.

However, another type of distinction does appear, in the opposition of "common sign" (*koinòn sēmeîon*) and "particular sign" (*ídion*). This distinction was not exclusively Stoic but belonged to Hellenistic philosophical *koiné* on which even schools of radically divergent thought concurred. A clear definition of the two types of sign is given in Philodemus' first-century semiotic treatise, *De Signis*:

> a sign is *common* (*koinón*) for no other reason than that it can exist whether the unperceived object (*tò ádēlon*) exists or not. We say that the person who believes this particular man to be good because he is rich is using an unsound and common sign, since many who are rich are found to be bad and many good. Therefore the *particular* (*ídion*) sign, if indeed it is cogent (*anankastikón*), cannot exist otherwise than with the thing that we say necessarily belongs with it, the non-evident object whose sign it is.

> (Philodemus, *De Signis*, I, 1-17)[23]

Almost all the post-Aristotelian schools consider the common sign not to be valid and accept only the particular sign. It is clear from Philodemus' definition that the particular sign has the characteristic of being "cogent or necessary" (*anankastikón*), a characteristic which is not shared by the common sign. It would thus seem that the *particular sign* is parallel to Aristotle's *necessary sign*, which required a necessary connection with the object to which it referred. The common sign is defined as the type of sign which refers to something existent, of which it is thus the sign, but which can also not refer to anything. On the basis of the example given by Philodemus, inferring the moral worth of individuals from their material wealth (an inference which works in some cases and not in others), it would seem possible to relate the common sign to Aristotle's signs in the second and third figures. For Aristotle, it was *possible* to infer from a woman's pallor that she had given birth (her pallor is a sign in the second figure) or that wise men are good from the fact that Pythacus is good (sign in the third figure), but these signs did not always, invariably, hold true.

We come therefore to an interesting conclusion. While for Aristotle, non-necessary (or weak) signs had no scientific validity but could be used in an epistemologically lower sphere such as rhetoric, the realm of opinion, for in the post-Aristotelian schools there was no place at all in any kind of knowledge for inference based on non-necessary, or weak, signs.

6.2.2.2 Sign types: (B) "commemorative" and "indicative"

Philodemus wrote his treatise around the middle of the first century B.C. Almost two hundred years later, Sextus Empiricus again takes up the distinction between signs in the particular sense (*idíōs*) and signs in the common sense (*koinôs*), in the context of his treatment of signs. Strangely, however, he connects this distinction to another distinction, that between *commemorative* signs and *indicative* signs:

> The term "sign", then, has two senses, the common (*koinôs*) and the particular (*idíōs*). In the common sense it is that which seems to make something evident—in which sense we are accustomed to call a sign that which serves to effect the renewal of the object observed in conjunction with it,—and in the particular sense it means that which is indicative of a non-evident object.
>
> (Sextus Empiricus, *Adversus Mathematicos*, VIII, 143)

It seems that Sextus wants to maintain the double distinction, even though this appears to be something of a contradiction, as he states, after having introduced the opposition between common sign and particular sign, that he intends to deal only with the latter (*ibid.*). Since the particular sign enables the discovery of things which are obscure, he proposes a preliminary distinction between manifest or evident things and things which are obscure, with a further subdivision of the latter into three categories. The result is a four-fold typology:

(i) *Manifest things*, or immediately evident things. These are things which can be known directly; Sextus proposes as an example "the fact that it is day and that I am speaking"[24] when I am actually doing this.

(ii) *Absolutely obscure things*. These are things which by their nature cannot be known to us (*katálēpsis*), for example, "whether the total number of stars is even or uneven" or "whether there are a certain number of grains of sand in Libya".[25]

(iii) *Temporarily obscure things*. These are things which, despite having a manifest nature, are not evident for a period of time due to special circumstances. The example given is that of the city of Athens, which, though quite certainly visible by nature, becomes temporarily invisible to someone at a distance from it.[26]

(iv) *Things obscure by nature*. These are things which by nature cannot be perceived, but only thought about (*noētoí*).[27] The examples given are "pores which must exist but cannot be seen" and "the void".

There is no need to consider signs in the first two categories, for manifest things can be understood directly and absolutely obscure things cannot be understood at all. It is, however, precisely by means of signs that things in the other two categories can be understood. But each of these last two categories has its own types of sign. Temporarily obscure things can be understood by means of *commemorative* signs whereas things which are obscure by nature can be understood by *indicative* signs. Sextus Empiricus explains these two types of sign as follows:

> Of the signs, . . . according to (the dogmatists), some are commemorative (*hypomnēstiká*), some are indicative (*endeiktiká*). They term a sign "commemora-

tive" when, being mentally associated with the thing signified, it by its clearness at the time of its perception, though the thing signified remains nonevident, suggests to us the thing associated with it, which is not clearly perceived at the moment—as for instance in the case of smoke and fire. An "indicative" sign, they say, is that which is not clearly associated with the thing signified, but signifies that whereof it is a sign by its own particular nature and constitution, just as, for instance, the bodily motions are signs of the soul.[28]

The commemorative sign is, basically, the product of a constant association between things commonly observed in empirical connection. The examples Sextus Empiricus gives to illustrate this type of sign seem to follow the tripartite distribution[29] *contemporary, future, past* between the sign and the thing it indicates. In the case of "smoke → fire", there is a contemporary relationship; in the case of "scar → wound" or "bandages → oiling of athletes", the fact indicated is prior to the sign; in the case of "heart wound → death", the thing referred to comes after the sign.[30]

The indicative sign, in contrast, cannot be observed along with the thing of which it is the sign, for in this case the thing has never been manifest and often is not even imagined. The examples given are "bodily motions" (which enable the understanding of "the soul") and "sweat" (which can be traced back to "skin pores").[31] Sextus Empiricus accepts the epistemological value of commemorative signs, but denies any epistemological value to indicative signs, which, he says, are an invention of "dogmatist philosophers" and "rationalist doctors".[32] Sextus Empiricus' classification of signs can be summarized according to Figure 6.2.

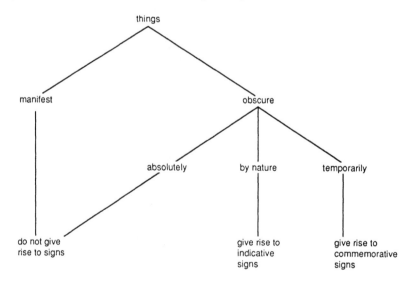

Figure 6.2

It should be noted, however, that there is some doubt whether the distinction which Sextus Empiricus makes between *commemorative* and *indicative* signs was really formulated by the Stoics. In truth, no traces can be found of such a distinction in other sources nor indeed elsewhere in Sextus' own treatment of signs. In addition, this distinction seems to contrast strongly with the overall direction of Stoic philosophy and particularly with the logico-formal orientation of their theory of the sign. Nonetheless, however interesting this distinction is from the epistemological point of view, from the logical point of view it must be considered irrelevant.

The distinction between the common sign and the particular sign reported by Philodemus does seem to be genuinely Stoic. The element of necessity attached to the particular sign indeed forms a characteristic point of Stoic thought in general. For the Stoics, the sign is always a "necessary" sign as a more detailed analysis of its structure will show.

6.2.3 THE STRUCTURE OF THE SIGN IN "THE CONDITIONAL"

Going back now to the Stoic definition of the sign given earlier, there are at least three elements which must be examined more closely. First of all we must consider the notion of *synēmménon*, which means literally "connected" or "connection". Its meaning in logic is made clear in a passage from Diogenes.[33] It is the conditional statement of the type "if *p*, then *q*", in which a first proposition gives rise to a second, as in the example "If it is day, it is light".

The next important point is the notion of the sound (*hygiés*, "sound") conditional. From the definition given in a passage from Sextus Empiricus, it may be seen that this idea is close to the modern truth-function interpretation "if *p*, then *q*". The validity or lack of validity of the "if *p*, then *q*" conditional depends on the truth value of its antecedent and consequent.

In two parallel passages,[34] Sextus Empiricus defines as valid only "that conditional which does not begin with truth and end in falsehood". He gives a table of truth values which conforms exactly to that which modern logic lays down for material implication (cf. Figure 6.3).

p	q	"if **p**, then **q**"
true	true	sound
false	false	sound
true	false	unsound
false	true	sound

Figure 6.3

Sextus Empiricus also mentions a dispute among Stoic logicians with regard to the criterion for judging a conditional to be valid.[35] This was what Kneale and Kneale (1962) have called "the debate on the nature of conditionals", a debate of central importance to treatments of logic during the Stoic period.

The third point which demands attention in the definition of the sign is connected to the idea of the sign as *antecedent* (*prokathēgoúmenon*) in a valid conditional. As Sextus Empiricus himself states,[36] there are three types of valid conditional in the table of truth values relating to material implication (TT, FF, FT); it is therefore a question of seeing whether the sign resides in each of these three types of conditional or only in special cases. It has to be said that a sign can be expressed only by a true proposition, as indeed the proposition to which it refers must be true. This therefore excludes the second and third types (FF, FT), which both have false antecedents. The only possibility remains therefore for the sign to relate to the first type of conditional, that which begins and ends with something true.[37]

There remains, however, an important observation to be made with respect to the Stoic definition of the sign with regard to the characteristic the sign must have of being *something which reveals* (*ekkalyptikón*) the consequent. For example, a conditional of the type "If it is day, it is light", when both conditions are manifest and it is day and light, consists of two true propositions. However, according to Sextus Empiricus,[38] we do not here have the conditions in which a sign appears, since both propositions refer to things which are *per se* evident. The first term of the conditional does not reveal anything about the second. In order to understand the true nature of the sign, the strictly logical sphere must give way to the more generally epistemological sphere. For the Stoics, the sign must not only have a correct logical construction, shown by the implication between two true propositions, but must also have the characteristic of being a means of increasing or gaining knowledge.[39]

As earlier with Aristotle, so with the Stoics the sign is founded on a logical basis but operates in a cognitive frame of reference. The many examples of a medical nature bear witness to the origins of this frame of reference. In general, the sign must enable the inferential passage from an easily accessible piece of knowledge, for example, "s/he has brought up bronchial cartilage", to much less easily accessible knowledge, such as, in this example, "s/he has a lung wound." But, what the theory of the sign acquires when it passes from the hands of the doctors to the hands of the philosophers is a solid logical-formal structure which serves to exclude any possibility of false inferences.

6.2.4.1 *The debate on the nature of conditionals*

The lively debate which existed on "the nature of conditionals" (Kneale and Kneale, 1962) serves to indicate the complexity and range of work which the philosophers had to undertake in the sphere of logic in order to establish a criterion capable of excluding false inferences. As Sextus Empiricus reports: "Now all the dialecticians agree in asserting that a conditional is valid when its consequent follows (*akoloutheî*) from its antecedent, but they disagree about when and how this follows and propose conflicting criteria of this 'following'." (*Adversus Mathematicos*, VIII, 112).

Sextus Empiricus lists four criteria which were proposed during this debate to establish the validity of a conditional statement: (i) Philo Megarian's criterion; (ii) Diodorus Cronus' criterion; (iii) the *synártēsis* criterion attributed to Chrysippus; (iv) the *émphasis* criterion.[40]

Before looking in detail at these criteria, we must make one general observation about this debate. As Martha Hurst (1935, p.492) points out, the starting point for the various contributions to the debate remains invariably an *already-known relation*, a relation which is recognizable in its instances. The aim, however, is always the *definition of this relation* of "following" (*akolouthía*) in formal terms. Throughout the whole course of the debate on the nature of conditionals, the Greek logicians focused their attention on the *definiendum* rather than on the *definiens*. The *definiens*, which could have an autonomous property (since it was endowed with meaning), was taken into consideration only with respect to the possibility of proving that it coincided with the *definiendum*. Confusion was therefore often created between the two levels, and very often unintentionally ambiguous examples were chosen which could equally illustrate both the recognized relation and the properties of the logical relation which they were attempting to identify with such a relation.

A comparison with the methods of contemporary logic may help us better understand the procedure used in the debate. In general, contemporary logic is interested only in the *definiens*, that is, in the relation which can be established through symbols, without regard to the question of whether this relation is identical with any logical relation which is widely known, easily recognized and little understood, such as the relation of an expression of implication ("following", cf. Hurst, 1935, p.492). Peirce and Russell, for example, were interested in the properties of *material implication* independent of the fact that, as they admitted, it does not reproduce the "usual" meaning of "implies". Lewis also examined the system of *strict implication* without feeling the need to state that this represents the accepted meaning of "implies".

This fundamental difference in approach between ancient and modern logic leads to a further difference between the two. While the theorists of ancient logic wanted to give a single definition of implication, modern theorists have to provide a double definition, one of "material implication" and one of "strict implication".

6.2.4.2 *Implication according to Philo*
Philo is the first member of the Megarian Stoic school cited by Sextus Empiricus and is the first to give a truth-function definition of the expression "if *p*, then *q*". According to Philo, a conditional expression is valid if

and only if it does not start from the truth and end with falsehood. As we have already seen, Philo's definition of the criterion of "following" (*akolouthías kritérion*) corresponds to the framework of material implication. There are in fact three cases where the conditional is valid, corresponding to the following three examples: (i) "If it is day, it is light" (TT); (ii) "If the earth flies, the earth has wings" (FF); (iii) "If the earth flies, the earth exists" (FT).

As Kneale and Kneale (1962) have pointed out, Philo was probably thinking of the use of the expression "if p, then q" in reasoning, and he probably wanted to call attention to the fact that the conjunction of the conditional statement with its antecedent always implies the consequent. Philo's interpretation is the weakest interpretation which satisfies such a requirement.

6.2.4.3 *Implication according to Diodorus Cronus*

Diodorus Cronus was Philo's teacher, and the reason Sextus Empiricus cites the pupil before the master is probably that Diodorus was able to confute Philo's theory, whereas Philo was not able to confute Diodorus' (cf. Hurst, 1935, p.485 note 2).

Diodorus' criticism of Philo's interpretation is based on the weakness which it displays. He gives examples of conditionals which, while satisfying Philo's requirement at one time (t_1), fail to satisfy it at another time (t_2). For example, the statement "If it is day, I am talking" would be considered true by Philo, given the conditions, at a t_1 time, that it was day and I was talking. Diodorus showed that this is in fact false and states that there is nothing in the nature of this statement which enables us to say whether it falls under Philo's definition or not. It could indeed be pronounced at a t_2 time too, when it was day but I was silent. In this case it would have the invalid form TF.

To solve this difficulty, Diodorus elaborates a conception according to which a conditional is valid when "(it) did not, and does not admit, the possibility of the antecedent being true and the consequent being false".[41] The example he gives is "If atomic elements of things do not exist, then atomic elements of things do exist". According to Diodorus, in this conditional the antecedent is always false and the consequent is always true. This is sufficient to exclude the possibility of a true antecedent with a false consequent, which is the only case in which the conditional is not valid.[42]

6.2.4.4 *Chrysippus' "connective implication" ("synártēsis")*

The third type of valid conditional given by Sextus Empiricus corresponds, according to some modern scholars (Mates 1949a; Bocheński, 1951, 1956), to Lewis' strict implication or at least to a form of necessary implication (cf. Kneale and Kneale, 1962). This conception of the valid conditional is given both in the passage from Sextus Empiricus quoted above and in a passage from Diogenes (*Vitae*, VII, 73): "A conditional is true in which the contradictory (*antikeímenon*) of its conclusion is incompatible (*máchetai*) with its premiss, as, for example, 'If it is day, it is light' ". Neither Sextus Empiricus nor Diogenes gives the name of the author of this conception, but there is evidence to suggest that it was first proposed by Chrysippus (cf. Mueller, 1978, pp.18-19).

This passage brings to the forefront the extremely interesting—but problematic, since it is not clearly defined—notion of "incompatibility". From the commentary given on this passage by Martha Hurst (1935, p.495), it seems that the relation of incompatibility and, more generally, the relation of "following" too, cannot be expressed in extensional terms. That is to say, they cannot be expressed by means of *external relations* which exist between propositions by virtue of the properties which these have outside the relation; on the contrary, they must be expressed by recourse to *internal relations* which exist by virtue of their meaning.

It is interesting to compare Martha Hurst's conclusion with Preti's (1956, p.13) observation that Sextus Empiricus' example when talking of *synártēsis* "seems to allude to something even stronger (than Lewis' strict implication): to absolute tautology".[43] Preti's observation is based on what Philodemus says about Stoic doctrine in *De Signis*. As we shall see in the chapter dedicated to this work, *De Signis* presents as genuinely Stoic the inferential method of "elimination" (*anaskeué*), which seems to be analogous to the *synártēsis* method.

In inference by "elimination", the negation of the consequent in turn causes the negation of the antecedent. It works in such a way that the truth of the conditional "If the first, then the second" is proved by the truth of the corresponding conditional "If not the second, not the first".[44]

Preti underlines the affinity between *synártēsis* (according to which the negation of the consequent is incompatible with the antecedent) and the *anaskeué* elimination method (in which the negation of the consequent results in the negation of the antecedent). In both cases he refers to Lewis' strict implication, stressing that Philodemus' examples seem to indicate an even stronger relation which tends to resolve inference into either a form of tautology or a form of *L-implication*.

6.3 CONCLUSION

As we have seen, in the passage from the Aristotelian theory of the sign to the Stoic theory of the sign, there is a shifting of emphasis from the terms on which the categorical propositions are constructed in the syllogism to the relationship between the propositions in the conditional statement. There is at the same time a notable increase in the importance which Aristotle gave to the nature of necessary consequentiality or "follow-ing", which the signic relationship is required to set up: inference from the known term to the unknown term must have a cogent nature.

There are two explanations for the emphasis given to the aspect of ne-cessity in Stoic semiotics, one linked to the analysis of the nature of reason and its processes and the other stemming from the structure of Stoic meta-physics (cf. De Lacy and De Lacy, 1978, p.208).

With respect to the first point, Sextus Empiricus informs us that the Stoics believed that humans differed from animals because of their capacity for "internal speech" (lógos endiáthetos) and their ability to combine concepts and to pass from one concept to another.[45] Humankind possesses the notion of consequentiality or "following" (akolouthía) and concom-itant with this is the notion of the sign in the form "If this, then this other". The existence of the sign is a direct result of the nature of human thought.

With regard to the second point, Stoic metaphysics was based on the idea that the real is built up by a continuous chain of events which are interconnected by cause-effect relationships. These relationships were understood to be necessary relationships in that they depended on a ratio-nal order imposed by the divinity. In this way, the necessary "following" of the valid signic relationship reproduces the same "following" which is present at the level of concatenation of events.[46] The Stoic insistence on the conditional statement and on inference from signs indicates the empha-sis they placed on the relation of necessity between concepts and proposi-tions at the logical level and between cause and effect at the metaphysical level.

The Stoics' reluctant acceptance of divination is itself based upon the same principles. Divination consists in grasping the relations which con-nect certain present events to certain future events.[47] Although human ra-tionality basically mirrors divine rationality, the gods nonetheless have an awareness of the entire causal chain which links events ("conligatio causarum omnium"),[48] whereas this is not available to humanity. Human individuals, therefore, cannot know the causes, but only the characteristic indications of the causes ("signa . . . causarum et notas") of events, on which they must base their predictions of the future. However, in contrast to the situation which prevails for the gods, human conditionals about the future cannot be necessary.

In the case of human science (which for the Stoics means dialectics), the sign must be based on a necessary implication. However, even though this is an essential characteristic of the sign, it is by no means sufficient on its own to serve as a definition of the sign. In a conditional such as "If it is day, it is light",[49] the day cannot be considered a sign of the light because both things are evident, thus the inference can *prove* nothing. The truth on which the inference is based is certainly both *a priori* and analytic, as seems to be required in the case of necessary truth, but this conditional is devoid of the characteristic of enabling the attainment of new knowledge.

The Stoic sign, therefore, must fit into a logical scheme (necessary implication), but at the same time it must also go beyond this to act within an epistemological framework, where it becomes a factor in the growth of knowledge. It must not be forgotten that the essence of the sign is an inference which goes from manifest things to things which are not perceived.

At this point, we run into what promises to be a very difficult problem in Stoic semiotics: How can signic inference be analytic (thinking of Preti's L-implication) yet simultaneously provide new knowledge (the discovery of a hidden fact)?

We can take as an example of this problem a proof (according to Sextus Empiricus, proof itself can be considered to be sign):[50]

—If sweat flows through the surface of the body, there are intelligible pores in the skin.
—The first.
—Therefore the second.

Here the inference is made from the perceptible fact of the flowing of sweat to the hidden fact of the existence of pores in the skin. The presence of pores in the skin is a fact which is obscure by nature: pores could be known only through the mind (*noētoî*), not through the senses, in a period which pre-dates the invention of the microscope. As a supportive argument to the premisses of the preceding reasoning, Sextus Empiricus adds a further reasoning:[51]

—It is impossible for a liquid to flow across a compact, non-porous body.
—Sweat flows through the body.
—It is therefore not possible that the body is compact, but it is porous.

The major premiss of this argument seems to be based on the application of the test of elimination ($\bar{q} \supset \bar{p}$) to the major premiss of the preceding argument. If we apply the test of elimination to the conditional:

p (if sweat flows through the surface of the body) $\supset q$ (there are intelligible pores in the skin),

we obtain:

$\bar{q}$ (if the skin is a compact, non-porous body) $\supset \bar{p}$ (a liquid cannot flow through it).

This expression is the basis of the premiss of the second reasoning offered by Sextus Empiricus. It enables the development of a reasoning corresponding to the *modus tollens*, which validates the conclusion of the first reasoning.

It is impossible to say whether the Stoics manage to avoid, by use of elimination, the contradiction between the requirement of a necessary *a priori* relation between the two propositions of the conditional and the necessity that the sign produce new knowledge. Elimination renders the relation a necessary one, even in the case of factual truths, since it begins from the assumption that the fact that is obscure by nature is linked to the evident fact in such a way that what is evident could not exist if the non-perceived fact were not what it is revealed to be.

SEVEN

Inference and Language
in Epicurus

7.0 INTRODUCTION

The contribution to the history of semiotics made by the Epicurean school belongs to the same period as the reflections on the sign of the Stoic school. One of the key points of Epicurean epistemology was the semiotic principle of making conjectures about facts which are by nature imperceptible to the senses from visible phenomena. The fundamental elements of Epicurean physics (that is, the existence of atoms and of the void, the forms and reasons for celestial phenomena) are established by means of semiotic inferences which start from perceptible phenomena:

> Some phenomena within our experience afford evidence (*sēmeîa*) by which we may interpret what goes on in the heavens. We see how the former really take place, but not how the celestial phenomena take place, for their occurrence may possibly be due to a variety of causes.
>
> (Epicurus, *Letter to Pythocles*, 87)

Epicurus rejected the deductive reasoning typical of Aristotle and the Stoics, judging it to be empty and devoid of use, but he accepted and believed in the importance of analogic inference, which takes signs as the starting point for its development. In the Hellenistic period, the Epicureans became the main exponents and promoters of a method of reasoning which could be termed "semiotic induction", and they entered into heated polemics with the Stoic philosophers on the subject of the method of inference. An entire first century B.C. treatise, *Perì sēmeíōn kaì sēmeiốseōn* (*On Signs and Inferences*) by the Epicurean Philodemus of Gadara, was devoted to the debate which took place between the Stoics and the Epicureans on the subject of semiotic inference.[1]

Epicurus and the Epicurean school as a whole propounded the possibility of making objectively valid judgements about phenomena not directly knowable through experience on the basis of inferences made from signs.

The central problem then became how to establish the criterion to check if and within what limits these judgements could be considered reliable or unreliable (that is, true or false) and to establish the basis on which to pronounce whether or not certain assertions indeed correspond to the facts which they describe. The notion of the "truth criterion" thus comes to the fore, and this provides the framework within which both the theory of semiotic inference and the theory of language were developed. There is not, in fact, a unique truth criterion, but many. According to what Diogenes Laertius records,[2] these include sensations (*aisthēseis*), affections (*páthē*) and preconceptions (*prolēpseis*), to which may be added, for reasons which will become clear below, immediate evidence (*enárgeia*). Truth criteria—and in particular *prolēpsis* ("anticipation", "preconception")—have a fundamental and creative role in both the theory of inference[3] and the theory of language.[4] In this way, they form a linking element between the two theories. Nonetheless, this is still not sufficient to allow a common analysis and explanation of the inferential sign and the linguistic sign, which are once again the objects of two separate investigations.

For the Stoics too, as will be recalled, the theory of the linguistic sign, termed *sēmaînon*, had its beginnings with the discussion of the truth criterion and the "true". In their conception, and that of the Epicureans, the inferential sign, termed *sēmeîon*, had no point of contact with the linguistic sign except through the part played by the notion of *lektón*, which had to be considered true or false. Epicurean semiotics, however, has one special feature which is worth noting: it also takes into consideration a theory of the perceptible image which is linked to the truth criterion but also anticipates several interesting problems from the point of view of a semiotic theory of iconism.

In the following sections we shall deal with the questions of the truth criterion, of prolepsis and of the perceptible image in Epicurus' philosophy, which we shall link both to the theory of semiotic inference and the theory of language. Because of their range and importance, the developments which Epicurean semiotic theory underwent in Philodemus' *De Signis* merit an individual investigation and will therefore be dealt with in a separate chapter (Chapter 8).

7.1 THE TRUTH CRITERION AND EPICUREAN EPISTEMOLOGY

From the point of view of epistemology, Epicurean philosophy is structured around the attempt to base knowledge on purely empirical foundations. Facts and objects are viewed as having the greatest importance, but words also constitute a mode of access to things. There are thus two possible methods of research for philosophy in this perspective: (i) one oriented towards the knowledge which comes from words; (ii) the other towards the knowledge which comes directly from things.[5] However, the second method is considered preliminary to the first, and knowledge which is obtained through language, such as that which is produced by means of propositions, is often empty and unreliable.[6]

The final basis for truth is represented by truth criteria, which can lead the inquiring human subject to nothing less that imperturbability.[7] Truth criteria therefore lie at the base of Epicurus' philosophy in general; they were dealt with in a lost work, entitled *Canon*, which contained all the preliminary matter to Epicurus' doctrinal system.[8] It is no use thinking of truth in modern terms, that is, as a function of propositions, if we wish to understand Epicurean thought correctly. It must be remembered that in Greek, in general, the adjective *alēthés* ("true") may be used both to qualify the truth of a proposition and to indicate what actually exists and is real. For Epicurus, in particular, the adjective "true" implies an effective awareness of something. This explains its application to sensations and affections, for saying that a certain sensation (or affection) is true is the same thing as saying that it gives an effective *indication* of a real fact, thereby making us aware of it.[9]

Before examining the different forms of truth criterion, perhaps we must first emphasize how the truth criterion is functional to a theory of semiotic inference. It tends to establish basic truths regarding perceptible objects, which in turn form a starting point from which to make inferences about the things which are not accessible through sense perception.[10]

7.2 THE FORMS OF TRUTH CRITERION

Epicurus therefore considered truth criteria to be: sensations, preconception (or prolepsis), affections (or sentiments).[11] Paragraph 82 of the *Letter to Herodotus* also mentions *enárgeia* ("immediate evidence" or "clear sight"). With reference to this passage, Long (1971b, p.116) makes an interesting proposal about the internal organization of the forms of truth criteria. He suggests that they are organized hierarchically. First of all, there are affections and sensations, then immediate evidence, then preconceptions. According to Long, affections and sensations have a purely subjective truth value when considered on their own. They must instead be coordinated with immediate evidence and prolepsis in order to constitute an objective criterion.

Affections and sensations carry the awareness of something, and their "truth" resides precisely in such awareness, even if it remains subjective. Figure 7.1 illustrates the relationships between the forms of truth criteria.

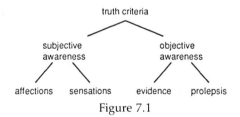

Figure 7.1

7.3 THE IDOLS THEORY

So far we have been considering the cognitive process from the point of view of the subject who feels a sensation or experiences an affection in relation to external stimuli. However, if we now look at the same process from the opposite point of view, that is, from the point of view of the object, we can see that Epicurus developed a fully fledged theory of the image which offers many points of interest for a semiotics of iconism. Epicurus begins to talk about the mechanics of sense perception in paragraph 46 of the *Letter to Herodotus*. According to his view, objects continually emit a fine stream of atoms which form configurations which are completely identical to the outer shape of solid bodies.[12] These configurations are called idols (*eídōla*) and they travel at extremely high speed to penetrate human sense organs and enter into the mind where they produce a more or less exact image (*phantasía*) of the body or object from which they were emitted. The process can be represented as in Figure 7.2.

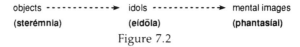

Figure 7.2

Epicurus' theory could thus be defined as a "causal" theory of perception (cf. Long, 1971b, p.117), since external objects are directly responsible for the existence of idols, and idols directly cause the formation of images in the mind. It must be said, however, that the images are a direct consequence of the idols and thus only secondarily a consequence of the external objects, from which they can also differ slightly.

In fact the continuity of the process can be interrupted at the level of the passage of the stream of atoms from the external objects to the idols. Sometimes the idols, although usually exact copies of the objects, can undergo modifications (caused by entering into collision with other atoms while travelling through the air), and they can also become reduced in size when they enter a person (this too because they collide with other atoms).[13]

This particular aspect of the theory reflects Epicurus' attempts to take into consideration the fact that objects seen close seem to have certain dimensions, whereas they have quite different (much smaller) dimensions when seen from a distance. Epicurus thus avoids the contradiction of the principle that sensation is always a guarantee of truth. The contradiction would be inevitable if the *phantasía* were an image of the object, but in fact it is an image of the idol (*eídōlon*).

Sextus Empiricus seems to have grasped Epicurus' thought correctly when he quotes the example of the tower in this context:

> . . . just so I should decline to say that eyesight is false because at a long distance it sees the tower as small and round but from close at hand as large and square, but I should say rather that it reports truly because, when the object of sense appears to it small and of a certain shape, it really is small and of a certain shape, as the limits belonging to the images (*eídōla*) are rubbed away by

their passage through the air; (and again when it appears large and of a different shape it is correspondingly large and of a different shape, since it is no longer the same object that is both at once.)

(Sextus Empiricus, *Adversus Mathematicos*, VII, 208-209)

The senses receive the stream of atoms which is given off by the object and which makes up its idol, not the object itself. The configuration of the stream of atoms can be altered in its passage through the air, and this is what produces the diversity of images of the same object. Thus every mental image (*phantasía*) is effectively true because it reflects not the object but one of its various idols, which differ according to the distance covered to reach the subject who perceives them. It is essential not to identify the idol which is produced close to the object with that which is seen when the observer is some distance from the object.

7.4 THE THEORY OF ERROR AND OF OPINION

The theme of semiotic inference becomes more central in the field of perception processes when we leave the safe ground of sensation to venture into the rough area of opinions, where error may occur. If human individuals paid attention only to their sensations and limited themselves to describing their mental images (*phantasíai*), there would be no possibility of error. But this, of course, does not happen, and error occurs when what Epicurus refers to in the *Letter to Herodotus* (51) as "second movement" (*állē kínēsis*) is added to sensation.

Long (1971b, p.118) identifies this "second movement" with the process of the formation of opinion. Epicurus says that it is "connected" to the first movement (that is, the simple apprehension of images), but that it differs from this in that it "admits a distinction", the distinction between true and false. The first movement, or apprehension of images, admits no such distinction, for it is produced by external causes, that is, by idols. The second movement, however, since it consists of adding a judgement we make about these images, can receive confirmation or proof of the opposite. The process can be schematized as shown in Figure 7.3.

If, on the basis of viewing from a distance or in bad light conditions, I say, translating my sensations into words: "That *has the appearance of* a round tower", I am speaking in a true manner. If, however, I say "That *is* a round tower", my judgement will be proved wrong when I come closer to the tower and receive an image of a square tower. Images are always true, whereas some opinions are true and some opinions are false.[14] The conclusion of this, of course, is the conjectural nature of opinion.

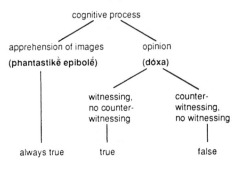

Figure 7.3

7.5 CONJECTURE

It is to be expected that a special place be dedicated to conjecture within the bounds of a theory of opinion. In general, conjecture consists precisely of a cognitive hypothesis on a dimension which goes beyond what can be perceived by the senses. Opinion, in Epicurus' use of the term, is associated precisely with this characteristic, for it is a judgement which requires the commitment of the subject to something which awaits confirmation.

There are several key terms which define the cognitive process affected through opinion. The first of these is *prosménon*, "that which awaits confirmation",[15] which is the object on which judgement is made.

The second and third key terms are linked by a relation of antonymia and are *epimartýrēsis* ("witnessing") and *antimartýrēsis* ("counterwitnessing"). However, Epicurus' system for verification or falsification of an opinion works on not just two terms, but on four. Verification is achieved when there is "witnessing" or "no counterwitnessing" and falsification is given when there is "counterwitnessing" or "no witnessing". Thus a proper semiotic square is created (cf. Figure 7.4).[16]

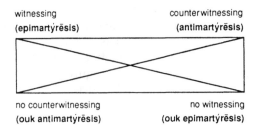

Figure 7.4

However, in reality each of the four terms is sufficient to establish the validity of an opinion. Later, in the semiotic theory expressed by Philodemus' *De Signis*, the criterion for deciding the validity of an inductive inference is simply no counterwitnessing, or the absence of conflict between the signic expression and perceptible phenomena.

In Epicurus' square, there is the problem of establishing a criterion to define in what the base term, that is, witnessing, consists. We can identify this criterion with *enárgeia* ("evidence", "clear sight") as Sextus Empiricus indicates:

> And witnessing (*epimartýrēsis*) is apprehension by means of evidence (*di' enargeías*) that the thing opined is of such a sort as it was opined to be—as when, for example, on the approach of Plato from afar I guess and opine, because of the distance, that it is Plato, and when he has drawn near the fact that he is Plato is further testified—the distance being reduced—and is confirmed by actual evidence of sense.

> (Sextus Empiricus, *Adversus Mathematicos*, VII, 212)

In fact, Epicurus was very well aware that error in identification or recognition of objects of perception could occur and, in all likelihood, he considered that every act of perception was marked not only by pure and simple sensation, but also by *dóxa*. In this way, conjecture becomes ubiquitous, for it is involved in all acts of perception. As a consequence, sensations and mental images take on the role of providing data on which to base conjecture.[17]

The *Letter to Herodotus* (38) seems to take into consideration two kinds of object on which semiotic inference operates:

(1) that which awaits confirmation (*prosménon*)

(2) that which is not available to the senses (*ádēlon*).

These give rise to two different kinds of inferential process.

The first type of inferential process involves the kind of conjecture which is formulated within the processes of perception themselves. It is illustrated by the example, which Sextus Empiricus repeats above, of seeing Plato approaching in the distance and being able only to conjecture that it is truly he. In this case the object on which conjecture is made is something which is perceived by the senses, but indistinctly. Nonetheless, the process concludes with a verification, in this case the confirmation of the conjectured fact, by means of clear sight.

The second type of conjecture is that which formulates an inference with respect to things which do not fall within the range of sense perception. This is conjecture in the classic sense. Sextus Empiricus gives us an example of this type of conjecture as well.[18] His example is that of tracing the existence of the void from the existence of motion, that is, moving from a perceptible element, a *phainómenon*, to an imperceptible element, an *ádēlon*. This is the typical logical relationship of implication (which Sextus Empiricus terms *akolouthía*) between an antecedent and a consequent. We can call this second type of inferential process *inference to the imperceptible*.

7.6 INFERENCE FROM SIGNS

Inference to the imperceptible is a typical kind of inference from signs. In many cases, as in the example given above, "If there is motion → there is the void", it is not possible to know directly the object about which the inference is made ("the void"), but it must be reached through a sign ("motion"). Thus, for Epicurus too, inference from signs is connected with the possibility of broadening the scope of knowledge beyond the sphere of sensible objects. It is indeed thanks to the theory of signic inference that the Epicurean school is able to go beyond the limits of its characteristic basic empiricism and to open the way to knowledge of phenomena not directly perceptible to the senses. In Philodemus' *De Signis* (fr. 2), there is an explicit invitation to consider knowledge achieved through inference to be as reliable as direct knowledge.

This kind of cognitive programme rests on an epistemology which divides objects into four categories, very much as in Stoic semiotics:

(1) *Evident objects or facts (enargê)*. These are "those things which are perceived involuntarily through representation or affection" (Sextus Empiricus, *Adversus Mathematicos*, VIII, 316). The examples given for this category include the fact that it is day or the recognition that a certain person is a man.

(2) *Absolutely obscure (phýsei ádēla) objects*. These are "those things which neither have been previously apprehended, nor are they now being apprehended, nor will hereafter be apprehended, but are eternally unknowable" (Sextus Empiricus, *Adversus Mathematicos*, VIII, 317-18). The example given is that of the impossibility of knowing whether the total number of stars is odd or even. Facts of this type are unknowable, Sextus Empiricus explains, not by their nature, but by our nature, given the limits of human understanding.

(3) *Obscure by their own nature (génei ádēla) objects*. These are "those things which in their own proper nature are hidden but are made known, it is claimed, by means of signs and proofs" (Sextus Empiricus, *Adversus Mathematicos*, VIII, 319). The examples given are atoms and the void. The existence of atoms and the void had been postulated by Leucippus and Democritus on a purely rational basis, but, in conformity with his general empiricism, Epicurus insists that they can be known through analogical inference.

(4) *Objects awaiting confirmation (prosménonta)*. These are objects immediately beyond our experience (cf. *Letter to Herodotus*, 38). The possibility of knowing these objects is limited by certain factors, such as distance in space or being situated in the future.

As may be seen from this classification, the only objects which can be known through inference are those belonging to the third and fourth category. These can be placed in correspondence with the two types of inference mentioned above.

Perceptive inference operates in the sphere of objects belonging to the fourth category, those "awaiting confirmation".

Inference to the imperceptible operates rather with respect to objects belonging to the third category, in the interest of gaining knowledge about objects which are "by their own nature obscure" and which can never be reached through the senses. In this case, the method of verification takes an indirect form of no counterwitnessing (*ouk antimartýrēsis*). As we have seen, the void is not verifiable through direct experience, but for the Epicureans, its existence is not in contradiction with any known fact,[19] while its negation would enter into conflict with the empirical experience of motion, which requires the void for its existence. The heart of reasoning based on no counterwitnessing consists in the fact that when there are two contradictory propositions about something which is imperceptible, and one of these is false according to empirical proof (in the example given above, the non-existence of the void, since this would conflict with the existence of motion), then the other can be considered to be true (cf. De Lacy and De Lacy, 1978, p.188).

7.7 PROLEPSIS

Prolepsis (or "anticipation", "pre-conception") is the second of the two truth criteria which we have defined as "objective". It has a decisive role in perceptive inference, as Diogenes shows:

> For example: the object standing yonder is a horse or a cow. Before making this judgement, we must at some time or other have known by preconception the shape of a horse or a cow.
>
> (Diogenes Laertius, *Vitae*, X, 33)

Indeed, prolepsis is necessary to the experience of perception *per se* in order that the subject move from the simple awareness of the fact that s/he is seeing an image to the objective judgement that this is an image of a specific thing. In other words, according to Epicurus, in order to perceive a horse or a cow, one must: (1) have already seen an image of these animals; (2) have stored this image in the mind; (3) compare the data provided by the present sensation with this stored image.

Prolepses are really mental images or concepts which have been formed as a result of numerous experiences of external objects. They have two basic characteristics: (i) they are firmly linked to memory of previous experiences; (ii) they are evident (*enargeîs*).

As concepts, prolepses do not necessarily correspond to individual external objects; instead, prolepses consist in individual perceptive experiences. This is strictly connected to the fact that prolepses are a test for truth. It is only through the possession of the general concept of "human being" that one can decide whether what one sees is a particular occurrence of this concept.

7.8 THEORY OF LANGUAGE

Prolepses also constitute a necessary condition of language and operate both on the level of decodification and on the level of codification. First of all, the act of uttering a name (for example |human|) brings to the mind of a listener an image or a concept, an underlying entity (*hypotetagménon*) of that name which is derived from prolepsis;[20] we could say, translating into Saussurean terms, that the presence of a signifier causes a listener to match this to a signified. In addition, a speaker must have a preconception of what s/he intends to express, otherwise it would be impossible to say anything; here the speaker codifies a signified which is present in his/her mind by means of an expressive device (a "name").

In Epicurean theory, prolepsis seems always to be involved in the formation of concepts. Diogenes Laertius says that "all concepts (*epínoiai*) stem from sensations, either by *direct experience*, or by *analogy*, or by *resemblance*, or by *combination*, with a certain contribution also on the part of reason" (*Vitae*, X, 32). Long (1971b, p.119) suggests that the first class of concepts—that is, those which stem from direct experience of sensations—should be identified with prolepses.

If prolepses then form the basis for all concepts, a theory of the linguistic sign begins to take shape which is very different from that usually attributed to the Epicurean school by Sextus Empiricus and Plutarch.[21] For these two writers claimed that Epicurus' theory of language involved only two factors: the signifying thing (*sēmaînon*, or "voice", *phōné*) and the designated thing (*tynchánon*). The reason Plutarch and Sextus Empiricus ignored prolepsis in the theory of linguistic meaning is that they could see nothing in Epicurean theory to match the Stoic *lektón*, which was simultaneously incorporeal and completely distinct from a mental image.

Nonetheless, this does not prevent prolepses from having precisely the same function as the Stoic *lektá*, that is, they form an element of mediation between words and things. As a result of this, the Epicurean theory of the linguistic sign could be represented as shown in Figure 7.5.

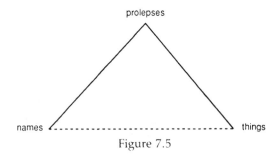

prolepses

names   things

Figure 7.5

To attribute to Epicurus a theory of language in which words refer directly to things, without the mediation of prolepsis, causes a contradiction with his doctrine of false beliefs. For example, if humans mistakenly believe that the gods are ill-disposed towards them, and express this belief in words, unless the conceptual level of prolepsis exists, there is nothing to correspond to the proposition "The gods are ill-disposed towards humans". The existence of prolepsis as a mediating element between words and things allows for false assertions and assertions about things which do not exist. When someone thinks that the gods are ill-disposed towards humans, this is a false supposition, or a concept which is not derived from the object, that is, from the gods themselves.

The centrality of prolepsis in the Epicurean theory of language is also shown by the fact that it can be identified also with the "basic" or "primary" meaning (*prôton ennóēma*) mentioned in the *Letter to Herodotus* (37-38), a meaning which stands apart from all other meanings which can be considered to be derived from it.[22]

7.9 THE ORIGIN OF LANGUAGE

In Epicurus' system of thought, the theory of language is linked to the theory of the origins of language itself, which are dealt with in the *Letter to Herodotus* (75-76).[23] Epicurus thought of language as an activity which humanity had developed during the course of its evolution, passing through two distinct phases. In the first phase, language expressed what could be defined as a natural relationship with reality, while in the second phase the relationship came close to what is usually termed conventional. Epicurus may in fact be seen to occupy a middle position, and a very particular one, in the *phýsis/nómos* debate, for he rejects both the idea that there was a single name-giver and the notion that words reflect things in a natural way (as the Stoics held). Let us now look more closely at how the birth and development of language are described in the *Letter to Herodotus*.

In its first phase, human linguistic activity was no different from other natural processes such as sneezing, coughing, groaning, etc. Humans emit sounds, which are similar to words, as a result of natural involuntary stimuli from the affections (*páthē*) they feel and the images (*phantásmata*) which are formed within their minds. Primitive language is thus an instinctive reaction to the environment, and Epicurus' hypothesis in this respect conforms perfectly to the naturalistic model. However, a closer analysis of the hypothesis reveals further considerations. Disciples of the naturalist theory of language have always had difficulty in accounting for the diversity of languages. Epicurus does not ignore this aspect of the problem[24] but manages to integrate it into his theory.

According to Epicurus, the diversity of languages is a direct result of the diversity of environments in which different peoples live and to which they react by emitting different sounds. In a nutshell, languages vary because things vary from one place to another. Furthermore, humans realize that they produce different sounds in relation to the affections and images which are produced by objects and therefore find it useful to use these sounds as name-labels for objects.

At this point, the second phase in the evolutionary process of language comes into play, whereby conventional elements are introduced. The introduction of conventional elements occurs under a two-fold impetus. First of all, it is the result of a rationalizing movement which takes ambiguous expressions that were created naturally and makes them "clearer" and "more concise". Then there is also the work of "the learned", who tend to introduce concepts related to things beyond the scope of perceptions, signifieds which therefore cannot have been named naturally. As Sedley (1973, p.19) points out, the deliberate attempt to introduce processes of simplification into the evolution of language corresponds to the desire to take into account the abstract processes in which a one-to-one relationship between words and things is no longer tenable. This occurs in two cases, both of which are linked to the entire problematic of language in Epicurus' thought: (i) in the formation of general terms and (ii) in the use of metaphors.

7.10 EPICURUS AND THE "PHÝSIS"/"NÓMOS" TRADITION

Having looked at the Epicurean theory of the origin of language, it is now possible to go back to the semiotic triangle and analyze what relationships it implies between the various terms it uses, in relation to earlier theories of language.

An immediate connection can be seen with Aristotle's position in this tradition. Scholars have often suggested that Epicurus' theory of language depended heavily on that of Aristotle (cf. Arrighett, 1960, p.476, and others), or at least that it is very similar to that of Aristotle (cf. Long, 1971b, p.121). In fact, in *De Interpretatione* (16 a), Aristotle considers affections of the soul to be images produced by sensorial expressions derived from external objects in a way very similar to that in which Epicurus' prolepses derive from objects.

However, even though this represents a point of contact between the two theories, as Sedley (1973, p.20) points out, the mutual differences are greater. Perhaps the most significant difference in the linguistic theories of Aristotle and Epicurus lies in the fact that for Aristotle, different peoples have exactly the same mental affections, but they represent them by means of different linguistic expressions. For Epicurus, in contrast (as we have seen with respect to his thoughts on the origin of language), linguistic forms are different because mental affections (*páthē* and *phantásmata*, both of which are covered by the Aristotelian term *pathēmata*) are different from one people to another as a consequence of differences in the natural environment. However, the differences between the two theories do not stop here. For Aristotle, no name can alone have an apophantic function, that is, no name can be said to be true or false *per se*, and an expression can become a symbol only as a result of convention. For

Epicurus, however, the names of individual objects can be true or false, as also is the case, for example, in the Platonic *Cratylus*. In addition, an expression, which could be simply a sound, can be used as a symbol when there are no conventional elements (as occurs, for example, in the primitive phase of communication).

A second useful comparison can be made with Plato's position on the theory of language. Certainly Epicurus does not propose anything remotely similar to Plato's first semantic theory[25]—which was subsequently adopted also by the Stoics—according to which a name is an abbreviated list of the properties of the object to which it refers. Plato considered primitive words to be the faithful representation of the properties of an object, almost as though vocabulary deliberately consisted entirely of onomatopoeia.

The naturalist position adopted by Epicurus does not go beyond stating that, within each language, a name is used correctly when it is used to denote the object, or the class of objects, with which it was associated at the moment of its natural origin. However, notwithstanding this distinction, there remain some strong points of convergence between the positions of Plato and Epicurus with respect to the theory of language. These may be seen in the way that for both thinkers names originally have a cognitive value which is partially obliterated by the changes in language over time.[26] For Plato, it was possible to recuperate the original meaning of words by means of etymology, and the Stoic school agreed with him in this. For Epicurus, in contrast, the original relationship between language and objects has been clouded principally through the processes of metaphor; to recuperate the original epistemological value of names, he suggests looking for "the first image" (*prôton ennóēma*, cf. *Letter to Herodotus*, 38). The first image can be identified with the prolepsis, that is, with the concept which was formed at the first perception of the object and which was then associated with that name.

It could therefore be said that Epicurus represents an intermediary position between Aristotle's theory of language and Plato's first semantic theory. For Aristotle, names are *symbols* and they are *conventional*. For Plato, names are *icons* of objects and they are *natural*. For Epicurus, names are *symbols* (as for Aristotle) in that they do not reproduce the properties of objects, but they are also *natural* (as for Plato) in their origin, which coincides with the first of the two phases in the evolution of language.

The conventional elements in language are developed only later, in the second evolutionary phase. The intermediary position adopted by Epicurus with respect to Aristotle and Plato explains why his theory has no need to refer to etymology, as Plato and the Stoics do, yet involves keeping "the first image" in mind. The biconditional correspondence between the name and "the first image" is based not on the *form*, but on the natural *origin* of the name.

EIGHT

Philodemus

De Signis

8.0 INTRODUCTION

After Epicurus, the theory of the sign was widely developed by later Epicureans. A first century B.C. treatise,[1] the *Perì sēmeíōn kaì sēmeiṓseōn* (*On Signs and Inferences*)[2] by Philodemus, demonstrates the depth and range which the theory of the sign reached in the Epicurean school. This was in all probability a work written for use in the Epicurean school at Herculaneum, where Philodemus was one of the most prominent members. *De Signis* is not strictly speaking a methodological treatise, nor is it a systematic exposition of the Epicurean theory of the sign, rather it records the polemic which raged between the Stoics and the Epicureans on the subject of inference from signs and on the various semiotic themes connected to this. The treatise is divided into four parts in which are set out the arguments of three Epicurean masters—Zeno of Sidon, Bromius and Demetrius Lacon[3]—in support of the Epicurean theory of the sign and criticizing the objections to this theory raised by exponents of the Stoic school.

The treatise is of prime semiotic importance, since both the Stoics and the Epicureans constructed their theories of logic around inference from signs. Put together like this, the two theories are mutually illuminating. In addition, *De Signis* deals with a series of problems which are still at the center of semiotic interest and debate. The relevance to semiotics of this text was noted by C.S. Peirce, who set his student Allan Marquand to investigate and analyze it. Marquand then wrote an article on the semiotic logic of the Epicureans.[4]

8.1 THE SIGN RELATIONSHIPS: "A PRIORI" OR "A POSTERIORI"

At the heart of Philodemus' treatise lies the fundamental contrast between the two schools with respect to the way of understanding the relation which exists between the two terms in the sign relationship. The Stoics claim that this relationship is *a priori*, formal and of a rational nature, whereas the Epicureans state that the relationship is *a posteriori* and entirely based on empirical considerations. The Epicurean point of view is that in order to establish a relationship between the sign and the thing to which it refers it is necessary to have observed the two terms many times in some kind of conjunction (be it spatial, temporal, causal, etc.). In this way, the relationship is set up following experience and not *a priori*, as the Stoics would have it. As a consequence of this, the semiotic method proposed by the Epicureans is that of *analogy* (*ho katà tền homoiótēta trópos*), or a "strictly empirical (method) and based on the observation of similarities in our experience and upon certain constant conjunctions, from which we infer like similarities and conjunctions in the sphere of the unknown." (cf. E.A. De Lacy, 1938, p.398).

In correspondence with their different ways of understanding the sign relationship, the Stoics and the Epicureans also develop two different theories on the verification of the logical validity of this relationship. The Stoics consider valid the sign relationship based on the elimination method (*anaskeuē*), according to which the elimination of the consequent implies the simultaneous elimination of the antecedent. For example, in the inference "If motion exists, the void exists", the Stoics claim that the elimination of the signified thing ("the void exists") would imply also the elimination of the sign ("motion exists"). This is a totally *a priori* and abstract method of verification, and the Epicureans contest it with a totally empirical method. The Epicureans claim that an *a priori* method is not possible until an inference has been built on empirical grounds. In the example quoted, the existence of the void is inferred from the *empirical observation* that motion is not seen without the conjoined existence of the void and from a consequent *generalization*.[5]

This means that the Stoic abstract principle can be formulated only after the inference has been constructed on empirical grounds and with the use of analogic reasoning. Thus, claim the Epicureans, the elimination method is based, unwittingly, on the foundations of Epicurean analogy. In this way, the necessary truths, which the Stoics consider to be analytical and *a priori*, are really established by means of induction. The Epicureans here propose a point of view by which deductive logic is subsequent to inductive logic in the order of development: the former in fact depends on the latter (cf. De Lacy and De Lacy, 1978, p.221). Even though this idea is clearly set out in *De Signis*, it would be mistaken to expect an articulate discussion on the relationships between formal, deductive logic on one side and inductive logic and empirical method on the other. In fact, as the treatise progresses, both sides of the debate tend to confuse two things which modern logic would keep quite distinct: the *method* for the construction of sign inference and the *criterion* for the verification of its validity (cf. Martinelli, 1988, pp.151-53). Thus the method of construction of inference for the Epicureans is analogy, while the criterion for the verification of validity is more precisely that of *inconceivability* (*adianoēsía*). However, the distinction is not that clear, since both the method and the criterion have an empirical

basis. In fact, during the debate the Stoics tend to attack the method in order to invalidate the criterion and *vice versa*.

8.2 ELIMINATION VS. INCONCEIVABILITY

Let us now analyze formally the opposition which exists between the Stoic
criterion of *elimination* and the Epicurean criterion of *inconceivability*.

For the inference

$$p \supset q$$

the criterion for its verification according to Stoic *elimination* can be ex
pressed as

$$\bar{q} \supset \bar{p}$$

That is to say, if the consequent is negated by hypothesis then the antecedent is also negated. The proof of the inference therefore is made on formal
and not empirical grounds.

The Epicurean criterion of *inconceivability*, in contrast, ignores formal
considerations and is based on empirical analogy. Philodemus explains it
as follows:

> But sometimes the proposition is not proved to be true in this way (= by elim-
> ination), but from the very impossibility of conceiving that the first is or is of a
> certain character, and the second is not or is not of such a character, as for
> example, "If Plato is a man, Socrates is also a man." If this is true, it becomes
> true also that "If Socrates is not a man, Plato also is not a man", not because by
> the denial of Socrates Plato is denied along with him, but because it is not pos-
> sible for Socrates not to be a man and Plato to be a man; and this inference
> belongs to the method of analogy.
>
> (*De Signis*, Col.XII, 14-31 = Chapt.17)

In formal terms the criterion of inconceivability can be expressed as

$$\text{impossible } (p \wedge \bar{q})$$

In truth, the two formulae—which reflect the verification criteria for the
Stoics and the Epicureans respectively—express a very similar logical context. Even the presence of a modal operator in the inconceivability-criterion
formula is counterbalanced by the equally modal nature of necessity which
we know was required by implication as the Stoics understood it.

Nonetheless, Philodemus presents the two methods as being counter-
opposed and indeed, in the passage quoted above, he seems to indicate
that they are used for different cases.

If the two methods are basically similar from the point of view of logical
content, what in fact renders them different from one another? An answer

to this question may be found by looking at the example which Philodemus offers of an inference verified with the inconceivability method.

"If Plato is a man, then Socrates is also a man"

According to Philodemus, this inference belongs to the method of analogy. Both sides of the inference share an element, that is the property which is attributed to the respective subjects of the two propositions. This could be expressed as

$$m(P) \supset m(S)$$

where "m" is the property "being a man", "P" is Plato, and "S" is Socrates.

This example is useful for understanding precisely what the Epicureans meant by "analogy" and "sign inference based on analogy". While for the Stoics it is not necessary to have a shared element between the two sides of the sign inference, this characteristic is essential for the Epicureans.[6] However, the fact that analogy, from a logical point of view, is being shown to be a situation in which there is a shared property between the subjects of the two propositions which form the inference demonstrates that the logic used by the Epicureans is significantly different from the logic used by the Stoics. While the Stoics use a logic of propositions, the Epicureans use a logic of predicates, which in some ways is more similar to Aristotelian logic.

What distinguishes the elimination method from the inconceivability method is therefore the context of its application, *propositions* for the former and *properties* for the latter. The aim of both methods is nonetheless the same, that of demonstrating that the inference has a necessary nature. Considering the Stoic relationship verified by elimination to be necessary presents no problems whatsoever, since it uses an *a priori* method. However, as the Stoics were quick to point out, there are certain difficulties in considering inference by analogy to be necessary.

For the Epicureans, sign-relationships are discovered empirically and, if the search is carried out efficiently, the relationship between the sign and the object to which it refers is necessary. However, the inconceivability method is itself an empirical method in that something can be inconceivable only in the terms of our own experience. Inferences verified by inconceivability are based on analogy between the sign and what it refers to: "an object having nothing in common with appearance is inconceivable" (Col.XXI, 27-29 = Chapt.36).

Even inferences which go beyond the scope of experience are based on analogy with properties presented by things within the realm of experience. If it is not possible to verify directly the presence of those properties in objects which cannot be perceived, then the indirect test of *non-incompatibility* (*ouk antimartýrēsis*) with empirical data can be used.[7] The inference used as an example of this situation is as follows:

How is it similar to pass from the fact that all people among us, when beheaded, die and do not grow new heads, to the inference that people everywhere, when beheaded, will also be affected in this way?

(Col. XIII, 8-15, Chapt.18)

The first member of the conditional is considered to be the sign of the second. A shared element is established between the two members, and the
inference is strictly speaking an induction. The repeated experience of the
association between beheading (on one side) and death, in addition to the
non-regrowth of the head (on the other), leads to the generalization of this
association so that inferences and predictions can be made even in cases
which have not been previously observed, or which are not observable.

Furthermore, since it is impossible to verify an inference in unobserv-
able cases, the Epicureans consider it to be verified if it is not incompatible
with cases which fall within the realm of experience. It is a question, however, of choosing the right cases, that is, those which belong to the same
type. For example, when attempting to infer the non-regrowth of heads, it
would not be correct to base oneself on the regrowth of hair or nails
(Col.XIII, 20–Col.XIV, 2 = Chapt.18).

8.3 COMMON SIGNS
AND PARTICULAR SIGNS

The dispute over methods of inference verification is also linked to the debate on the possible types of sign. Both the Stoics and the Epicureans made
a distinction between the *common sign* (*koinòn sēmeîon*) and the *particular
sign* (*ídion sēmeîon*). The *common sign* was defined as an entity which can
exist even in the absence of an entity to which it ought to refer (for example, in the inference "If this particular person is rich, then s/he is good",
richness can exist even if goodness does not exist).[8] The *particular sign* was
defined as an entity which can exist only if an imperceptible object to which
it refers exists (for example, in the inference "If motion exists, the void exists", motion can exist only if the void also exists).[9]

The Epicureans agreed with the Stoics in not accepting common signs
as reliable bases of inference, but they disagreed on the fact (claimed by the
Stoics) that all cases of particular signs were also cases of signs established
by *elimination*, that is signs established *a priori*. For the Epicureans it was
possible to set up particular signs by using an empirical criterion, such as
that of *inconceivability*.[10] If we consider the inference:

"If Epicurus is a man, then Metrodorus is also a man"

we find a particular sign based on analogy, that is, on the observation of a
property in Epicurus which it is inconceivable that Metrodorus does not
possess in the same terms. In other words, both schools agreed about the

validity of particular signs, but while the Stoics considered an object to be a sign beginning from the consequent (or rather from what was referred to), the Epicureans considered it from the point of view of the antecedent.

In Epicurean semiotics, it is the object which appears in the antecedent which is associated with certain (constantly observed) properties which becomes the sign of another imperceptible object to which are attributed the properties of the first object. However, the first object (X) must have at least two properties (p_1 and p_2), and the second object must have at least one of these. The property they have in common then becomes the sign of the second property, which may not be directly perceptible in the second object. For example, if a certain individual (X) has the two properties:

p_1 = "being a person"

p_2 = "not being able to re-grow a head once it has been cut off"

it will be sufficient for another individual (X_1) to have the property p_1 to attribute him or her the property p_2 as well.

There are two conditions of general validity for this inference: (i) that association between two properties of the first member is constant; (ii) that this association is not between chance properties. As will be seen below, it is a question of choosing "essential" properties.

There is one last general observation to make about the type of sign proposed by the Epicureans. It seems to take the form of an *iconic sign* since, as Peirce terms it, it refers to its object thanks to a resemblance to the object or to having certain properties in common with it (cf. Peirce, II, p.143; Eco, 1973, p.51).[11]

8.4 STOIC CRITICISM OF EPICUREAN INDUCTION

The Stoics did not accept the validity of inference based on inductive criteria proposed by the Epicureans. They suggested in opposition to this sign inferences based on two general types of criterion: (i) tautology; (ii) L-implication.[12] We can now examine the Stoic reasoning with respect to these. They chose as a starting point for their criticism of the Epicurean method a typical inductive or analogic inference:

"If the people among us are mortal, then all people are mortal."

Formulated in this way, the inference is not acceptable for the Stoics. In order to become acceptable it must be re-formulated according to one of the two criteria mentioned above. We can look first at the *tautology* criterion. The Stoics held that in order to make the inference valid—in their terms, to make the relationship between the two members necessary—

both properties first considered must be contained in the premiss.[13] The inference contained in the example would thus have to be re-formulated as follows:

> Since the people among us are mortal, if people in other places are similar to the people among us in all other respects, and also in being mortal, they would be mortal.

> (Col.II, 37–Col.III, 4 = Chapt.5)

The Stoics themselves admitted the tautological nature of this inference and expressly stated that "The conclusion apprehended by this sign will not differ from the sign from which we also infer (*sēmeioúmetha*)".[14] What happens in fact is that the premiss assumes that both series of entities (that is, both the people among us and the people in places unknown to us) have not only the shared property of being "people", but also simultaneously, the shared property of being "mortal".

In the premiss, the assumption of the very nature of "mortality" — which ought also to be the object of the inference — is for the Stoics *condicio sine qua non* of the necessity of the inference. An inference is valid, therefore, only if it is totally analytical or tautological.

Let us now examine the Stoic reasoning based on the *L-implication* criterion against induction. For this method the Stoics re-formulate the Epicurean inference in such a way that the nature of "mortality" which is to be inferred is contained in the very definition of "people". In order to express the idea that the word |person| semantically implies a series of properties which a definition would reveal, they introduce the expressions *hêi* "insofar as" and *kathó* "according as". Re-formulated according to this principle, the inference in question takes on the following form:

> Since the people among us, insofar as (*hêi*) and according as (*kathó*) they are people, are mortal, people everywhere are also mortal.

> (Col.III, 30-34 = Chapt.6)

Here the expression |person| is given as containing the implicit meaning of "mortality", which was to be inferred.

According to the Stoics, the attribution of the property of being "mortal" to |person| in any way other than that which they propose here (as in the Epicurean method, for example) would render the inference invalid.

8.5 THE EPICUREAN RESPONSE
IN FAVOR OF INDUCTION

The basis of the Epicurean reply to the Stoic criticism is that the Stoic system, even though it might appear to be analytic and *a priori*, is really founded on inductive grounds. According to the Epicureans, the necessity of inferential relations is built upon the observation of constant conjunctions. It is because we never see smoke without fire, nor motion without void, that we can say that smoke is a sign of fire and motion a sign of the void.[15] Thus the *a priori* system of logical necessity which the Stoics use is based on empirical grounds. In addition, even the necessary connection between two terms—a connection which is expressed by means of the elimination method—can be verified only once experience has demonstrated the constant conjunction of these two terms.

As Estelle De Lacy (1938, p.405) puts it: "Hypotheses on the logical and theoretical level are formed on the basis of information about connections of terms arrived at by the observation of sense experience. The validity of these hypotheses, accordingly, is dependent upon their correspondence with facts and their adequacy in comprehending these facts, as well as their internal coherence or consistency with each other."

Though this is the general Epicurean reponse to the Stoic criticism of induction, it is nonetheless worthwhile to look at the specific reply they make to the second Stoic criticism.[16] With respect to L-implication, the Epicureans overturn the Stoic argument and raise an extremely interesting question in the process: the definition of "person" as being mortal is not the starting point for a deductive inference, but the terminus of repeated inductive inferences. To put it another way, the definition of "person" as being such, and as including the property of being "mortal", is constructed as a consequence of two sets of information: (i) information which history provides about the lives of people who have lived before us; (ii) information which derives from the direct experience of our contemporaries. Thus the Epicureans propose the following two propositions as being equivalent:

(a) "People, insofar as they are people, are mortal"

(this is the formula suggested by the Stoics and it indicates the fact that the concept "person" includes the "mortal" property)

(b) "People with this property (of being mortal) are people"[17]

This latter formula is the Epicurean formula which suggests how the definition came to be made. Basically, the Epicureans seem to claim that the definition of "person" is constructed through an accumulation of properties which are discovered by means of an analogical method into entities which are denoted in a certain way, in this case, |people|.[18]

8.6 ESSENTIAL PROPERTIES AND INCIDENTAL PROPERTIES

Another interesting point which emerges from the debate between the Stoics and the Epicureans is the distinction between primary and secondary properties. This distinction goes back to Democritus, who was the first to use it (cf. E.A. De Lacy, 1938, p.403). This problem is far from being banal and can still be seen today in many semantic theories which operate a similar distinction.

The Epicureans deal with this argument in response to the Stoic criticism of their method of analogy, a criticism which called attention to the inherent risk of applying this approach to properties which did not all have the same qualities or belong to the same general type. The Stoics had pointed out that if the concomitance observed between the properties "person" and "mortal" can be generalized, then so too could the concomitance observed between "person" and "short-lived". The risk is that by universalizing this concomitance the property of being short-lived would be applied even to the inhabitants of Mount Athos, famous throughout the ancient world for their proverbial longevity.[19]

In response to this type of criticism, the Epicureans make a distinction between properties which are *variable* (that is, peculiar to certain individuals) and properties which are *constant* (that is, observable in all individuals). Correct inferences would therefore be inferences which are made from constant properties. The Epicureans claim, however, that the very existence of variable properties, far from undermining the analogical inference theory, in fact strengthens it. Given the fact that the people known to us have differing life spans (since some are short-lived and others long-lived), it is possible, because of this existence of variations, to make the correct inference that elsewhere there exist people of exceptional longevity, such as, for example, the inhabitants of Mount Athos.[20]

The Epicureans are forced to go even further along this road of reasoning by the attack the Stoics make on inferences which affect their theory of physics. The Stoic provocation concerns the theory of atoms. According to the Epicurean physical theory, atoms have the properties of being "colorless" and "indestructible"; however, atoms also have the property of being "bodies", and bodies are usually associated with the opposite properties of being "colored" and "destructible". According to the Stoics, the Epicureans would have to make the following two inferences for a correct application of the analogical method:

(1) "Since all bodies in our experience have color, and atoms too are bodies, atoms too have color."

(2) "Since all bodies in our experience are destructible, and atoms too are bodies, atoms must be said to be destructible."[21]

The Epicurean reply to this is particularly interesting for two motives. First of all it once again stresses the necessity of making distinctions between properties to which the analogical method is applicable and those to which

it is not. The analogical method works selectively and in a precisely or-
dered way on properties.[22]

The second point of interest of the Epicurean response lies in the way it
modulates the previous distinction into theoretically stronger terms. It becomes a distinction between properties which we could term *essential* properties and properties which we could term *incidental*. The Epicureans talk
about certain properties which bodies have precisely "insofar as they are
bodies" (*hệi sōmata*), and which they always maintain. The most important
of these is the property of "offering resistance to the touch". This is therefore an essential property. There are also properties which are not strictly
linked to the nature of bodies which vary according to circumstances.
These are incidental properties which bodies have "insofar as they partake
of a nature opposed to the corporeal and non-resistant".[23] Examples of
such properties are being able to be destroyed or color, the latter of which
is so incidental that it disappears entirely in the dark.

These two series of properties can be expressed as a table (Figure 8.1).

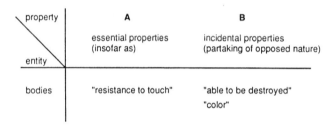

property \ entity	A essential properties (insofar as)	B incidental properties (partaking of opposed nature)
bodies	"resistance to touch"	"able to be destroyed" "color"

Figure 8.1

The Epicureans state quite clearly that generalizing inductive inferences
cannot start from properties in column B, but that it is quite possible to
make generalizing inferences, using the analogical model, starting from the
properties in column A.[24]

As a demonstration of this method of division we can look at the example of "fire";[25] "fire" has the essential property of burning and a series of
variable properties which belong to particular types of fire (cf. Figure 8.2).

In the section of *De Signis* dedicated to Bromius' replies,[26] a sort of classification system is suggested to identify the types of properties. In order to
ensure that inferences are correct, essential (or common, *koinótēta*) properties and incidental (or particular, *idiótēta*) properties must be analyzed in
the various fields or categories which are relevant to a particular object: in
substances, powers, qualities, attributes, dispositions, quantities, numbers. This
classification system seems to have been drawn up in order to justify the
use of generalizing inferences within homogeneous categories. For example, if we consider that even though there exists an infinite variety of human beings and of foods which can nourish them, when we look at straw

property entity	essential properties (koinótēta)	incidental properties (idiótēta)
fires	"burning"	"long or short-lasting" "not all substances burn in the same way" "easy or hard to put out" "hard or soft" "variable colors according to types of fuel"

Figure 8.2

with respect to the category of "powers", we can see that it has two invariant properties: "does not nourish human beings" and "cannot be digested by human beings".[27]

In this way, notwithstanding the different characteristics which this object can present (different colors, different size, different degrees of ripeness, etc.), we can make the inference in all safety that we shall never find anywhere straw which has the properties of being able to nourish and be digested by human beings.

The question remains, however: Just what are, for the Epicureans, the properties of objects "insofar as" (which we have defined as essential properties)? From the examples examined above (and from similar examples), it seems clear that they are the defining properties of an object, the properties which go to make up an object's essential definition.

We saw earlier that for the Stoics a definition was constructed analytically, working through a recognition of the properties implicit in the concept to be defined. For example, an individual, insofar as s/he is a human being, has the property of being mortal.

For the Epicureans, however, things worked in the opposite way. The definition of a concept is constructed through the accumulation of the properties which are common to certain individuals. As a consequence of this, there is no difference between the common (or essential) properties discovered empirically and the properties which make up the definition. The use of the particle *hēi* ("insofar as"), which is used (as we shall see later) in defining expressions, is a further demonstration of this. The problem remains, however, whether it is possible to construct a definition empirically by noting the properties shared by a class of objects or if this method is not in fact suspect (at least in part) due to the preliminary existence of definitions which refer to language as a self-defined and/or historically stratified global structure.

The latter hypothesis seems to come into play with the definition of

|person|. For the Epicureans, the property "mortal" is, as we have seen, an essential or defining property of |person|. The fact cannot be ignored, however, that "mortal" had already formed part of the definition of |person| in a tradition dating back at least to Aristotle. Aristotle had defined |person| as "mortal animal endowed with reason" (*Topics*, V, 1, 128 b, 35–36). The Stoics later defined |person| as "mortal capable of practical wisdom" (*De Signis*, Col.XXII, 22-24 = Chapt.37).[28]

It is therefore probable that definitions of this kind provided an implicit guide for the empirical recognition of properties shared by a series of objects (perceptible people) which could be analyzed with the scope of making an inference about something outside the range of sense perceptions.

8.7 MODALITIES OF INHERENTNESS OF ESSENTIAL PROPERTIES TO THEIR SUBJECTS

In *De Signis*, common or essential properties are linked to their subjects by means of the particles *hêi*, *kathó* or *paró*, which are the equivalents of the English expressions "insofar as", "according as". These are used to indicate a restrictive condition of the inference to the imperceptible, as we have seen with regard to the example of the nature of atoms as "insofar as they are bodies" or of people as mortal "insofar as they are people".

In the section of the treatise dedicated to Demetrius' arguments, four basic meanings of these particles are listed, referring to four methods by which properties are inherent in their subjects.

(i) According to the first meaning, properties can be seen as *necessary consequences* (*ex anánkēs synépetai*). For example, necessary consequences of the fact of being humans are the fact of having a body and being subject to illness and old age.[29] This example seems to suggest a type of property which in certain contemporary semantic theories is termed *factual* or *synthetic* properties,[30] or *π-mode* properties.[31]

(ii) The second meaning sees properties as *essential to the definition* of a certain object or to the basic conception (prolepsis)[32] of it. This may be seen in examples such as: "Bodies, insofar as they are bodies, have volume and resistance", or, "A human individual, insofar as s/he is a human being, is a rational animal". Here the relationship seems to be of an equivalent type. The extension of the first term coincides with that of the second. In the example of |human individual|, the equivalence of definition is given in terms of type ("animal") plus specific difference ("rational").

(iii) The third meaning gives properties as being always *concomitant* (*synbebēkénai*) to the subject, as in the example, "A human individual, insofar as s/he is a human individual, will die".[33] Here contemporary theories term this kind of property *semantic* or *analytic* or *Σ-mode* properties. "Human individual" is included in the wider class of "being mortal". This latter expression then comes back in the form of a semantic marker to make up the sentence which corresponds to the term |human individual|.

(iv) The precise definition of the fourth meaning is unfortunately lost because of a lacuna in the text, but may be hypothesized from the examples which the text preserves. "A human individual is wretchedly unhappy according to the fact that s/he is mad", "A knife cuts according to the fact that it is sharp", "Insofar as they are solid, atoms are indestructible", "A body, insofar as it has weight, falls downwards". Marquand (1883, 9) interprets these as examples of properties which imply gradation of proportions. De Lacy and De Lacy (1978, p. 125) advance the conjecture that what is being dealt with here is properties of properties. Certain of these examples call to mind the semiotic relationship of connotation, understood in the sense of a meaning which depends on another meaning and which is fixed by a code.

The four ways in which properties can be linked to their subject can be set out either according to Marquand's interpretation and terminology or according to that of contemporary semiotics, as shown in the Figure 8.3.

	Marquand	Contemporary semiotics
1.	necessary consequence	factual or synthetic properties
2.	definition or essential conception (prolepsis)	properties equivalent to subject by extension
3.	concomitance	semantic or analytic properties
4.	gradations or proportions	codified connotations

Figure 8.3

8.8 CONCLUSION

Whereas the Stoics had given semiotics a solid logical infrastructure, the Epicureans enrich the consideration of the sign with a series of specifications which have notable practical value in concrete research.

We have already seen how they introduced distinctions between types of sign, types of property and the ways of linking properties to their subjects. In addition to these problems, the Epicureans also took on the problem of the range of variation to which phenomena are subject and the consequent problem of the limits of this variation as a necessary condition for inferences to be correct. They admit the existence of properties which vary from individual to individual, but they refuse to accept that there could be an unlimited range of variation in imperceptible phenomena or even that there could be a range of variation greater than that to be observed in known phenomena. In this way, it cannot be inferred that people outside our experience could be so resistant as to be invulnerable, or that they could be made of iron, or that they could walk through walls in the same way that those we know walk through air. This negation of such inferences is the result of the inconceivability method: "An object having nothing in common with appearance is inconceivable."[34]

De Signis also deals with the problems connected with different types of inference: from class to class, from identical objects, from rare cases, from unique cases. All these problems are linked to one of the constant themes of Epicurean semiotics, the proof of validity of an inference.

For example, an incorrect inference is one that leads to the conclusion that all people are white, starting from the observation that Greek people are white, or *vice versa*, that all people are black, starting from the observation that Ethiopians are black. This kind of inference is mistaken because "anyone who makes inferences of this kind fails because he has not properly made the rounds of all appearances."[35] From the logical point of view, what happens in cases of this type is that a property is applied to a whole class or genus (that of "people") which in fact is a property which occasionally applies to a sub-class or species ("the Greeks" or "the Ethiopians").

In order to guarantee maximum reliability for their method, the Epicureans base their method of inference construction on a theory of progressive semantic inclusion between individuals, species and genuses, that is, a theory of classes. It is legitimate to make inferences between members (classes or a particular individual) which are ranked on an analogous level or which are as close and similar to one another as possible. Of course, this does not mean that inferences can be made exclusively between members ranked at exactly the same level, otherwise induction would have little effect or usefulness, but in most cases an ascending movement of generalizations is envisaged.[36]

The Epicurean treatment of *unique cases* also features a theory of classes. Once again, their treatment of this problem arose in response to criticism from the Stoics. The Stoics had attacked the analogical method by referring to the existence in nature of unique cases, which have no analogy with any other phenomenon. For example, among the great number of types of rock in our experience, only one, lodestone, is able to attract iron; in the same way, only amber has the property of attracting straw and only for the square with side measurements of four units is the perimeter and the area expressed by the same number.[37]

However, according to the Epicureans, the Stoic criticism rather than weakening analogical inference in fact strengthens it. This they demonstrate by reducing unique cases to classes in themselves. Thus, they say, if some lodestones attracted iron and others not, then analogical inference would be undermined, but since this is not the case, it *is* possible to infer the properties of other lodestones from the lodestone under observation.[38]

There are many other points we could list to illustrate the Epicurean achievement in adding breadth and practical applications to the theory of the sign. However, suffice it to say here that the characteristic theme of Epicurean semiotics is its connection to a complete empiricist programme (such as that held by empiricist doctors). There are three basic stages in this programme: (i) observation, (ii) history, (iii) inference from like to like. The first two stages enable the identification of "essential properties", which then allows the passage to the third stage: reconstructing the true semiotic process.

The first two stages place certain conditions on the observation of phenomena in order to discover constant properties: they must be "many", they must be different from one another ("varied"), yet, at the same time, "homogeneous".[39] The third stage then combines the properties of the semantic encyclopedia with the laws of logic (which for the Epicureans are those of the logic of classes).

It is this compromise between the concrete, practical indications stemming from empirical faith and the attempt to maintain maximum formal rigor which constitutes the originality of the Epicurean proposal.

NINE

Latin Rhetoric

9.0 INTRODUCTION

The interest of the Roman world in learning about semiotic arguments formed part of a constant, progressive transfer of the Greek cultural heritage, beginning in the third century B.C. However, in the passage from the Greek world into the Roman world, the semiotic paradigm moved away from the field of philosophy in the strict sense and into the area of judicial rhetoric, where it assumed a central position.

Knowledge through signs had become in Greece, above all in the post-Aristotelian schools, the model for knowledge in general. From the Stoics onwards it had found its setting within the sphere of dialectic, one of the most abstract branches of philosophy, being a subdivision of logic. In contrast, the Romans were more interested in matters which tended principally to the pragmatic, and, although they recognized and appreciated the potentiality of the semiotic paradigm, they immediately channeled it into what were for them the more attractive ends of political and judicial debate, a debate which was conducted with instruments supplied by rhetoric.

This change in prospective can be made clearly apparent by a comparison of Aristotle's and Cicero's attitudes toward rhetoric. Aristotle had indeed used rhetoric as the subject for an important treatise (*Rhetoric*) where he dealt with the theme of signs, but, as he had already done in *Prior Analytics*, he here attempted to reduce the form of the various types of sign to that of the types of syllogism. In doing this, he had laid down a very precise path which indicated that the basic forms of reasoning are established by logic and that these basic forms must remain as a point of reference even when interest shifts from scientific discourse to persuasive discourse, from referential signs to effective signs, as it does in the case of rhetoric.

In Cicero, as with the other Roman writers on rhetoric, there is a notable reversal of the orders of priority. Rhetoric no longer occupies second place after logic, but, in contrast, it is philosophy as a whole which becomes an ancillary science whose role is to contribute towards the making of a fine orator. In the Roman context, eloquence is the highest expression of intellectual activity. A passage in *De Oratore* (II, 159-60) clearly demonstrates Cicero's opinion about the relationship between dialectic and rhetoric. In this passage, Antonius states that those who study dialectic are capable only of criticizing utterances, not of producing them themselves.

Rhetoric in fact is the highest accomplishment of philosophy—from which it cannot be dissociated (cf. *De Oratore*, III, 59-61)—and should not be considered simply the technical ability to add an elegant expression to an already-formed thought. As Marc Baratin and Françoise Desbordes (1981, p.50) point out, Cicero is working on a somewhat ill-defined but frequently reiterated view that if you speak well, you also think well, or, to put it another way, that you can think well only when you can speak well.

Nonetheless, rhetoric does possess an indisputable technical side, and all the Roman writers of rhetorical treatises show how this is organized along two planes of reference. The first of these concerns *types of discourse*, that is, the discourse of courtrooms (judicial), the discourse of public assemblies (political) and the discourse of public ceremonial (demonstrative or epideictic). The second plane of reference regards the parts of rhetoric or the *types of procedure* which must be put into play in order to structure a discourse progressively. These are *inventio* (the search for arguments); *dispositio* (ordering of what has been discovered); *elocutio* (rendering of the arguments in decorated form); *memoria* (mnemonic techniques); *actio* (the delivery or performance of the discourse, gestures and diction).

The consideration of signs rests at the heart of *inventio*, that is, when proofs must be "found" to convince the court of the guilt or innocence of the accused. In rhetoric, proofs have a special force; they start off from reasoning and become part of the procedure used to *convince* (*fidem facere*), the first of the two procedures which form the field of operation of *inventio*. The second of these procedures is to *move* or *touch* the hearers (*animos impellere*), and this consists in concentrating not on the message or on its probatory force, but rather on the emotions of the intended receiver of the message. However, as Barthes (1970) points out, there is some difficulty in using the term "proof" when talking about rhetorical *probationes* (*písteis*), since the word "proof" today has a scientific connotation which is entirely lacking in rhetorical "proofs". (The absence of "scientific" proof is in fact a defining element of rhetorical proof.) Nonetheless, it seems right to acknowledge a certain positive achievement which rhetoric accomplished in its attempt to classify the different degrees of probatory strength and the different argumentative powers of "proofs" or clues.

Different writers, unfortunately, had their own diverse views on how this classification system should be drawn up, and rarely did one coincide with the others any more than very partially. In the following sections of this chapter we shall try to illustrate the ways in which the three main Roman writers on rhetoric—Cornificius (the supposed author of *Rhetorica ad Herennium*), Cicero and Quintilian—reconstruct the evidential paradigm in their works, each in a different way.

9.1 CORNIFICIUS AND
RHETORICA AD HERENNIUM

Direct records of Latin rhetoric begin with treatises written in the first century B.C., among which may be found the *Rhetorica ad Herennium*. This text was formerly attributed to Cicero, following certain statements within the manuscripts themselves, but it is now generally considered to be the work of Cornificius (cf. Calboli, 1969).

Semiotic material is dealt with by Cornificius within the context of *constitutio coniecturalis* in which, for the purposes of verifying whether a certain action was performed by a certain accused individiual, signs are sought which will demonstrate his or her guilt or innocence. The object which is not directly knowable (and to which the signs must refer) is not the fact or the deed of the crime itself, which is already known, but the agent responsible for that action, or the relationship between a certain individual and a certain act. This specific aspect is particular to judicial semiotics and may be well illustrated by an example from Cornificius:

> The issue is Conjectural when the controversy concerns a question of fact, as follows: In the forest Ajax, after realizing what in his madness he had done, fell on his sword. Ulysses appears, perceives that Ajax is dead, draws the bloody weapon from the Corpse. Teucer appears, sees his brother dead, and his brother's enemy with the bloody sword in hand. He accuses Ulysses of a capital crime. Here the truth is sought by conjecture.
>
> (*Rhetorica ad Herennium*, I, 18)

For Roman rhetoric, what is in question in the example (that is, Ulysses' guilt or innocence) cannot be established by spontaneous intuition or rapid abduction.

In the classical period, as Barthes has shown (1970), rhetoric was founded wholly on method and totally rejected the idea that spontaneous or unmethodical insights could lead to anything of worth. Cornificius, therefore, with his typical, minutely detailed classificatory procedure, divides the conjectural state into six parts, which are the six different ways of arriving at the truth (II, 3): *probabile* (probability); *conlatio* (comparison); *signum* (evidential procedure); *argumentum* (sign); *consecutio* (consequence) and *adprobatio* (confirmation).

9.1.1 PROBABILITY

It seems here that we are confronting familiar terminology, for *probabile* could be considered the Latin transcription of *eikós*, and *signum* could be the Latin transposition of *sēmeîon*, considering just these two cases. However, a word of warning: the contents of the Latin expressions are in no way similar to the corresponding Greek concepts!

Probabile is "that through which one proves that the crime was profitable to the defendant, and that he has never abstained from this kind of foul practice" (II, 3). There is very little of the Aristotelian *eikós* in this definition. The concept of *probabile* seems to be linked instead to the psychological make-up of the individual under suspicion ("if the prosecutor contends that the motive for the crime was money, let him show that the defendant has always been covetous; if the motive was public honor, ambitious; he will thus be able to link the flaw in the defendant's character with the motive for the crime." [II, 5]) and, as may be seen from the further division into *causa* ("cause") and *vita* ("life"), it ranges from the concept of "motive" to that of "precedents".

9.1.2 EVIDENTIAL PROCEDURE

Cornificius defines the concept of *signum* as "that which shows that the accused sought an opportunity favorable to success" (II, 6). There is nothing of the Greek concept of *sēmeîon* here either. The *signum* stands for the whole series of procedures for gaining evidence which are carried out by the investigator and which enable the reconstruction of the fact by breaking it down into its component parts which, as Cornificius indicates, are the objects of separate investigations: the scene of the crime, the time, the opportunity, the hope of carrying out the fact, the hope of keeping the fact undiscovered.

9.1.3 THE SIGN

The *argumentum* is an altogether more interesting concept. Although the definition of this concept is hardly encouraging ("*Argumentum* is that through which guilt is demonstrated by means of signs [*argumentis*] that increase certainty and strengthen suspicion"), the examples of this concept clearly indicate that we are now dealing with a sign understood as a single, perceptible phenomenon which refers to a fact that is not directly knowable. It has an inferential structure which is expressed by a hypothetical period: "If the body of the deceased is swollen and black and blue it signifies that the man was killed by poison" (II, 8); if blood is found on the accused's clothing or if s/he has been seen at the scene of the crime, this means that s/he is guilty (ibid.), and so on.

The *argumentum* is, characteristically for Cornificius, sub-divided into three types according to the time relationship existing between the antecedent and the consequent of the sign (prior, contemporary or subsequent). This is in fact a classification which goes back to pre-Aristotelian rhetoric (it is contained in the *Rhetorica ad Alexandrum*, 1430 b, 30 ff., for example) and reaches down also to Quintilian.

9.1.4 UNCONTROLLABLE PHYSICAL REACTIONS

Another extremely interesting concept is that of *consecutio*, which Calboli (ed., 1969, p.232) compares to the *sýmptoma* of medical terminology, *Consecutio* consists of "signs (*signa*) which usually accompany guilt or innocence" (II, 8) such as, for example, when the accused, on interrogation, "blushed, paled, faltered, spoke uncertainly, collapsed, or made some offer, which are all signs of a guilty conscience" (ibid.). What we are dealing with here therefore are uncontrollable physical reactions, involuntary signs which can be compared, in a highly schematic way, with states of mind (such as that of feeling guilty). Even though these signs are not easily displayed with conscious intent to subvert the course of justice, they are nonetheless very open to manipulation at the level of interpretation. The defense may comment on their appearance by saying that the accused is overcome by the danger of the case rather than by having the crime on his or her conscience. On the other hand, the prosecution could comment on the absence of such signs by claiming that the accused had so premeditated the event as to display great confidence and thus that the absence of seeming upset is a "sign of confidence, not of innocence" (ibid.).

9.1.5 CLASSIFICATION AND ARGUMENTATIVE FORCE OF CORNIFICIUS' SIGNS

As we have seen, the procedure of gathering evidence which operates within the area of judicial rhetoric works on several levels: (i) most importantly, there are the *signs of premeditation* which in Cornificius' classification are divided between the *probabile* and the *conlatio* (which involved demonstrating that the accused had had more potential reason for and possibility of committing the crime than anyone else) and the *signum*; (ii) there then follow the *signs of the fact itself*, which are dealt with in the *argumenta* and which relate the accused directly to the crime; (iii) finally there are those signs which are almost experimentally produced, or the signs which relate to the accused's behavior as observed after the crime.

The scheme in Figure 9.1 gives an overall view of Cornificius' classifica-

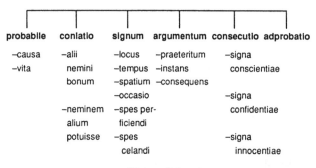

Figure 9.1

tion of conjectural material (cf. Curcio, 1900). When compared with Aristotle's *Rhetoric*, Cornificius' classification appears certainly less philosophically coherent and betrays rather shaky foundations. It nonetheless seems more appropriate for the material of its intended application and not without a certain internal logic in its way of following the accused's signs along a path which stretches right from the time before the crime to the trial.

Cornificius also deals with the argumentative force of signs when he suggests organizing the evidence into a logical structure. He points out that there are signs which do not guarantee certainty, such as "She must have given birth because she is holding a small child" or "Since he is pale, he must be ill" (II, 39). As may be noted, these are signs which correspond to those in Aristotle's second figure. They are not reliable signs because, for example, pallor can of course indicate illness but also a great number of other causes. The interesting point here is that Cornificius does not reject these signs, but accords them an argumentative value when they appear in great numbers ("if, however, all the others are added to them, this kind of sign has a certain importance in increasing suspicion").

9.2 CICERO

Cicero deals with semiotic material and effects significant developments in the treatment of signs in two principal areas of his theoretical works: (i) works dealing with rhetoric; (ii) works dealing with divinatory signs.

If we look at the first of these two areas, we find that interest in signs does not occupy an equally prominent position in all these works. First of all, there are works such as *De Oratore*, *Orator*, *Brutus*, *De Optimo Genere Oratorum*, which deal with a more socio-political argument concerned with defining the figure of the perfect orator, his role in Roman society and his position in relation to the Attic and the Asian schools. In these works the traditional technical apparatus of rhetoric (and, within this, material relating to signs and proofs) is not so much ignored as taken for granted. These more practical matters remain a vast field of implicit competence which serves as background to the argument and comes to the fore only when the author or the characters in the dialogue use its technical terms.

Then there are works such as *De Inventione*, *Partitiones Oratoriae*, and *Topica*, works which—although different from one another in form and purpose—resemble one another in their characteristic of considering and making systematic the huge mass of concepts and ideas which make up the technical apparatus of rhetoric. A weakness in these works may in fact be seen in their excess of classificatory zeal, which comes close to mania at times (especially in *De Inventione*) and which is not always supported by adequate theoretical justification. However, it is within these particular works that we can find the hints and material for a reconstruction of Cicero's theory of the sign.

9.2.1 DE INVENTIONE

De Inventione is one of Cicero's early works and condenses the preceding rhetorical tradition from Aristotle up to Hermagoras. It is entirely natural, therefore, that we should find reproduced in this work certain aspects of the conception of the sign which had been developed and laid down within this tradition. Most noticeably we can find the conception of the sign in propositional form, that is, as an antecedent which enables the discovery of a consequent. Cicero also gives a lot of attention to involuntary signs (blanching, blushing or stuttering of the accused) as evidence of guilt. We can also find the classical division of clues or proofs according to their chronological relationship to the crime (prior, contemporary or after the fact).

De Inventione thus includes many traditional features of the concept of the sign. Nonetheless, it must be said that Cicero offers a classification of signs which is to a very great extent different from the earlier classification. Cicero's classification appears within the context of a theory of the *argumentatio* ("the bringing forward of proof") or the procedure by which elements of proof are adopted in order to confirm a certain hypothesis: "Argumentation seems to be something which can be derived from some kind of thing and which reveals something else in a probable way (*probabiliter ostendans*), or demonstrates it in a necessary way (*necessarie demonstrans*)" (*De Inventione*, I, 44). Even though the usual semiotic vocabulary is not being used here, this definition is in fact referring to the mechanism of the sign. Something which has been found (a clue which has been recorded in the lawyer's brief) refers to something else. We have here also the Aristotelian distinction between a weak argumentative force (*probabiliter ostendans*) and a necessary inference (*necessarie demonstrans*).

9.2.1.1 *Necessary and weak reference*

Necessary signs are defined as follows: "Something is demonstrated in a necessary way which cannot be verified or proved except by the way it is said" (ibid.). Examples of necessary signs are "If a woman has given birth, then she has been with a man" (ibid.), "If a person is breathing, that person is alive", "If it is day, it is light" (*De Inventione*, I, 86). Cicero explains that in cases of this kind the antecedent and the consequent are linked by a binding relationship (*cum priore necessario posterius cohaerere videtur* [*De Inventione*, I, 86]).

Unnecessary or weak relationships between signs and their referents are defined in this way: "That is probable which for the most part usually comes to pass, or which is a part of the ordinary beliefs of mankind, or which contains in itself some resemblance to these qualities, whether such resemblance be true or false."

Cicero draws attention to two important characteristics with this latter definition: the probable and the debatable. Aristotle had attributed the first of these to *eikós* (verisimile). Cicero's first two examples are of precisely the kind that Aristotle classifies as *eikós*: "If a woman is a mother, she loves her child", "If a person is avaricious, then that person will pay little respect to the oath" (*De Inventione*, I, 46).

These two examples also illustrate the relationship of generalization which for Aristotle constitutes the verisimile (*eikós*; cf., Aristotle, *Rhetoric*, 1357 a). Cicero's third example, however, seems to be of a very different type and to be much closer to Aristotle's *sēmeîon*: "If there is a great deal of dust on a person's shoes, that person must have been on a journey" (*De Inventione*, I, 47).

9.2.1.2 *Clues*

The category of *signum* appears as a subdivision of non-necessary or weak signs, along with that of *credibile* (credible), *iudicatum* (judgement) and *comparabile* (comparable). These last three concepts seem to differ on the basis of extrinsic criteria and do not in fact appear in later treatments, but the *signum* represents a very particular category of phenomenon: "A *sign* is something apprehended by one of the senses and indicating (*significat*) something that seems to follow logically as a result of it: the sign may have occurred before the event or in immediate connection with it, or have followed after it, and yet needs further evidence and corroboration" (*De Inventione*, I, 48). Examples of *signa* are "blood", "pallor", "flight" and "dust".

These are *clues*, understood as perceptible, barely codified, generally involuntary, phenomena. Here they are given in a non-propositional form but there is nothing to prevent them from being developed into propositions, as may be seen in the case of the "dust" clue: "If there is a great deal of dust on a person's shoes, then that person must have been on a journey". Clues are then subdivided according to the standard time relationship with the crime.

The classification offered in *De Inventione* can therefore be represented as shown in Figure 9.2.

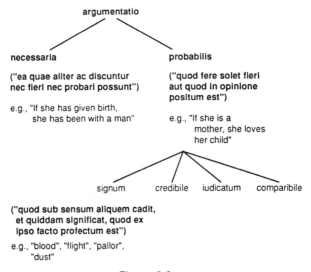

Figure 9.2

9.2.2 *PARTITIONES ORATORIAE*

The *Partitiones Oratoriae* is a mature, late work by Cicero and presents a classification of semiotic material which reveals certain significant differences and original features with respect to his earlier treatise. Most importantly, the terminology used in this work sheds its similarity to the Greek models and is completely Latinized. In addition, *clues* (here called *vestigia facti*) are no longer placed as a subdivision of another category but are now given an autonomous role. The final important innovation is that in this work the Aristotelian distinction between "extrinsic topics" (which correspond to Aristotle's "extratechnical proofs" *átechnoi*) and "intrinsic topics" (which correspond to the "technical proofs", *éntechnoi*) which was criticized in *De Inventione* (II, 47) is now accepted. This distinction is further developed in Cicero's *Topica*.

It is interesting to note that along with human witnesses, "divine" witnesses such as oracles, auguries, presages, soothsayers and sacred responses (as made by priests, interpreters of entrails and interpreters of dreams) (cf. *Partitiones Oratoriae*, 6) are also included in the extrinsic topics. This is no doubt a vestige of the very ancient, sacred conception of the administration of justice. It is also evidence of a continual resurfacing of the divinatory model within the context of semiotic concerns, even when signs have been operating in the secular sphere for a very considerable period of time.

Cicero's use of divinatory echoes is by no means an isolated case within the judicial sphere. An example from Greek culture may be found in *The Murder of Herodes*:

> Whatever proof is to be found in human evidence and testimony has now been presented. But in casting your vote in such a case as the present one you ought also to attach great weight to the signs provided by the gods.
>
> (Antiphon, *The Murder of Herodes*, V, 81)

9.2.2.1 *Verisimiles and characteristic signs*

Human signs are dealt with in the context of intrinsic topics and in particular in the context of the state of conjectural motivation. Conjecture can be made from two types of sign: *verisimilia* (verisimiles) and *notae propriae rerum* (characteristic signs of things).

Cicero states that *verisimile* is "that which usually occurs in such and such a way — for example that youth is more prone to self-indulgence" (*Partitiones Oratoriae*, 34). This type of sign corresponds to the Aristotelian *eikós*, with which it shares the probabilistic and generalizing nature.

The *nota propria rei* is defined as "a proof that is never otherwise and that supplies an indication that is certain, as smoke is a certain indication of fire" (ibid.). This seems to be the familiar necessary sign, as is suggested both by the example and by the adjective *proprius*, which reflects the idea of *ídion sēmeîon* (particular sign). For Aristotle, the particular sign was the specific characteristic of a particular genus; for example, the fact that lions have large extremities is a sign of their courage (cf. *Prior Analytics*, 70 b, 11-38). The later schools considered the particular sign to have the nature of necessity and defined it as a sign which cannot exist unless the thing to which it refers exists (cf. Philodemus, *De Signis*, I, 12-16).

9.2.2.2 *Indications of the fact, or clues*

Cicero also considers the *vestigia facti* (indications of the fact, or clues), of which he provides the following examples: "a weapon, blood, a cry, a stumble, change of color, stammering, trembling, or anything else that can be perceived by the senses: also some sign of preparation or of communication with somebody, or something seen or heard or hinted later on" (*Partitiones Oratoriae*, 39). The only definition Cicero gives of this type of sign is to say that it deals with "phenomena (which can be) perceived by the senses", a characteristic shared with the *signa* mentioned in *De Inventione* (I, 48) (which lists similar examples) and with the *argumenta* used by Cornificius (*Rhetorica ad Herennium*, II, 8).

Scholarly debate has attempted to discover whether the *vestigia facti* can be more closely related to necessary signs (*notae propriae rerum*) or to the verisimile (*verisimile*) (cf. Crapis, 1988, pp.184ff). In actual fact, the *vestigia facti* would seem to represent a fairly autonomous category which reflects neither the necessity of the necessary signs nor the typical features of the verisimile. It is plausible that the category of *vestigia facti* corresponds to the Aristotelian category of *sēmeîon*, which is different from both *tekmērion* and *eikós*.

In a section of the *Partitiones Oratoriae* (114), similar examples are given to those used above and the *vestigia facti* (which in this passage are also called *signa*) are defined as *consequentia*. *Consequentia* are inferences drawn from the consequent, a characteristic which for Aristotle defined non-necessary or weak signs. However, while Aristotle condemned *sēmeîa* on epistemological grounds because of their lack of certainty, Cicero is quick to recognize the usefulness of this kind of sign when it appears in large numbers of examples (*coacervata proficiunt*, 40).

The classification of signs given by Cicero in the *Partitiones Oratoriae* may be represented as shown in Figure 9.3.

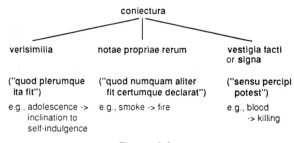

Figure 9.3

9.2.3 CICERO'S WORKS ON DIVINATION

Judicial rhetoric can be linked to divination in several ways. The most evident of these is the fact that both fields use signs in order to attain knowledge of facts which are not directly accessible to sense perception. Another similarity lies in the distinction which both judicial rhetoric and divination make between purely conjectural elements and natural or obvious elements. The dichotomy which holds in rhetoric between *technical proofs* (or conjectural proofs) and *extra-technical proofs* is matched in divination by the distinction between *artificial divination* and *natural divination*. Cicero himself points out a further similarity between these two fields when he notes that signs in divination are sometimes interpreted in diametrically opposed ways, just as in a trial the prosecution and the defense sometimes offer two very different, yet both plausible, interpretations of the same fact (cf. *De Divinatione*, II, 55).

However, there is a notable difference in approach for Cicero's treatment of judicial rhetoric and divination. For Cicero respects the methods of judicial investigation whereas he holds divination in barely disguised contempt. Like many of the intellectuals of his time—people who had been trained in the essentially rationalist methods of Greek philosophical investigation and who were also actively involved in political life—Cicero felt the need to establish a clear distinction between religion and superstition, of which, in his view, divination formed part. Religion belonged to the ancient Roman tradition, and, because it formed part of the very foundations of the state, it had to be conserved, lest the state itself disintegrate. Superstition, however, represented the irrational accumulation of spurious elements which polluted and undercut the credibility of religion; this had to be rejected, or the freedom of the individual Roman citizen would be restricted with regard to responsibility in the governing of the Republic.

Cicero treats these arguments in *De Natura Deorum*, in *De Fato* and particularly in *De Divinatione*. *De Divinatione* is written in the form of a dialogue between Cicero and his brother Quintus, who defends divination by using the traditional theories which linked divination to the existence of the gods. The comments Cicero makes in opposition to the views put forward by Quintus are of interest not only because they can be seen as a fully fledged criticism of a sectorial semiotic mechanism but also because they present a contribution to a general conception of the sign.

9.2.3.1 *"Artificial" divination*

According to the theory proposed by Quintus, the gods can be seen as sources of information and as senders in a process of divinatory communication in which humankind is the intended receiver. However, there are two different types of divination and consequently two different forms of communication process.

The first type is that of *divinatio artificialis*, that is, a professional technique of decoding entrusted to specialists who each have her or his own branch of expertise: *extispices* (interpreters of entrails), *interpretes monstrorum et fulgurum* (interpreters of monstrous births and of lightning), *augures* (interpreters of the flight of birds), *astrologi* (interpreters of stars), *interpretes sortium* (interpreters of combinations of blocks mixed in an urn and drawn out at random). In this kind of divination, the information sent by the god first takes the form of a perceptible expressive substance which—through the *ars* of the interpreter—can then be matched to a semantic content.

Interpretations of this type are based on assumptions taken from the Stoic theory that all phenomena are linked one to another in a continuous chain of cause and effect. This chain starts from the divine *lógos* and represents fate (*heimarméné*). It cannot be fully known by humankind since omniscience is a divine rather than human prerogative (*De Divinatione*, I, 125-27).

Nonetheless, the existence of cyclic time is envisaged: it "is like the unwinding of a cable: it creates nothing new and only unfolds each event in its order" (*De Divinatione*, I, 127). Humankind can thus, by careful observation, grasp the way in which events repeat themselves and—even though it remains impossible to know the causes of events directly—the characteristic evidence of these can be seen (*signa tamen causarum et notas cernunt* [ibid.]).

Given the fact that it is possible to transmit memories of past connections through time, a code based on repetition is created. The process can be illustrated as shown in Figure 9.4.

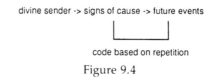

divine sender -> signs of cause -> future events

code based on repetition

Figure 9.4

9.2.3.2 *"Natural" divination*

The second type of divination is *"naturalis"*, deriving from direct divine inspiration without passing through the mediation of an external sign. The forms of foresight which arise from prophetic possession (that is, *vaticinationes*) and those which occur in *dreams* form part of this type of divination. The philosophical background to this type of divination is provided by the theories of the Peripatetic school (cf. *De Divinatione*, II, 100), according to which the soul has a natural link with the divinity and—once it is moved by divine frenzy or liberated (in sleep) from the chains which bind it to the body—participates directly in the knowledge of the god. In this case, the role of the code is much reduced and is more or less replaced by a partial identification between the sender and the receiver of the communication, according to the scheme in Figure 9.5.

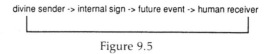

divine sender -> internal sign -> future event -> human receiver

Figure 9.5

9.2.3.3 *"Semiological" criticisms of divinatory signs*

Cicero's objections to divination are based on specifically semiotic grounds. Cicero's general thesis in denying value to divination is that divination is not really semiotic in nature, that is, that the phenomena which it interprets as signs are not truly such, or, at least, they do not behave as antecedents with respect to consequents.

In order to distinguish true signs from the so-called signs of divination, Cicero sets up a comparison between scientific techniques (such as medicine, meteorology, navigation, the farmer's and the astronomer's forecasting techniques) and divination. In both cases, there is an attempt to predict a future event from some kind of evidence. However, whereas the professional techniques adopt a proper methodology which involves "science (*ars*), reasoning (*ratio*), experience (*usus*) and conjecture (*coniectura*)" (*De Divinatione*, II, 14), divination technique is based rather on "chance, thus it seems to me that it is not in the power of the god himself to know what event is going to happen accidentally and by chance" (*De Divinatione*, II, 18).

This opposition between what is *code* (even if this is created by natural links based on statistical frequency)[1] and what is *chance* is identical to the opposition which the Hippocratic doctors tended to see as distinguishing their professional science from divination and magical medicine (cf. *Ancient Medicine*, Chapter XII).

Cicero demolishes the theory whereby artificial divination also uses repeated observation of coincidences in strong rationalist terms, stating that it is both ridiculous and untenable (cf. *De Divinatione*, II, 74).

9.3 QUINTILIAN

By the time of Quintilian, the transformation of the Republic into the Empire meant that rhetoric was no longer of any use as a means of social or political agitation. Thus, instead of the pragmatic tool which it had represented for Cicero, rhetoric had become principally a theoretical subject. Against this background, Quintilian illustrates the principles of the art of rhetoric more clearly and more completely than any other writer, yet he is basically recording the fossilization that eloquence was undergoing at the time of writing.

Quintilian's *Institutio Oratoria* (c.93-95 A.D.) presents a complete programme for the training of an orator, a course in which semiotic abilities play an important part. Much of Quintilian's work contains elements of indisputable semiotic relevance, but the *Institutio Oratoria* contains a whole section devoted to signs, as indeed was the practice now for all treatises on rhetoric.

As with the earlier authors of treatises on rhetoric, it must be clearly stated that, for Quintilian as well, any discussion of the concept of the sign is firmly embedded in the area of judicial considerations, and it is dealt with uniquely from this perspective. Signs form part of the *probationes arti-*

ficiales, the evidence which the ability (*ars*) of the orator will reveal in order to achieve the acquittal or conviction of the accused. The *probationes inarti- ficiales* are those elements which derive from events outside the trial itself and which are delivered to the orator as a part of his brief.

The orator's inventory can be illustrated as in Figure 9.6.

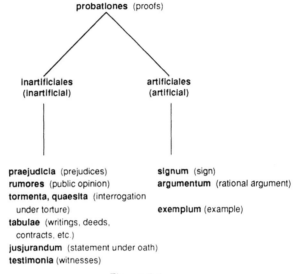

Figure 9.6

9.3.1 FORMAL AND EPISTEMOLOGICAL
NATURE OF QUINTILIAN'S RHETORIC

In addition to its judicial context, Quintilian's rhetoric is remarkable for its strong theoretical basis. This tends to set its concerns as much as possible within the formal terms of logic (even though Kennedy [1969] has shown that Quintilian is not entirely at ease in this field).

The three types of *technical* evidence (*signa, argumenta, exempla*) are thus placed in a network of logical relations which are very close to those of implication, that is, the relation "if *p*, then *q*". The mechanism for evaluating the strength of the evidence has to take on a logical form which reflects one of the following four types: (i) concluding from the existence of one thing that another thing does not exist ($p \rightarrow \sim q$) ("It is day, therefore it is not night"); (ii) concluding from the existence of one thing that another thing exists ($p \rightarrow q$) ("The sun is shining therefore it is day"); (iii) concluding from the non-existence of one thing that another thing exists ($\sim p \rightarrow q$) ("It is not night, therefore it is day"); (iv) concluding from the non-existence of one thing that another thing does not exist ($\sim p \rightarrow \sim q$) ("This is not a rational being, therefore this is not a human being") (cf. *Institutio Oratoria*, V, 8, 7).

Looked at within the context of this kind of network, signs tend to be seen as antecedents in respect to consequents. Quintilian does not feel it necessary to state this idea explicitly, for it forms part of the rhetorical and logical tradition which stretches back to the Greeks. Quintilian indeed draws on many examples from this tradition, including the (by now famous) "If a woman has given birth, then she has had sexual intercourse with a man"; this example, with slight variations turns up again and again in all writers who concern themselves in some way with signs.

Like Aristotle, to whom he makes constant reference, Quintilian deals with signs in an epistemological rather than a logical framework. He is interested above all in the possibility of acquiring knowledge by means of signs.

> Aristotle, who was interested in finding arguments capable of explaining the necessary links between facts, posited a number of epistemological distinctions between necessary signs and weak signs. The Stoics, who were interested only in the formal mechanisms of inference, avoided the problem. Only Quintilian (*Institutio Oratoria*, V, 9), who was interested in the reactions of a forensic audience, tried to account for every type of persuasive sign according to an epistemological hierarchy.[2]

With respect to the persuasive nature of *signa*, Quintilian makes a preliminary distinction: *signa* have much in common with extra-technical evidence, in the way that, for example, a piece of blood-stained clothing, screams and cries, or pallor are not produced by the skill of the orator, but are delivered to him as part of his brief. In addition, if *signa* refer to an incontestable meaning, then there is no possibility of reasoning through debate, whereas if they are ambiguous they are not proofs, but they themselves require proofs (*Institutio Oratoria*, V, 9, 1).

It is for this reason that signs must be divided first of all into *necessary* and non-necessary or *weak signs*.

9.3.2 NECESSARY SIGNS

Quintilian defines *signa necessaria* as signs which "aliter se habere non possunt" (*Institutio Oratoria*, V, 9, 3), that is, they are antecedents which refer in a necessary way to consequents. He indicates that they correspond to the *tekmḗria* of the Greek tradition. They are irrefutable signs (*ályta sēmeîa*), that is, they are irrevocably linked to their consequents. Information obtained from these signs is certain, reliable and incontrovertible.

With typical ancient-world classificatory zeal, Quintilian goes on to subdivide this type of sign into three groups according to whether their consequents are to be found in the *past* ("If a woman has given birth, she has had sexual intercourse with a man"), in the *present* ("If a strong wind is blowing on the sea, there are waves") or in the *future* ("If a person has been wounded in the heart, that person will die") (cf. *Institutio Oratoria*, V, 9, 5).

Quintilian next subjects this type of sign to a further form of classification based on the criterion of the *reversibility* of the terms. Some signic relationships, such as "If one breathes, one is alive", maintain the relation of necessity even when the antecedent and the consequent are inverted: "If one is alive, one breathes". However, there are some types of signic relationship in which such reversibility is not possible, for example "If a person walks, that person moves", "If she has given birth, she has had sexual intercourse with a man", "If someone is wounded in the heart, that person will die", "If the harvest has been gathered in, the seed was sown", "If someone has been wounded with a sword, then there is a scar" (cf. *Institutio Oratoria*, V, 9, 7). Quintilian here seems to be raising the question of *"conversion" (antistréphein)*, which for Aristotle (cf. *Prior Analytics*, 70 b, 32 ff.) provides the condition for the particular sign, that is, "the existence of a single sign for a single thing".

9.3.3 NON-NECESSARY OR WEAK SIGNS

Quintilian places *signa non necessaria* in correspondence to the Greek *eikóta*, that is, verisimilitudes or facts which form part of common opinion, facts which, as Eco points out (cf. Eco, 1984a, p.38), are technically able to be as convincing as necessary signs but depend on codes and scripts which a certain community defines as "good".

Quintilian distinguishes three basic types of weak sign according to the strength of the link which is set up between the antecedent and the consequent: *firmissimum* (almost certain), this corresponds to the statistical norm, as in "If they are parents, they love their children"; *propensius* (highly probable), as in "If a person is in good health, that person will survive until the next day"; *non repugnans* (not contradictory), i.e., something which does not contradict common sense, as in "If there has been a theft within a house, then it has been perpetrated by someone who was in the house" (cf. *Institutio Oratoria*, V, 10, 16).

None of these inferences offers a fully acceptable degree of certainty. However, from the point of view of persuasion and convincing argument, they can be extremely effective, especially when many of them can be provided—for quantity will make each of them more convincing (cf. *Institutio Oratorio*, V, 9, 8)—and because they recreate a pattern which reflects public opinion.

9.3.4 MATERIAL CLUES

When dealing with *signa non necessaria* (*Institutio Oratoria*, V, 9, 8), Quintilian also talks about *signum* without qualifying the noun in any way, and he places this in correspondence both with *indicium* and *vestigium* and with the Greek *sēmeîon*. It is not entirely clear whether this is intended as a distinct category with respect to the preceding categories (necessary signs and verisimilitudes), as occurs, for example, in Aristotle's works, or if Quintilian simply considered *eikóta* and *sēmeîa* to be analogous. If the latter hypothesis is true, then we can speak of a real mistake on Quintilian's part, as indeed Cousin would believe (cf. J. Cousin, 1936/67, p. 232). However, the fact that Quintilian considers the word *vestigium* to be synonymous with *signum* and that he uses the example of blood stains which enable a murder to be discovered leads us rather in the direction of understanding his conception of *signum* to be parallel to that of the *vestigia facti* which appear in Cicero's *Partitiones Oratoriae* (39), where the same example is used.

This would mean that Quintilian is here referring to the standard category of material, non-verbal, clues (bruises, swellings, wounds, etc.) (cf. *Institutio Oratoria*, V, 9, 11) which are accessible to sense perception. Quintilian defines these as things "which enable us to infer that something else has happened" (*per quod alia res intelligitur* [V, 9, 9]) and emphasizes that with this type of sign a relation of signification is set up which begins from a sense perception and leads to something else.

The preceding category (that of *signa non necessaria* = *eikóta*) classified facts or properties which provided somewhat unreliable knowledge, in the sense that it was information which could not be proved scientifically (for example, if someone is in good health, it is not *scientifically* certain that she or he will survive until tomorrow). The category of *signa* deals rather with facts which are unreliable because they are *ambiguous* (for example, a blood stain on a piece of clothing could indeed indicate a murder, but could equally well have been caused by a nose bleed or a splash of blood from a sacrificial animal).

The final classification of Quintilian's idea of signs is therefore as shown in Figure 9.7. This would explain why Quintilian terms *signa non necessaria*,

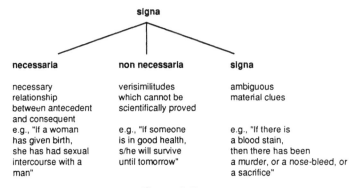

Figure 9.7

rather than *signa*, clear cases of verisimilitude such as the examples he takes (and comments critically upon) from Hermagoras: "Hermagoras would include among such signs, but not necessary signs, an argument such as the following: 'Atlanta cannot be a virgin, as she has been roaming the woods in the company of young men' " (*Institutio Oratoria*, V, 9, 12). Quintilian is not very willing to consider this and other extremely weak verisimilitudes as acceptable evidence in a trial: "If we accept this view, I fear that we shall come to treat all inferences from a fact as signs. Nonetheless, such arguments are in practice treated exactly as if they were signs." (ibid.). What we have here is the typical situation of judicial semiotics, caught in a perennial quandary between the objectively acceptable proof of arguments and the skill of the lawyer in making convincing use of even the weakest signs.

Of course, from the general semiotic point of view, there is no objection whatsoever to considering "all inferences from a fact" as signs. The properties recorded in the encyclopedia with respect to a certain object or fact are all perfectly valid signs of that object or fact. It is circumstantial or contextual relationships which bring about the differences in probatory force. For example, a gun can be the sign of a crime, but things are put under a very different light if it is found in the home of a suspected terrorist, or a police officer, or a gunsmith (cf. Eco, 1984a, pp.37-38).

This last point seems to have been, perhaps unconsciously, understood by the ancient practitioners of rhetoric—to some extent by Aristotle, but even more so by Quintilian. While making a clear-cut distinction between "scientific certainty" and "certainty according to the socio-cultural codes", Quintilian nonetheless admitted and used both, but recommended (in the second case) that one gather as many mutually enhancing pieces of evidence as possible.

TEN

Augustine

10.0 UNIFICATION OF THE THEORY OF SIGNS AND THE THEORY OF LANGUAGE

With Augustine we reach for the first time an explicit fusion of the theory of the sign with the theory of language. Such a rigorous and important theoretical development remains unmatched for at least the following fifteen centuries, until Saussure's *Cours de linguistique générale* is written.

The central importance of semio-linguistic matters in Augustine's works derives principally from his reading of the Stoics, as his early work *De Dialectica* (387 A.D.) clearly demonstrates. This work summarizes many of the main Stoic semiotic themes, including the principle that knowledge is, on a simple level, knowledge gained by means of signs (cf. Simone, 1969, p.95).

However, there are certain elements which differentiate Augustine's treatment of semiotic material from that of the Stoics. The Stoics collected and formalized a long tradition rooted principally in medicine and divination; they considered to be truly signs (*sēmeîa*) only non-verbal signs, such as the smoke which reveals a fire or the scar which refers to a previous wound. Augustine—in his most important departure from the Stoics—is the first in the ancient world to include in the category of *signa* not only non-verbal signs such as gestures, military insignia, fanfares, mime, etc., but also the expressions of spoken language ("We call sign in general everything that means something, and among these we may include words too" [*De Magistro*, 4.9]).

The second important point of divergence between Augustine and the Stoics is that the Stoics had identified the utterance as the point of conjunction between the signifier (*sēmaînon*) and the signified (*sēmainómenon*), an element which did not coincide with the sign (*sēmeîon*). In contrast, Augustine identifies the individual linguistic expression, that is the *verbum* ("word") as the element in which signifier and signified are united, and considers this unification to be a sign of something else ("Thus, after having sufficiently demonstrated that words [*verba*] are nothing else but signs [*signa*] and that something which does not mean something cannot be a sign, you have proposed a verse in which I have struggled to show what the individual words might mean" [*De Magistro*, 7.19]).

In a third important area of difference, the Stoics had formulated a theory of language characterized by the features of being formal (the *lektón* corre-

sponded to no actual substance) and centered on signification; Augustine proposes instead a theory of the linguistic sign which has a psychological (signifieds are to be found in the mind) and communicative (signifieds pass into the
mind of the hearer) nature (cf. Todorov, 1977, Eng. tr., pp.36-37; Markus,
1957, p.72).

10. 1 THE SEMIOTIC TRIANGLE AND TERMINOLOGICAL STRATIFICATION

De Dialectica begins with an analysis of the very concept of "word" (*verbum
simplex*), and starting from here Augustine makes a series of very interesting terminological distinctions.

In Chapter V of this work, Augustine makes a three-fold distinction which
may be compared to the modern concepts of signifiers, signified and referent.
First of all he identifies the *vox articulata* (or *sonus*) of the word, which is what
is heard by the ear when the word is pronounced. He then identifies the
dicibile[1] (which corresponds, even from the point of view of the linguistic
transposition, to the Stoic *lektón*), which he defines as what is apprehended by
and contained in the mind. The third element is the *res*, which is defined as
any object which either (i) can be perceived by the senses or by the intellect, or
(ii) is not accessible to the senses (*De Dialectica*, Chapter V) (cf. Figure 10.1.).

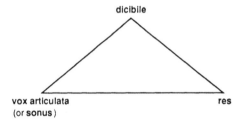

Figure 10.1

However, Augustine does not consider signs merely from the point of
view of signification, but also from that of their powers of designation. This
consideration prompts him to operate a further terminological subdivision
according to the two possible aspects of the referent of a word: (i) the word
can refer back to itself as its own referent (as happens with quotations, or
metalinguistic designations), in which case it takes the name *verbum*;[2] (ii)
the word, understood as the combination of signifier and signified, which
has something other than itself as referent (as happens in the denotative
use of language) in which case it takes the name of *dictio*.[3]

It is precisely this concept of *dictio* which, as Baratin (cf. 1981) has noted,
constitutes the element of conjunction between the theory of language and
the theory of the sign. This occurs because the Stoic concept of *léxis* (articu-
lated signifier, but not necessarily a carrier of meaning) had undergone a shift

in meaning in the course of investigations of language in the intervening centuries. *Dictio* is the translation of *léxis*, but it does not have the same meaning as the Stoics gave to *léxis*. Here it carries meaning it was given by the grammarians of Alexandria, in particular Dionysius Thrax, who defined *léxis* as "the smallest part of the elaborated utterance" (*Grammatici Graeci*, I, 22, 4). Thus it is halfway between letters and syllables on the one side and the utterance on the other. In this position, *léxis* becomes a carrier of meaning (in contrast to letters and syllables, which do not have meaning), but of only partial meaning (whereas the utterance has complete meaning).

Since the Alexandria grammarians had moved the individual word into the position of central importance (whereas the Stoics had held the utterance to be centrally important), the word now takes on the functions which were formally attributed only to the utterance. Most importantly, the word can now be a sign.[4]

Augustine defines the word definitely as a sign in Chapter V of *De Dialectica*: "A word is a sign (*signum*) of any sort of thing. It is uttered by a speaker and can be understood by a hearer". A sign is defined as "something which is itself sensed and which indicates to the mind (*animus*) something beyond the sign itself." (ibid.).

10.2 THE RELATION OF EQUIVALENCE AND THE RELATION OF IMPLICATION

As a result of focusing attention on the word rather than on the utterance, Augustine invokes the Platonic opposition between word and thing. There is nothing fortuitous in this parallel as Plato is the only thinker prior to Augustine who had a semiotic conception of language. For Plato, a name was *délōma*, a discovery of something not directly accessible to sense perception, or the essence of a thing. While in *Cratylus* the issue was whether or not the relationship between name and thing was an iconic relationship (with the solution which we have already encountered in Chapt. 4), for Augustine, the relationship is immediately conceived of as a relation of signification: a name "signifies" a thing (an idea which is equivalent to "being a sign of a thing").

Once Augustine has proposed his conception of words as signs, this change of perspective results in a series of inevitable modifications. In earlier theories of language, the relationship between linguistic expressions and their contents was conceived of as a *relation of equivalence*. As we have seen, the motivation for this was epistemological and concerned the possibility of working directly on language, rather than on objects of reality, since language was understood to be a system for the representation of reality (even though inevitably mediated through the mind). In contrast, the relationship between a sign and the thing it referred to was understood to be a *relation of implication*, thanks to which the first term, by the mere fact of existing, enabled the passage to knowledge of the second term. Umberto Eco (cf. 1984a, pp.33-34) has suggested that within the Stoic utterance the relations between the signic and the linguistic relationships can be illustrated by a scheme in which the implicational level is based on the level of equivalence. The relationships can be illustrated as shown in Figure 10.2. Here **E** indicates expression, **C** context,

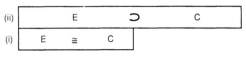

Figure 10.2

⊃ stands for "implies" and ≅ indicates "is equivalent to". In Augustine, the unification of the two perspectives is achieved at the level of the individual word without any need to resort to equivalence relations. At most, *dictio*, represented by level i, is made up of the union (or logical product) of a *vox* (signifier) and a *dicibile* (signified), and the resulting unit becomes a sign of something else (level ii).

10. 3 CONSEQUENCES OF THE UNIFICATION OF PERSPECTIVES

The first consequence of Augustine's process of unification is, as Umberto Eco has pointed out (cf. 1984a, p.33), that the position of language within the implicative context is no longer altogether comfortable or convincing. Language is too strong and too highly structured a system to bend itself to a theory of signs which had been developed to describe very elusive, generic relationships such as those found, for example, in the classifications of Greek and Roman rhetoric. Semiotic implication was conceived of as being broad enough to encompass the entire range of the necessary and nonnecessary relations.

Language, as Augustine makes clear in *De Magistro*, has a special characteristic not shared by other sign systems; language is a "primary modeling system",[5] that is, a system into which any other semiotic system can be translated. The strength and importance of language mean that relations with other sign systems are inverted, and that language, rather than being a species, becomes a genus. Slowly but surely the model of the linguistic sign will end up as the semiotic model *par excellence*.

However, by the time this process of evolution reaches its apex in Saussure, the implicative nature of language has been lost along the way, and the linguistic sign has crystallized in the degraded form of the dictionary model, in which the relationship between a word and its content is understood as a relationship of synonymy or essential definition.

The second important consequence of Augustine's unification of the two theories concerns the problem of the foundation of dialectic and of science (cf. Baratin, 1981, pp.266 ff.). While the relationship between language and real objects was understood in terms of equivalence, the former did not seem to be responsible for knowledge of the latter. However, once the word has been granted the nature of being a sign, the knowledge of a word seems to imply, in itself and *a priori*, the knowledge of the thing it signifies. The whole semiotic tradition, after all, agreed in considering the sign as a means of access, without further mediation, to knowledge of the object to which it referred.

Augustine thus has to deal with the problem of taking a firm position on the question of whether or not language provides, in itself and by its very nature, information about the things it signifies.

10.4 LANGUAGE AND INFORMATION

Augustine faces the problem of the informative nature of linguistic signs in his *De Magistro* (389 A.D.). This work is in the form of a dialogue with his son Adeodatus and begins by establishing two basic functions of language: (i) teaching (*docere*) and (ii) recalling to memory (*commemorare*), either to one's own, or other people's memory. These functions are simultaneously informative and communicative as they centrally involve the presence of an addressee at the moment of providing information.

The first portion of the dialogue demonstrates that these two functions, particularly the informative function, are carried out by language in that it is a system of signs. It is words, in the quality of signs, which give information about things, and nothing else can achieve this function.

In the second part of the dialogue, however, Augustine returns to the argument again and approaches it from a completely different point of view. Using the fact that language is a system of signs as basis, he shows that there can be two types of circumstances for these signs. The first set of circumstances is that in which a speaker produces a sign which refers to something unknown to the addressee. In such a situation, the sign is not able, in itself, to give information. Augustine gives the example of the word *saraballae*, which, unless previously known, cannot lead the addressee to understand the reference to "headdress" which it contains. The second set of circumstances is that in which the speaker produces a sign which refers to something which is already known to the addressee. Yet even here, Augustine claims, it is not really appropriate to speak of a true process of acquiring knowledge (*De Magistro*, 10.33).

Augustine concludes the argument by inverting the cognitive relationship between sign and object and states that one must first have knowledge of the object of reference to be able to say that a word is a sign of this object. It is the knowledge of the thing which is responsible for the presence of the sign rather than *vice versa*. This solution has clear Platonic overtones, and to this may be linked the equally Platonic-inspired statement

that knowledge of things is more important than knowledge of signs because "whenever a thing stands for something else, it must needs be worth
less than the thing for which it stands" (*De Magistro*, 9.25).

However, even though for things accessible to sense perception
(*sensibilia*) it is external objects which enable us to reach knowledge, this
is not the case for things which are accessible only to the intellect (*intel-
ligibilia*). For these, Augustine identifies a "theological" solution,
whereby knowledge of such things derives from revelations which
conscience—which stems from God—grants within the human mind, the
conscience being a guarantee both of information and of truth (*De Magistro*,
12.39).

Even within this "theological" solution of the language problem, language in some ways still coincides with the function of the commemorative
sign, but in other ways it extends beyond commemorative sign: when we
already know the object of reference, words recall information, but when
we have no prior knowledge of the object, words prompt us to seek out
such knowledge (*De Magistro*, 12.36).

10.5 EXPRESSION AND COMMUNICATION OF THE INNER WORD

The theological solution is by no means merely a convenient way out of a
theoretical impasse for Augustine. On the contrary, it introduces a whole
new series of theoretical concerns. *De Trinitate* (415) deals with the idea of
the expression of the inner word after it has been conceived of in the re-
cesses of the mind. In order to communicate with others, human beings
must use words or some kind of sign which is accessible to the senses in
order to stimulate within the mind of the person being spoken to a word
which matches the word which lies in the speaker's mind while he or she is
speaking (*De Trinitate*, IX, VII, 12).

Augustine emphasizes the pre-linguistic nature of the inner word. This
word does not belong to any natural language but has to be encoded by
means of a sign if it is to be expressed and presented to the comprehension
of intended addressees.

The inner word has a two-fold origin. On the one hand it represents
immanent knowledge, the source of which is God, while on the other it is
determined by the impressions made on the mind by the objects of knowledge. Even in this case, however, the inner word stems from God, in that
the world is the language through which God expresses himself. We find
here the seeds of the universal symbolism which was so important in medieval thought and culture.

It may thus be seen that Augustine's semiology is primarily communicative in nature, as the overall scheme proposed by Todorov (cf. 1977, Eng.
tr., p.44) shows (Figure 10.3).

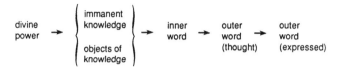

Figure 10.3

10.6 CLASSIFICATIONS

While it is undeniable, as Simone (1969, p.96, note 2) points out, that Augustine's semiology has a strong theological tendency (linked to the problem of the divine word), it nonetheless also has a clear-cut and well-defined secular aspect which may be seen when Augustine turns his attention to the inherent specific characteristics of the sign. Included in this aspect are the various classifications of signs which appear most notably in *De Doctrina Christiana* (397 A.D., with later additions), but which also feature in other works.

Todorov (1977, Eng. tr., p.44 ff.) has identified and analyzed five types of classification which Augustine imposes on the sign:

(1) According to the mode of transmission: visual/aural
(2) According to origin and use: natural signs/intentional signs
(3) According to social function: natural signs/conventional signs
(4) According to the nature of the symbolic relation: proper/transposed (*translata*)
(5) According to the nature of the designatum: sign/thing

Todorov is disappointed that Augustine juxtaposes what he could in fact have put in relation, for such oppositions are generally not interrelated. However, this complaint is not entirely justified since (especially in *De Magistro*) Augustine does make an attempt to give a combined classification of certain aspects of the sign.

It is possible to reconstruct this classification according to a tree diagram (cf. Bernardelli, 1987), following the model of the Porphyrian tree (cf. Eco, 1984a, pp.91 ff.) (Figure 10.4).

Augustine's classification does not in fact totally follow logical inclusion, as the Porphyrian-tree version tends to do. As may be noted, if the collateral branches were to be developed, by developing the side branches, some of the categories on the principal branch would appear again. However, Augustine himself points us towards an inclusive classification from genus to species when he defines the relationship between noun and word as "the same as that between horse and animal" and when he includes the category of words in the wider category of signs (*De Magistro*, 4.9).

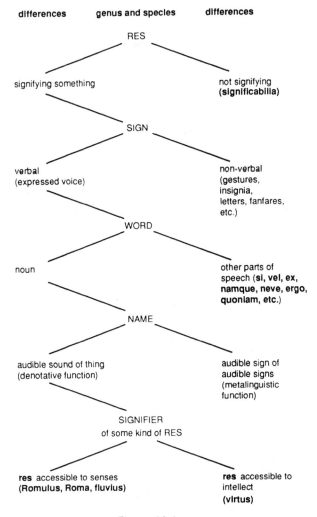

differences   genus and species   differences

RES

signifying something

not signifying
(**significabilia**)

SIGN

verbal
(expressed voice)

non-verbal
(gestures,
insignia,
letters, fanfares,
etc.)

WORD

noun

other parts of
speech (**si, vel, ex,
namque, neve, ergo,
quoniam, etc.**)

NAME

audible sound of thing
(denotative function)

audible sign of
audible signs
(metalinguistic
function)

SIGNIFIER
of some kind of RES

res accessible to senses
(**Romulus, Roma, fluvius**)

res accessible to
intellect
(**virtus**)

Figure 10.4

10.6.1 "RES" AND "SIGNA"

The first interesting relationship in Augustine's classification is that between *res* and *signa*. Although the world is basically thus divided into
things and signs, Augustine sees this distinction as functional and relative
rather than ontological.

Signs are also types of *res*, and it is quite possible to take as a sign a *res*
which had previously not been endowed with this status. The idea of *res* is
defined in thoroughly semiological terms (cf. Simone, 1969, p.105):
"Strictly speaking I have called things (*res*) those objects which are not used
as signs of something: for example, wood, stone, farm animals" (*De Doc-*

trina Christiana, I, II, 2). However, realizing that the processes of semiosis are extremely pervasive, Augustine immediately qualifies this statement: "But not that wood which, as we read, Moses threw into the bitter waters to dissipate their bitterness (*Exodus*, 15:25), nor that stone on which Jacob rested his head (*Genesis*, 28:11); nor that sheep which Abraham burnt instead of his son (ibid., 22:13)".

The relationship which exists between signs and things is analogous to that of the two essential processes "use" (*uti*) and "enjoy", "take benefit from" (*frui*) (*De Doctrina Christiana*, I, IV, 4). Things which are used are transitive, like signs, which are instruments through which something else may be reached; things which are enjoyed are intransitive, that is, they are considered simply for themselves (cf. Todorov, 1977, p.39).

In *De Magistro* (4.8), Augustine proposes a name for things which are not used as signs, but which are signified by means of signs: *significabilia*. However, there is nothing to prevent these from being given a signifying function at a future date.

Having established the relationship between signs and things in this manner, in *De Doctrina Christiana* (II, I, 1), Augustine offers the following definition of a sign: "The sign is a thing (*res*) which above and beyond the impression it produces on the senses on its own account, makes something else come to mind (*in cogitationem*)".

10.6.2 VERBAL AND NON-VERBAL SIGNS

In constructing the Porphyrian tree for Augustine's classification of signs, I decided to express Augustine's principal division of signs according to the dichotomy *verbal/non-verbal*, even though other possibilities, equally evident in the texts, could have been used. I would justify my choice by quoting a passage from *De Doctrina Christiana* (II, III, 4), in which, at the end of an analysis of various types of sign, Augustine states "I could express the meaning of all signs of the type here touched upon in words, but I would not be able at all to make the meanings of words clear by these signs."

This statement makes explicit reference to a special characteristic that verbal language possesses, that of being a primary modeling system, and this characteristic is taken as the criterion for the basic division of signs.

10.6.3 CLASSIFYING SIGNS ACCORDING TO CHANNELS OF PERCEPTION

An intersecting classification in comparison with the previous one is that which is made according to the channel of perception employed. Augustine states "among the signs which people use in order to communicate what they feel to each other, some pertain to the sense of sight, more to the sense of hearing and very few to the other senses" (*De Doctrina Christiana*, II, III, 4).

Signs perceived through the sense of hearing include the basically aes-
thetic signs produced by musical instruments such as the flute or the lyre,
and the essentially communicative signs produced by military fanfares and
soundings of the trumpet. Of course, words form part, and indeed a dominant part, of signs which are perceived through hearing: "Words, indeed,
have obtained the most important position among human beings for the
expression of thoughts of all kinds which anyone wants to convey" (*De
Doctrina Christiana*, II, III, 4).

Augustine lists the following as signs which are perceived through
sight: nodding and shaking the head, gestures, bodily movements of ac-
tors, flags, military insignia and letters.

Augustine also turns his attention to signs which concern the other
senses, such as smell (for example, the perfume of the ointment applied to
Christ's feet), taste (for example, the sacrament of the Eucharist) and
touch (the gesture of the woman who touched Christ's robe and was
healed).

10.6.4 "Signa naturalia" and "signa data"

Even though it cannot be directly integrated with the inclusive tree
we have constructed out of Augustine's classification of signs, the classification which he suggests based on the opposition of *signa naturalia* with *signa data* is of fundamental importance to Augustine's conception of the sign.
Signa naturalia include "(signs which) without any intention or desire of
signifying, make us aware of something beyond themselves, as for example, smoke which signifies fire" (*De Doctrina Christiana*, II, I, 2). Other examples of this type of sign are animal tracks and facial expressions which
reveal, unintentionally, irritation or pleasure. Having defined this type of
sign, Augustine then says that he has no wish to deal any further with
them.

Augustine is much more interested in the *signa data*, for this category
includes Scriptural signs. This type of sign is defined as "(signs which) all
living creatures make, one to another, to show, as much as they can, the
motions of their spirits, that is, everything that they feel and think" (*De
Doctrina Christiana*, II, II, 3). The prime examples of this type of sign are
human linguistic signs, that is, words.

Somewhat curiously, Augustine also includes animal sounds in this category, as, for example, the sounds the cock uses to inform the hen that he
has found food (ibid.). In this respect there is a very marked difference between Augustine and Aristotle, who placed animal noises among natural
signs (*De Interpretatione*, 16 a).

Aristotle made a binary distinction between "natural" and "conventional" signs; however, Augustine's *signa data* are not "conventional
signs", as Markus has suggested (cf. Markus, 1957, p.75) (and indeed as
the French translation of Augustine by G. Combès and J. Farges suggests).
Signa data are rather "intentional signs" (cf. Engels, 1962, p.367; Darrel

Jackson, 1969, p.14) and correspond to a very clear communicative intention (*De Doctrina Christiana*, II, III, 4). It is indeed the intentional nature of animal noises which causes Augustine to include them among *signa data*, even though he does not make any precise comments on the nature of animal intentionality (cf. Eco, 1987, p.78).

Indeed, as Todorov has pointed out (1977, Eng. tr., p.47), focusing attention on the idea of intention corresponds exactly to Augustine's general semiological system, which is based on communication. Intentional signs — or rather, signs created expressly with a view to communication — can be placed in correspondence with Aristotle's *sýmbolon* and with the Stoic combination of a signifier with a signified. Natural signs, that is, signs which already exist as things, would correspond rather to the *sēmeîa* proposed by both Aristotle and the Stoics.

10.7 UNLIMITED SEMIOSIS AND "INSTRUCTIONAL" MODELS

One of the fundamental points of Augustine's semiology is the search for methods by which the meaning of signs can be established. This search appears particularly in *De Magistro*, where a semantic conception very similar to Peirce's "unlimited semiosis" can be seen at work. As Markus points out (cf. Markus, 1957, p.66), for Augustine the meaning of a sign can be established or expressed by means of other signs, such as by using synonyms, by pointing at something with the index finger, by using gestures, or by means of demonstration (*De Magistro*, 2; 7).

This conception of meaning is possible only once the *equational* model of the symbol has been abandoned in favor of the *implicational* model of the sign which Augustine uses. Augustine's semiological theory, as Eco demonstrates (cf. Eco, 1984, pp.34 ff.), thus moves towards an "instructional" model of semantic description. An example of this model is given in the analysis which Augustine makes, in collaboration with Adeodatus, of the line from Vergil's *Aeneid* "si nihil ex tanta superis placet urbe relinqui" (cf. *De Magistro*, 3.3). Augustine states that this line is made up of eight signs, for which the meaning is then sought.

The inquiry begins with |si|, which is recognized as expressing a quality of "doubt", after we have been shown that no other term could be substituted to express the same concept. Next |nihil| is considered, and its meaning is identified as the "affection of the soul" which occurs when, on not seeing something, its absence is noted.

Augustine then asks Adeodatus what the meaning of |ex| is, and he replies by offering a synonymous definition, that is, |ex| is the same as |de|. However, this definition does not satisfy Augustine, who argues that while the latter term *is* an interpretation of the former, it nonetheless requires in its turn an interpretation. The final solution offered is that |ex| means "a separation" from an object. Augustine then adds an *instruction* for the contextual decodification of this solution. |Ex| can mean a separation from something which no longer exists, as in the line from Vergil under consideration, where the city of Troy to which it refers no longer exists. However, the term can also mean a separation from something which is still in existence, as, for example, when it is said that there are some traders in Africa who come from (*ex*) Rome.

The meaning of a term, then, is "a set (a series, a system) of instructions for its possible contextual insertions and for its different semantic outputs in different contexts (all registered by the code)" (Eco, 1984a, p.35).

The implicative structure allows rules of the type "*If* A appears in the contexts x, y, *then* it means B; but *if* B, *then* C; etc.". These are rules which the instructional model and unlimited semiosis share.

It may thus be seen that it is precisely due to the generalized adoption of the implicational model that Augustine's semiology can be considered to be both a synthesis of the semio-linguistic developments of the ancient world (theory of the word as sign) and a striking anticipation of some of the most recent semantic research tendencies (instructional model) in the contemporary world.

Notes

Unless otherwise stated, translations of texts are taken from current versions, with occasional modifications on the part of the author.

ONE. MESOPOTAMIAN DIVINATION

1. It is not yet possible to establish precisely how much Greek culture owes to Mesopotamian culture with respect to the idea of the sign; however, with respect to the implicative scheme in general, it is possible to distinguish a historically documented connection between the two cultures in certain areas of sign use. For example, in medicine, the implicative sign scheme ("If . . . , then . . . ") is used in the presentation of aetiological situations both in Mesopotamian treatises and in Greek treatises. Medicine was an area in which it is known that there were positive contacts between the two cultures. Cf. Di Benedetto and Lami, 1983: 11.

2. Barthes and Marty (1980, p.71) place the earliest traces of writing in Mesopotamia around 3500 B.C. Other scholars, such as Cardona (1981, p.70), claim that the invention of the cuneiform characters themselves may be dated to 3500 B.C. Bottero (1974) thinks that this occurred much later and claims that cuneiform writing was invented in lower Mesopotamia around 2850 B.C. Cf. also Barthes and Mauriès (1981, p.602).

3. Cf. sumerogram no. 73 in Labat's manual (1948, p.69). It is interesting to note here a similarity to the homographic play in Greek between *bíos* ("life") and *biós* ("bow"): as the fragment from Heraclitus puts it (Diels-Kranz, 1951, 48): "The bow (*biós*) has life (*bíos*) as its name and death as its work". (In subsequent references, Diels-Kranz, 1951, will be abbreviated as D-K.)

4. In each example, the protasis is divided from the apodosis by means of a dash (−), in order to show the distinction between them more clearly. These examples, like most of the Mesopotamian texts quoted or referred to in this chapter, come from the extremely full and well-researched essay by Bottero (1974). The reader is referred here and throughout the present chapter to Bottero's essay for details of primary sources and critical editions. I acknowledge the debt to this essay for much of the information contained in this chapter.

5. Each tablet contains over a hundred oracles, and some collections contain around twenty tablets.

TWO. GREEK DIVINATION

1. Crahay (1974), in an analysis of the words used with respect to oracles, has demonstrated that certain words present the text of the revelation as a sign, often as a sign in advance, since they direct action towards the future. Among these words, the two verbs *sēmaínō* and *prosēmaíanō* (that is, "to inform in advance through signs") and the verbal adjective *próphanton* (which expresses the idea of information before the event) stand out in particular.

2. This is shown very clearly through a comparison with the role played by divination, for example, in the Mesopotamian civilization, where the central position held by divination meant that its formal model extended also into other spheres of public and cultural life, such as medicine and justice.

3. Cf. also *Iliad*, III, 277. Translation by Richmond Lattimore, *The Iliad of Homer*, University of Chicago Press, Chicago, 1951.

4. L. Romeo, "Heraclitus and the Foundations of Semiotics", *Versus*, 15 (1976), pp.73-90; p.86.

5. Divination is very strongly linked to Apollo, and Apollo is very strongly linked to wisdom. The wisdom of Apollo is total and simultaneous and has no need to be broken down and fragmented into words. However, the god concedes to humanity only the fragments of oracular words, which are obscure and incomprehensible, for in them the divine wisdom appears as the madness of the possessed individual mouthpiece. Plato holds that madness is the very essence of divination and in *Phaedrus* (244 a–c), he links the etymology of *mantikē* ("divination", "soothsaying") to *manikē* ("mad art"). Madness is only wisdom seen from the outside.

6. Amandry (1950) suggests that cleromancy (telling the future through throwing dice) was also practised at Delphi.

7. Natural phenomena could undergo a complex process of classification and institutionalization. This was the case, for example, with the oracle at Dodona, where the signs given by the rustling of the wind through the branches of an oak tree sacred to Zeus were interpreted, as were also very probably the cooing and the flights of the sacred doves, the gurgling of a spring and the echoes of a gong. For oracles in general, cf. Ferri (1916) and Parke (1967). For an examination of the various types of divination, the fundamental texts are Bouché-Leclercq (1879–82) and Halliday (1913).

8. The "lobe", the "bladder" and the "doors" were the technical terms used to designate parts of the liver which the specialists in this type of divination considered to furnish signs from which interpretations could be made. Cf. Aristotle, *Historia Animalium*, I, 17, 496 b 32, and Euripides, *Electra*, 826-28.

9. Our knowledge of the forms of oracular consultation and response comes principally from a number of epigraphic inscriptions which have survived mainly from Delphi and Dodona. Cf. Parke and Wormell (1956) and Fontenrose (1978).

10. The latter category is intentionally linked to the notion of enigma as it existed in Greek culture, where it involved, as we shall see below, both an element of challenge (on the part of the god towards the human individual), the hidden presence of a second meaning and the idea that the first, obvious meaning had to be discounted. The term "mode" is used to emphasize the fact that we are not dealing with a single mechanism, but with a myriad of very different expressive procedures, ranging from banal homonymy to metaphor (metasemes), to changes of perspective (metalogisms), etc. The phrase "enigmatic mode" is a conscious echo of, and a reference to, the term "symbolic mode" propounded by Eco (1984). It is not possible to use that precise concept here because, although the processes have many points in common, there are important differences. The specific characteristics of close relationship between signifier and signified, nebula of potentially coexistent multiple senses which go to define the category of "symbolic mode", do not form part of the process we are dealing with here. It would have been fitting to define the way of speaking of the god as "symbolic", but, given these important differences, this is not possible.

11. The rhetorical device of the enallage recalls the oracular device used by the Cumaean Sibyl, as described by Vergil (*Aeneid*, VI): the Sibyl (priestess of Apollo) would write the parts of the response on leaves, following the normal syntagmatic order of human speech. She would then cast the leaves to the wind so that the initial order was lost and a new order created which rendered the meaning of the text obscure and hindered its interpretation.

12. The ambiguity of Apollo is represented in his two antithetical attributes. The lyre represents the benign face of the god (that which appears in Nietzsche's interpretation), whereas the bow represents the malignant and destructive side of Apollo. The very etymology of the name Apollo suggests the meaning "he who de-

stroys totally", and this is the aspect of Apollo which appears at the beginning of the *Iliad*, where his arrows carry death and destruction into the camp of the Achaians (Cf. Colli, 1975, p.18).

13. For a thorough and lucid account of the conception of "truth" in the ancient world, cf. Detienne (1967). Detienne also deals with the idea of *alḗtheia* as "synthesis of the past, present and future", which was used with respect to inspired poets, to soothsayers and to philosophical and religious matters.

THREE. SIGNS AND SEMIOSIC PROCESSES IN GREEK MEDICINE

1. From here onwards the *Corpus Hippocraticum* will be referred to in the short form *CH*. Of course, for a complete investigation of early Greek medicine, at least the works of Galen should also be taken into consideration. However, since these belong to a much more recent period (2nd century A.D.) and reflect a philosophical tradition (Aristotelian and Stoic) which had advanced the study of the sign considerably, they do not really come within the context of the present investigation. The interested reader should consult Manuli (1980).

2. The general attribution of medical treatises of the 5th and 4th centuries B.C. to Hippocrates occured within the environment of the Alexandria library in the 3rd century B.C. Cf. Di Benedetto (1986, p.81).

3. It is possible to distinguish within the *CH* certain homogeneous groups of treatises. The most striking of these is the group of therapeutic techniques (*On Internal Affections*, Book II of *Diseases A*), Book III of *On Diseases*, the oldest parts of the treatise *On the Diseases of Women*, which are all characterized by a very marked archaic flavor, and particular attention to the therapeutic and treatment aspects of medicine (cf. Di Benedetto, 1986 pp.5, 80). There is then the very noticeable group of treatises which deal in greater depth with the theoretical and methodological aspects of medicine. Vegetti (ed., 1976, p.21 ff.) has proposed to define as "Hippocratic thought" what emerges from this latter group of works (even though they are written by several different authors, none of whom in all probability was the Hippocrates who lived from 460 to 370 B.C.). These texts can all be chronologically assigned to the second half of the 5th century B.C., and they include *On Ancient Medicine*; *On Airs, Waters, Places*; *Prognostic*; *On Regimen in Acute Diseases*; *The Sacred Disease*; *Epidemics I and II*; as well as the principal surgical works (*Head Wounds*, *Articulations* and *Fractures*).

4. Cf. Jaeger (1934).

5. Cf. Vegetti (ed., 1976, p.65 ff.; 1967, p.78).

6. As Lloyd (1979) has pointed out, however, Hippocratic medicine can never be considered experimental in the true sense.

7. Translations from Hippocrates given here are from current published versions with an occasional modification on the part of the author.

8. It is only later in the Alexandrine School that a formal distinction was made between *anámnēsis*, which concerned the past history of the illness, *diágnōsis*, which concerned the present state and *prógnōsis*, which concerned the likely future progress of the illness. Cf. Di Benedetto and Lami (1983, p.166). With respect to *prógnōsis*, cf. also Grmek (1983). Irigoin (1983, p.179) however, offers a different interpretation of the prefix *pro-* in conjunction with the verb "to say", linking it to the sense of "publicly" rather than the sense of "advance prediction".

9. Cf. Detienne (1967).

10. Sometimes the vocabulary used for medical predictions is identical to that of divination. For example, in Chapter 9 of *Articulations* it is stated that the doctor's task is to *foretell* (*katamanteúsasthai*) certain processes relative to the body's health.

11. It should be noted that this conception has its roots in an animistic, demonic type of pre-Olympian religion. Cf. Lanata (1967), Detienne (1963), Dodds (1951), Lloyd (1979) and Parker (1983). In the 19th century, Rohde's studies (1890-94) had given a panorama of the cathartic, magic movement.

12. Cf. Diogenes Laertius, *Vitae*, VIII, 32 = D-K, 58 B 1a. It is worth noting that the primitive nature of the concept expressed in this passage is evident from the mention of animals within the context of human affairs such as illness and health. We have here the representation of a rural community in which people and animals form a unified whole. Cf. Detienne (1963, p.32).

13. A similar example is provided in Chapter 21 of the treatise *On Airs, Waters, Places*, which refutes, using the *modus tollens*, the thesis that the impotence which certain members of the Sciite community suffer from is due to divine intervention, since it affects only the rich (who have the habit of riding on horseback, which is thus, according to the author of the treatise, the real cause of the condition) and not the poor. If the impotence were of divine origin, it would affect the rich and poor equally.

14. A similar notion is expressed in Plato's *Timaeus* (71 e), which talks about the weakening of the senses during sleep, and in Aristotle's *De Divinatione per Somnum*, which claims that the lessening of the turbulence in the air enables the onset of dreaming.

15. The page number given is to the Italian edition of this work, as the section referred to does not appear in the English edition.

16. Diogenes Laertius VIII, 83 = D-K, 24 B 1; cit. Eco (1984, pp.26-27).

17. Cf. Eco (1975, p.295). Eco defines this concept as the phenomenon whereby "the object, seen as a pure expression, is made *of the same matter* as its possible referent".

18. Cf. also Lichtenthaeler (1983) and Wenskus (1983).

19. Cf. Vegetti (1976, p.48) and Manuli (1985, p.233).

20. With respect to abduction, cf. Thagard (1978), Proni (1981), Eco (1983), Bonfantini and Proni (1983), Bonfantini (1985), Peirce (1984) and Eco (1984).

21. Translated from the Italian of Vegetti, 1976, p.49.

22. Di Benedetto (1986) has shown very effectively the relationship between illness presentation modules in Greek medicine and those used in Mesopotamian and Egyptian medicine. Cf. also Di Benedetto and Lami (1983).

23. R. Campbell Thompson, "Assyrian Prescriptions for the Head", in *The American Journal of Semitic Languages and Literatures*, 53 (1937), pp.217-38, 235.

24. The term is coined from that used by A.G. Conte (*praxeologico*) in his study "Fenomeni di fenomeni" presented at the 7th Colloquium on Interpretation held in Macerata, 25–27 March 1985, and later published (1986) in the proceedings. Cf. G. Galli (ed.), *Interpretazione e Epistemologia*, Atti del VII Colloquio sulla Interpretazione, Macerata, 25–27 marzo 1985, Marietti, Turin, 1986, pp.167-98.

25. Translated from the French version of Littré, 1839, 7, 186, 3-10.

26. Cit. in Di Benedetto, *Il medico e la malattia: La scienza di Ippocrate*, Einaudi, Turin, 1986, p.91.

FOUR. PLATO

1. Cf. Hjelmslev (1943).

FIVE. LANGUAGE AND SIGNS IN ARISTOTLE

1. Cf. Aristotle, *Prior Analytics*, II, 70 a–b; *Rhetoric*, I, 1357 a–b.

2. Cf. Aristotle, *Rhetoric*, I, 1358 a, 36 ff.

3. Cf. Aristotle, *De Interpretatione*, 16 a; *Prior Analytics*, 70 a-b.

4. With respect to this argument, cf. Di Cesare, 1981, p.161.

5. Cf. Eco, 1984, p.16; 1987, p.75.

6. Cf. Heinimann, 1945.

7. Cf. Eco, Lambertini, Marmo and Tabarroni, 1984; Eco, 1987.

8. We may see here the beginnings of an awareness of the double articulation of human language which is developed in the present century by André Martinet (1960).

9. "Quando, una cosa essendo, un'altra è, oppure quando una cosa divenendo, un'altra diviene anteriormente o posteriormente, *queste ultime* sono segni del divenire o dell'essere" (Preti, 1956, p.5).

10. Even though Aristotle does not explicitly give this definition, there is in the *Rhetoric* (I, 1357 a, 14-22) a passage which suggests the idea of the enthymeme as a shortened syllogism. Furthermore, in a passage in *Prior Analytics* (II, 70 a, 24-25) Aristotle seems to attempt to distinguish the *sign* from the *syllogism* according to the number of premisses assumed in each (a single premiss in the former, two in the latter).

11. In *Rhetoric*, *tekmérion* is explicitly defined as "necessary" (*anankaîon*), while *sēmeîon* is defined as "not necessary" (*mḕ anankaîon*) (cf. *Rhetoric*, I, 1357 b, 4).

12. The same point of view and the same terminology reappear in the parallel passage in *Rhetoric* (I, 1357 b, 16-18).

13. With respect to the refutable nature of this type of sign, Aristotle makes the following comment on the example given in *Prior Analytics*: "A syllogism in the middle figure is always and in every way refutable (*lýsimos*), since we never get a syllogism with the terms in this relation; for it does not necessarily follow, if a pregnant woman is pale, and this woman is pale, that she is pregnant." (*Prior Analytics*, II, 70 a, 34-37).

14. "As to signs, some are related as the particular to the universal, others as the universal to the particular. Necessary signs are called *tekmḗria*; those which are not necessary have no distinguishing name. I call those necessary signs from which a logical syllogism can be constructed, wherefore such a sign is called *tekmḗrion*; for when people think that their arguments are irrefutable, they think that they are bringing forward a *tekmḗrion*, something as it were proved and concluded; for in the old language *tékmar* and *péras* have the same meaning (limit, conclusion)" (*Rhetoric*, I, 1375 b, 4-10). It should be noted that while in *Prior Analytics* and in *Rhetoric* a very strict distinction is made between *tekmḗrion* and *sēmeîon*, the use Aristotle makes of these two terms in his scientific treatises is considerably more flexible, without there being any apparent distinction between the two terms. Another term, *martýrion* is also used in the same sense as *sēmeîon* (cf. Le Blond, 1939/1973, note p.241).

15. Cf. Aristotle, *Prior Analytics*, II, 70 b, 7-14.

16. Cf. Aristotle, *Posterior Analytics*, II, 98 b, 25-30.

SIX. THEORY OF LANGUAGE AND
SEMIOTICS IN THE STOIC PHILOSOPHERS

1. For the Stoics, the "criterion of truth" is based on images produced in the mind by external objects, and in particular by certain types of images, which they call *katalēptikaì phantasíai*. The criterion of truth is "that on the basis of which we assert that certain things exist and others do not, and that the former are the case (literally 'are true', *alēthê*) and the latter are not the case (literally 'are false', *pseudê*)" (Sextus Empiricus, *Adversus Mathematicos*, VII, 29). Cf. Mignucci (1965 and 1966); Sandbach (1971a and 1971b) and the chapter "The criterion of truth" in Rist (1969).

2. The translation given is that by Long (Long, 1971a, pp.76-77). Cf. also Sextus Empiricus, *Adversus Mathematicos*, VIII, 69-70.

3. It should be noted that *lektón* is the *verbal* adjective from the verb *légein*. In this respect the Stoics make a distinction between "to utter" (*prophéresthai*), which was simply producing sounds, and "to say" (*légein*), which was to emit sounds in order to sig-

nify (*sēmaínein*) the state of affairs in the mind (cf. Sextus Empiricus, *Adversus Mathematicos*, VIII, 80). Long (1971a, p.77) prefers to translate *lektón* with "what is said" rather than by "what is meant" as Mates and the Kneales do, since the former translation is more general and makes it possible to interpret *lektón* as having both a logical and a grammatical function.

4. There is a tradition which goes back to Plato's *Cratylus* according to which naming X is the same as saying "this is the name of X". In this case Sextus' example should be understood in the terms of an implicit proposition such as "Dion is the name of this person", or "this is Dion". Cf. Long (1971a, p.107, note 11).

5. The Stoics classified *lektá* as "complete" or "incomplete", and each of these two types had a further complex sub-classification, which is not relevant to our discussion here. The interested reader is referred to Mates (1953, pp.11-26).

6. The translation given is again that by Long (cf. Long, 1971a, p.82).

7. Cf. Diogenes Laertius, *Vitae*, VII, 51; Long (1971a, p.83).

8. Cf. Sextus Empiricus, *Adversus Mathematicos*, VIII, 11-12.

9. Cf. Sextus Empiricus, *Adversus Mathematicos*, VIII, 70.

10. Cf. Diogenes Laertius, *Vitae*, VII, 63.

11. Cf. Mates (1953, pp.11-12). Mates understands *lektá* as the meaning of words and brings their definition close to Frege's *Sinn* and Carnap's *intension*.

12. Cf. Zeller (1865, pp.78-79).

13. Cf. Bréhier (1909, pp.114-25).

14. Cf. Mignucci (1965, p.96).

15. Sextus Empiricus gives a definition of the criterion of truth in *Adversus Mathematicos*, VII, 29: "that on the basis of which we assert that certain things exist and others do not, and that the former are the case and the latter are not the case". With respect to the criterion of truth, cf. Rist (1969, pp.133-51); Sandbach (1971a, p.9 ff.) and Mignucci (1966).

16. Cf. Plato, *Theaetetus*, 190 a (206 d); *The Sophist*, 263 a.

17. "Internal speech" (*endiáthetos lógos*), in contrast to materially produced expressions or sounds (*prophorikòs lógos*), is the feature distinguishing human beings from animals. Sextus Empiricus states in this regard: "(The Stoics) say that man differs from irrational animals by reason of internal speech (*endiáthetos lógos*), un-uttered speech (*prophorikòs lógos*), for cows and parrots and jays utter articulate sounds" (*Adversus Mathematicos*, VIII, 275-76; the translation is by Long, 1971a, p.87; cf. also Pohlenz, 1948, 1, pp.61-62).

18. Cf. also Sextus Empiricus, *Adversus Mathematicos*, VIII, 245-57.

19. Cf. Diels-Kranz, 75 B 2.

20. There is a very thorough discussion of this terminological problem in the introduction by the editor of the Italian version, W.C. and M. Kneale, *The Development of Logic*. Cf. A.G. Conte (ed.), *Storia della logica*, Einaudi, Turin, 1972, xxxv.

21. Cf. Sextus Empiricus, *Outlines of Pyrrhonism*, II, 95-96.

22. Ibid.: "for indeed proof seems to be a kind of sign". Cf. also *Adversus Mathematicos*, VIII, 180, quoted in note 50, below.

23. The text of *De Signis*, along with an English translation is given in Ph. & E.A. De Lacy (1978).

24. Cf. Sextus Empiricus, *Adversus Mathematicos*, VIII, 144; *Outlines of Pyrrhonism*, II, 97.

25. Cf. Sextus Empiricus, *Adversus Mathematicos*, VIII, 147; *Outlines of Pyrrhonism*, II, 97.

26. Cf. Sextus Empiricus, *Adversus Mathematicos*, VIII, 145; *Outlines of Pyrrhonism*, II, 98.

27. Cf. Sextus Empiricus, *Adversus Mathematicos*, VIII, 146; *Outlines of Pyrrhonism*, II, 98.

28. Cf. Sextus Empiricus, *Adversus Mathematicos*, VIII, 151-55.

29. This three-part division will be explicitly theorized in Roman rhetoric. Cf. Chapter 9.

30. Cf. Sextus Empiricus, *Adversus Mathematicos*, VIII, 152-53.

31. Cf. Sextus Empiricus, *Adversus Mathematicos*, VIII, 154.

32. Cf. Sextus Empiricus, *Adversus Mathematicos*, VIII, 156. Apart from the polemics it demonstrates, this observation is interesting in that it cites "doctors" and "philosophers" as though setting the two terminal points of the process of growth of interest in the sign. The cycle begins with the interest shown by doctors (as is attested to by the numerous medical examples which appear in all the treatises) and ends with the systematic study of the sign by philosophers.

33. Cf. Diogenes Laertius, *Vitae*, VII, 71.

34. Cf. Sextus Empiricus, *Outlines of Pyrrhonism*, II, 104-105; *Adversus Mathematicos*, VIII, 245-47.

35. Cf. Sextus Empiricus, *Adversus Mathematicos*, VIII, 245.

36. Cf. Sextus Empiricus, *Adversus Mathematicos*, VIII, 248; *Outlines of Pyrrhonism*, II, 106.

37. Cf. Sextus Empiricus, *Adversus Mathematicos*, VIII, 249-50; *Outlines of Pyrrhonism*, II, 106.

38. Cf. Sextus Empiricus, *Adversus Mathematicos*, VIII, 250-51.

39. Cf. Sextus Empiricus, *Outlines of Pyrrhonism*, II, 106-107; *Adversus Mathematicos*, VIII, 252-53.

40. Cf. Sextus Empiricus, *Outlines of Pyrrhonism*, II, 110-12. I shall take into consideration only these three criteria since it seems that the fourth criterion did not originate with the Megarian school of Stoicism.

41. Cf. Sextus Empiricus, *Outlines of Pyrrhonism*, II, 110-12; *Adversus Mathematicos*, VIII, 115-17.

42. Various interpretations of Diodorus' conditional have been proposed, but it is not within the scope of the present work to consider all of them. The interested reader is referred to the works by Hurst (1935), Mates (1949a), W.C. and M. Kneale (1962) and Mignucci (1966), where the topic is discussed in a progressive theoretical context.

43. Cf. Preti (1956), p.13: "sembra alludere a qualcosa di ancora più forte: alla vera e propria tautologia".

44. Cf. Philodemus, *De Signis*, Col.XIV, 11-14 = Chapt.19; Col.XI, 32–Col. XII, 1 = Chapt.17. The Roman numerals here refer to the columns of the Greek text and have been linked with an "equals" sign to the corresponding chapter of the English translation produced by P.H. and E.A. De Lacy (1978).

45. Cf. Sextus Empiricus, *Adversus Mathematicos*, VIII, 275-76, 287.

46. Cf. Goldschmidt (1953, p.79 ff.), Verbeke (1978, pp.401-402), Manuli (1986, p.262).

47. Verbeke's comment on the Stoic view of the relationship between philosophy and divination is illuminating here: "(le philosophe) est le médecin de cet organisme vivant qu'est le monde; il est aussi une sorte de prophète, un devin, un exégète, un interprète des signes qu'il observe" (cf. Verbeke, 1978, p.402).

48. Cf. Cicero, *De Divinatione*, I, 125-27.

49. Cf. Sextus Empiricus, *Outlines of Pyrrhonism*, II, 140; *Adversus Mathematicos*, VIII, 305.

50. Cf. Sextus Empiricus, *Adversus Mathematicos*, VIII, 180: "And, moreover, proof is, generically, a sign; for it serves to reveal its conclusion."

51. Cf. Sextus Empiricus, *Adversus Mathematicos*, VIII, 309.

SEVEN. INFERENCE AND LANGUAGE IN EPICURUS

1. This text by Philodemus has survived in the papyrus from Herculaneum and is now available in an admirable critical edition prepared by P.H. and E.A. De Lacy (1978). From here onwards I shall refer to this work using its Latin title, *De Signis*. Chapter 8 of the present work deals extensively with this work.

2. Cf. Diogenes Laertius, *Vitae*, X, 31. Cf. also Epicurus, *Letter to Herodotus*, 38; *Kyriai Doxai* (*Ratae Sententiae, Principal Doctrines*), XXIV.

3. Cf. Philodemus, *De Signis*, fr. 1.

4. Cf. Diogenes Laertius, *Vitae*, X, 33; Epicurus, *On Nature*, XXVIII, fr. 4, col. III, in Arrighetti (1960, pp.296-97). Long (1971b, p.114) claims that a similar relationship between language and *prólepsis* is assumed also in the *Letter to Herodotus*, 37-38.

5. Cf. Diogenes Laertius, *Vitae*, X, 34.

6. Cf. Epicurus, *Letter to Pythocles*, 86-87.

7. Cf. Epicurus, *Letter to Herodotus*, 82.

8. Cf. Diogenes Laertius, *Vitae*, X, 31.

9. Cf. Sextus Empiricus, *Adversus Mathematicos*, VIII, 9.

10. Cf. Diogenes Laertius, *Vitae*, X, 32.

11. Cf. Diogenes Laertius, *Vitae*, X, 31.

12. Cf. Epicurus, *Letter to Herodotus*, 46.

13. Cf. Epicurus, *Letter to Herodotus*, 48.

14. Cf. Sextus Empiricus, *Adversus Mathematicos*, VII, 211.

15. Cf. Sextus Empiricus, *Ratae Sentetiae, Principal Doctrines*, XXIV; Diogenes Laertius, *Vitae*, X, 34.

16. Cf. Sextus Empiricus, *Adversus Mathematicos*, VII, 211.

17. Semiotic conjecture is expressed by the verb *sēmeióō* (*Letter to Herodotus*, 38) and takes the form of induction in Epicurean theory. The noun which derives from this verb, *sēmeíōsis*, does not appear in Epicurus' writings but is treated extensively by Philodemus.

18. Cf. Sextus Empiricus, *Adversus Mathematicos*, VII, 213-14.

19. As will be seen in the following chapter, the concept of "non-incompatibility" with known facts is central to the theory of inference as it is expounded by Philodemus in *De Signis*.

20. Cf. Diogenes Laertius, *Vitae*, X, 33.

21. Cf. Sextus Empiricus, *Adversus Mathematicos*, VIII, 13, 258; Plutarch, *Adversus Colotem*, 1119f.

22. For a treatment of the semantic problem in Epicurus in terms very different from those used in the present study, the reader is referred to the article by Glidden (1983a), which takes up the position of Sextus Empiricus and Plutarch, claiming that there is not a specific level of signified understood in intensional terms in Epicurean linguistic philosophy.

23. Cf. Sedley (1973, pp.17-18); Sedley's text varies in part from that of Arrighetti (1960, pp.66-67).

24. This problem was avoided both by Cratylus and by Socrates in Plato's *Cratylus*.

25. See Chapter 4, above.

26. Cf. Plato, *Cratylus*, 421 d, 435 c; cf. Sedley (1973, p.20).

EIGHT. PHILODEMUS

1. The precise date of composition of the treatise remains controversial but

would seem to lie somewhere between 54 and 40 B.C. Cf. P.H. and E.A. De Lacy (1978, pp.163-64).

2. Due to the partial corruption of the Greek text, the Greek title of this work is mainly the result of conjecture by T. Gompers. Other conjectured titles have also been proposed, cf. P.H. and E.A. De Lacy (1978, pp.11-14).

3. The first section of the treatise deals with Zeno of Sidon's replies to Stoic criticisms; the second section gives Bromius' version of Zeno's listing and refutation of arguments against empirical inference; the third section gives Demetrius Lacon's listing of the errors of opponents of the analogical method; the fourth section is anonymous, but in all probability is also to be attributed to Demetrius, and gives a second list of the errors of the opponents of the analogical method.

4. Cf. Marquand, 1883; Deledalle, 1987.

5. Cf. Philodemus, *De Signis*, Col.VIII, 32-Col.IX, 3 = Chapt. 13. References to *De Signis* are given using first the column and line numbers of the Greek text of the papyrus, followed by the chapter number of the P.H. and E.A. De Lacy English translation of the text (1978).

6. This point is repeated frequently in the third section of the treatise, which gives Demetrius' thoughts on the subject. Cf. Col.XXVIII, 13-25 = Chapt.45, and Col.XXXVII, 12-24 = Chapt.57.

7. Cf. Col.XIII, 1-15 = Chapt.18.

8. Cf. Col.I, 1-12 = Chapt.2, and Col.XIV, 4-11 = Chapt.19.

9. Col.I, 12-16 = Chapt.2.

10. Col.XII, 14-31 = Chapt.17.

11. It would seem that Peirce's consideration of the concept of the *icon* is very similar to the Stoic and Epicurean distinction between common signs and particular signs. For Peirce "an *Icon* is a sign which refers to the Object that it denotes merely by virtue of characters of its own, and which it possesses, just the same, *whether any such Object actually exists or not. It is true that unless there really is such an Object, the Icon does not act as a sign: this has nothing to do with its character as a sign.*" (2, 247 = 1960, p. 143).

12. Cf. Preti, 1956, p.13; see also Chapter 6 above.

13. Cf. Col.II, 25-36 = Chapt.5.

14. Col.III, 4-8 = Chapt.5.

15. Cf. Col.XXXV, 35-Col.XXXVI, 7 = Chapt.53.

16. The replies to the Stoic objections are, in Zeno's section, Col.XVI, 4-Col.XVII, 28 = Chapts.23-24, and in Bromius' section, Col.XXII, 28-Col.XXIII, 7 = Chapt.38.

17. Cf. Col.XVII, 3-7 = Chapt.24.

18. There is a discussion which is attributed to the "Dogmatists" on the problem of definition as *combinations of attributes*, for example, "animal", "mortal", "rational" for people, in Sextus Empiricus, *Adversus Mathematicos*, VII, 276-77.

19. Cf. Col.IV, 3-5 = Chapt.6.

20. Cf. Col.XVII, 11-28 = Chapt.24.

21. Cf. Col.V, 1-7 = Chapt.7.

22. Col.XVII, 29-36 = Chapt.25.

23. Col.XVII, 37-Col.XVIII, 3 = Chapt.25.

24. Col.XVIII, 10-16 = Chapt.25.

25. Col.XXIII, 13-Col.XXIV, 8 = Chapt.39.

26. Col.XXIV, 10-17 = Chapt.40.

27. Col.XXVI, 6-9 = Chapt.41.

28. The tradition continued after the Epicureans, too; sometimes in late antiquity the two definitions are combined to give Galen's, "rational animals, that is (animals) endowed with reason" (*De Plac. Hipp. et Plat.*, IX, 3), and Sextus Empiricus' definition, "mortal rational animals, endowed with intelligence and rationality" (*Adversus Mathematicos*, VII, 269).

29. Cf. Col.XXXIII, 35–Col.XXXIV, 5 = Chapt.52.
30. Cf. Eco, 1984b, p.130 ff. This reference is to the Italian edition of this work since the English edition does not include this passage.
31. Cf. Groupe μ (1970, p.100).
32. Cf. Col.XXXIV, 5-7 = Chapt.52.
33. Cf. Col.XXXIV, 11-15 = Chapt.52.
34. Cf. Col.XXI, 27-29 = Chapt.36.
35. Cf. Col.XXX, 27-31 = Chapt.47.
36. Cf. Col.XVIII, 23-29 = Chapt.26.
37. Cf. Col.I, 19–Col.II, 3 = Chapt.3.
38. Cf. Col.XIV, 28–Col.XV, 13 = Chapt.20.
39. Cf. Col.XX, 32–Col.XXI, 3 = Chapt.35.

NINE. LATIN RHETORIC

1. Cicero talks about the "regularity of reason" (*ratio et constantia*) being opposed to "chance" (*fortuna*) (*De Divinatione*, II, 18).
2. Cf. Eco (1984a, pp.36-37).

TEN. AUGUSTINE

1. In other works, Augustine uses the term *significatio* in place of *dicibile*. Cf., for example, *De Magistro*, 10, 34.
2. It should be noted that Augustine uses the term *verbum* in two different senses: (i) a technical, specific sense which is that of the metalinguistic use of the word; (ii) a general sense which corresponds to that of the broader sense of the idea of "word" as "a sign of any sort of thing which, spoken by a speaker, can be understood by the hearer" (Chapter V).
3. The definition of *dictio* given in Chapter V of *De Dialectica* clearly indicates the nature of this term as a combination of signifier and signified: "What I have called *dictio* is a word, but a word which signifies simultaneously both the preceding units, the word (*verbum*) itself and that which is produced in the mind by means of the word (*dicibile*)". *Dictio* is "what is spoken not for its own sake, but for the sake of signifying something else" (ibid.).
4. The Stoics understood the sign in propositional terms as an antecedent which referred to a consequent. Cf. Sextus Empiricus, *Adversus Mathematicos*, VIII, 245.
5. Cf. Lotman and Uspenskij, 1971.

Bibliography

Allan, D.J.
1970 *The Philosophy of Aristotle*, Oxford University Press, Oxford.

Amandry, P.
1950 *La mantique apollinienne à Delphes. Essai sur le fonctionnement de l'oracle* (diss.), Bibliothéque des Ecoles Françaises de Athènes et de Rome, Vol. 170, Paris.
1959 "Oracles, littérature et politique", in *Revue des études anciennes*, 61, 1-2, pp.400-413.

Arens, H. (ed.)
1984 *Aristotle's Theory of Language and Its Tradition: Texts from 500 to 1750*, John Benjamins, Amsterdam & Philadelphia.

Aristotle
1956 *The Works of Aristotle* (translated under the editorship of J.A. Smith & W.D. Ross), Oxford.

Arrighetti, G. (ed.)
1960 *Epicuro Opere*, Einaudi, Turin.

Asmis, E.
1984 *Epicurus' Scientific Method*, Cornell University Press, Ithaca.

Avila Belloso, I.
1984 "Le discours divinatoire", in *Actes sémiotiques – Bulletin*, 32, pp.33-38.

Baratin, M.
1981 "Les origines stoïciennes de la théorie augustinienne du signe" in *Revue des études latines*, 59, pp.260-68.

Baratin, M., & Desbordes, F.
1981 *L'analyse linguistique dans l'antiquité classique*, 2 vols., Klincksieck, Paris.

Barnes, J.
1980 "Proof Destroyed", in M. Schofield, M. Burnyeat & J. Barnes (eds.), *Doubt and Dogmatism*, Clarendon, Oxford, pp.161-81.
1988 "Epicurean Signs", in J. Annas & R.H. Grimm (eds.), *Oxford Studies in Ancient Philosophy*, supplementary volume, Clarendon Press, Oxford, pp.91-134.

Barnes, J., Brunschwig, J., et al. (eds.)
1982 *Science and Speculation: Studies in Hellenistic Theory and Practice*, Cambridge University Press, Cambridge.

Barthes, R.
1970 L'ancienne rhétorique – Aide-mémoire", *Communications*, 16, pp.172-229.

Barthes, R., & Marty, E.
1980 "Orale/Scritto", in *Enciclopedia*, Einaudi, Turin, Vol. 10, pp.60-86.

Barthes, R., & Mauriès, P.
1981 "Scrittura", in *Enciclopedia*, Einaudi, Turin, Vol.12, pp.600-627.

Belardi, W.
1975 *Il linguaggio nella filosofia de Aristotele*, K. Libreria Editrice, Rome.

Benveniste, E.
1969 "Le vocabulaire latin des signes et des présages", in *Le vocabulaire des institutions indo-européennes II: Pouvoir, droit, religion*, Les Editions de Minuit, Paris, pp.255-63. (English translation by Elizabeth Palmer, "The Latin Vocabulary of Signs and Omens", pp.508-15, Book 6, Chapter 6 of *Indo-European Language and Society*, Faber, London, 1973.)

Bernadelli, A.
1987 *Teorie del segno in S. Agostino*, University of Bologna, manuscript.

Berrettoni, P.
1970 "Il lessico tecnico del I e III libro delle *Epidemie* ippocratiche", in *Annali della Scuola Normale Superiore di Pisa*, 1/2, pp.27-106; 3/4, pp.217-311.

Blasi, G.
1992 "Segno ed esperimento. Un problema di storia della semiotica", in P. Magli, G. Manetti & P. Violi (eds.), *Semiotica: Storia, teoria, interpretazione*, Bompiani, Milan, pp.43-58.

Bloch, R.
1963 *Les prodiges dans l'antiquité classique*, Presses Universitaires de France, Paris.

Bocheński, I.M.
1951 *Ancient Formal Logic*, North-Holland, Amsterdam.
1956 *Formale Logik*, K. Alber, Freiburg. (English translation by Ivo Thomas, *A History of Formal Logic*, University of Notre Dame Press, Notre Dame, Indiana, 1961).

Boisacq, E.
1907 *Dictionnaire étymologique de la langue grecque*, C. Winter, Heidelberg (4th edn. 1950).

Bonfantini, M.A.
1985 "Pragmatique et abduction", in *Versus*, 40, pp.51-56.

Bonfantini, M.A., & Proni, G.P. (eds.)
1983 *L'abduzione*, special number of *Versus*, 34.

Bonomi, A. (ed.)
1973 *La struttura logica del linguaggio*, Bompiani, Milan.

Bottero, J.
1974 "Symptômes, signes, écritures en Mésopotamie ancienne", in J.-P. Vernant (ed.), *Divination et rationalité*, Seuil, Paris.

Bouché-Leclercq, A.
1879-82 *Histoire de la divination dans l'antiquité*, 4 vols., E. Leroux, Paris.

Bourgey, L.
1953 *Observation et expérience chez les médecins de la Collection hippocratique*, Vrin, Paris.
1955 *Observation et expérience chez Aristote*, Vrin, Paris.

Brătescu, G.
1975 "Eléments archaïques dans la médecine hippocratique", in *La Collection hippocratique et son rôle dans l'histoire de la médecine*, "Colloques de Strasbourg (23–27 octobre 1972)", Brill, Leiden, pp.41-49.

Bréhier, E.
1909 *La théorie des incorporels dans l'ancien stoïcisme*, 2nd edn., Vrin, Paris, 1928.

Brisson, L.
1974 "Du bon usage du dérèglement", in J.-P. Vernant (ed.), *Divination et rationalité*, Seuil, Paris.

Brunschwig, J.
1980 "Proof Defined", in M. Schofield, M. Burnyeat & J. Barnes (eds.), *Doubt and Dogmatism*, Clarendon, Oxford, pp.125-60.

Burnyeat, M.F.
1982 "The origins of non-deductive inference", in J. Barnes, J. Brunschwig, et al. (eds.), *Science and Speculation: Studies in Hellenistic Theory and Practice*, Cambridge University Press, Cambridge, 1982, pp.43-58.

Bury, R.G. (transl.)
1935 Sextus Empiricus, Vol.2, *Against the Logicians*, The Loeb Classical Library, Heineman, London.

Calabrese, O.
1975 "Lineamenti per una storia delle idee semiotiche", in O. Calabrese & E. Mucci, *Guida alla Semiotica*, Sansoni, Milan.

Calabrese, O., & Mucci, E.
1975 *Guida alla Semiotica*, Sansoni, Milan.

Calboli, G. (ed.)
1969 *Cornifici, Rhetorica ad C. Herennium*, Patron, Bologna.

Cambiano, G. (ed.)
1986 *Storiografia e dossografia nella filosofia antica*, Tirrenia Stampatori, Turin.

Campbell Thompson, R.
1924 *Assyrian Medical Texts*, John Bale, Sons & Danielson, London.
1937 "Assyrian Prescriptions for the Head", in *The American Journal of Semitic Languages and Literatures*, 53, pp.217-38.

Cardona, G.R.
1981 *Antropologia della scrittura*, Loescher, Turin.

Carlier, J.
1978 "Divinazione", in *Enciclopedia*, Einaudi, Turin, Vol.4, pp.1226-38.

Carnap, R.
1947 *Meaning and Necessity*, The University of Chicago Press, Chicago.

Celluprica, V.
1980 "La logica stoica in alcune recenti interpretazioni", in *Elenchos*, 1, pp.123-50.

Chantilly, Colloque de
1978 *Les Stoïciens et leur logique*, "Actes du Colloque de Chantilly, 18-22 septembre 1976", Vrin, Paris.

Chiesa, C.
1986 "Symbole et signe dans le *De Interpretatione*", in A. Joly (ed.), *Philosophie du langage et grammaire*, Ousia, Brussels, pp.202-18.

Colli, G.
1975 *La nascita della filosofia*, Adelphi, Milan.
1977 *La sapienza greca*, Vol.1, Adelphi, Milan.

Conte, A.G.
1972 "Premessa del curatore", in W.C. & M. Kneale, *Storia della logica*, Einaudi, Turin (Italian translation of *The Development of Logic*, Clarendon Press, Oxford, 1962).
1986 "Fenomeni di fenomeni", in G. Galli (ed.), *Interpretazione ed Epistemologia*, "Atti de VII Colloquio sulla Interpretazione, Macerata, 25–27 marzo 1985", Marietti, Turin, pp.167-98.

Conte, M.E.
1983 "La pragmatica linguistica", in C. Segre (ed.), *Intorno alla linguistica*, Feltrinelli, Milan, pp.94-128.

Cortassa, G.
1978 "Pensiero e linguaggio nella teoria stoica del *lekton*", in *Rivista di Filologia*, 106, pp.385-94.

Cosenza, G.
1988 "Peirce and Ancient Semiotics", in *Versus*, 50/51, pp.159-64.

Cousin, J.
1935-36 *Etudes sur Quintilien I et II*, Boivin, Paris; repr. Schippers, Amsterdam, 1967.

Crahay, R.
1956 *La littérature oraculaire chez Hérodote*, Liège & Paris.
1974 "La bouche de la vérité", in J.-P. Vernant (ed.), *Divination et rationalité*, Seuil, Paris.

Crapis, C.
1988 "Théories des indices dans la rhétorique latine", in G. Manetti (ed.), *Signs of Antiquity/Antiquity of Signs*, special number of *Versus*, 50/51, 1988, pp.175-97.
1990-91 "Momenti della paradigma semiotico nella cultura latina. Indizio giudiziario e segno divinatorio", in *Ausidus*, 11/12, pp.141-87; 13/14, pp.55-89.

Crookshank, F.G.
1923 "The importance of a theory of signs and a critique of language in the study of medicine", in C.K. Ogden & I.A. Richards, *The Meaning of Meaning*, Kegan Paul, Trench, Trubner & Co., London, pp.511-37.

Curcio, G.
1900 *Le opere retoriche di M. Tullio Cicerone: Studio critico*, Acireale; repr. L'Erma di Bretschneider, Rome, 1972.

De Lacy, E.A.
1938 "Meaning and Methodology in the Hellenistic Philosophy", in *The Philosophical Review*, 47, pp.390-409.

De Lacy, P.H.
1939 "The Epicurean Analysis of Language", in *American Journal of Philology*, 60, pp.85-92.
1986 "Plato", in T.A. Sebeok (ed.), *Encyclopedic Dictionary of Semiotics*, Mouton/de Gruyter, Berlin, New York & Amsterdam, pp.735-36.

De Lacy, P.H. & E.A.
1938 "Ancient Rhetoric and Empirical Method", in *Sophia*, 6, pp.523-30.
1978 *Philodemus: On Methods of Inference*, Bibliopolis, Naples.

Del Corno, D.
1985 "Mantica, magia, astrologia", in M. Vegetti (ed.), *Il sapere degli antichi*, Boringhieri, Turin, pp.279-94.

Delcourt, M.
1955 *L'oracle de Delphes*, Payot, Paris.

Deledalle, G.
1987 "Quelle philosophie pour la sémiotique peircienne? Peirce et la sémiotique grecque", in *Semiotica*, 63, pp.241-51.

Deleuze, G.
1969 *Logique du sens*, Les Editions de Minuit, Paris.

De Mauro, T.
1965 *Introduzione alla semantica*, Laterza, Bari.
1971 *Senso e significato: Studi di semantica teorica e storica*, Adriatica, Bari.

De Rijk, L.M.
1986 *Plato's Sophist: A Philosophical Commentary*, North-Holland, Amsterdam, Oxford & New York.

Detienne, M.
1963 *De la pensée religieuse à la pensée philosophique. La notion de Daïmon dans le pythagorisme ancien*, Les Belles Lettres, Paris.
1967 *Les maîtres de vérité dans la Grèce archaïque*, Maspero, Paris.

Detienne, M., & Vernant, J.-P.
1974 *Les ruses de l'intelligence – La métis des Grecs*, Flammarion, Paris. (English translation by J. Lloyd, *Cunning Intelligence in Greek Culture and Society*, Hassocks, London, 1978.)

Di Benedetto, V.
1966 "Tendenza e probabilità nell'antica medicina greca", in *Critica storica*, 5, pp.315-68.
1986 *Il medico e la malattia: La scienza di Ippocrate*, Einaudi, Turin.

Di Benedetto, V., & Lami, A.
1983 *Ippocrate: Testi de medicina greca*, Rizzoli, Milan.

Di Cesare, D.
1980 *La semantica nella filosofia greca* (preface by Tullio De Mauro), Bulzoni, Rome.
1981 "Il problema logico-funzionale de linguaggio in Aristotele", in J. Trabant (ed.),
    Logos Semantikos I, de Gruyter, Berlin; Gredos, Madrid, pp.21-30.
1989 "Language and Dialectics in Plato: Reflections on the Linguistic Foundation of
    Philosophical Enquiry", in *Kodikas/Code/Ars Semeiotica*, 12, 1/2, pp.3-19.

Diels, H., & Kranz, W. (eds.)
1951 *Die Fragmente der Vorsokratiker*, 6th edn., Weidmann, Berlin. (English transla-
    tion by Rosamond Kent Sprague (ed.), *The Older Sophists: A Complete Translation
    by Several Hands of the Fragments in* Die Fragmente der Vorsokratiker, *edited by
    Diels-Kranz*, University of South Carolina Press, Columbia, 1972.)

Diller, H.
1932 "*Opsis adēlōn ta phainomena*", in *Hermes*, 67, pp.14-42.

Dinneen, F.P.
1967 *An Introduction to General Linguistics*, Holt, Rinehart and Winston, New York.

Dodds, E.R.
1951 *The Greeks and the Irrational*, University of California Press, Berkeley & Los An-
    geles.

Dubarle, D.
1980 "Logique et épistémologie du signe chez Aristote et chez les Stoïciens", in E.
    Joós (ed.), *La Scolastique, certitude et recherche: en hommage à Louis-Marie Régis*,
    Bellarmin, Montreal, pp.27-83.

Duchrow, V.
1961 "Signum und superbia beim jungen Augustin (386-390)", in *Revue des études
    augustiniennes*, 7, pp.369-72.

Dumont, J.-P.
1982 "Confirmation et disconfirmation", in J. Barnes, J. Brunschwig, et al. (eds.),
    Science and Speculation: Studies in Hellenistic Theory and Practice, Cambridge Uni-
    versity Press, Cambridge, pp.273-303.

Ebert, T.
1987 "The Origin of the Stoic Theory of Signs in Sextus Empiricus", in *Oxford Stud-
    ies in Ancient Philosophy*, 5, pp.83-126.

Eco, U.
1973 *Il Segno*, ISEDI, Milan.
1975 *Trattato di semiotica generale*, Bompiani, Milan. English edition:
1976 *A Theory of Semiotics*, Indiana University Press, Bloomington. English edition
    of the above.
1983 "Corna, zoccoli, scarpe. Alcune ipotesi su tre tipi di abduzione", in U. Eco &
    T.A. Sebeok (eds.), *Il segno dei tre*, Bompiani, Milan, pp.235-61. (English edition
    "Horns, Hooves, Insteps: Some Hypotheses on Three Types of Abduction", in
    The Sign of Three: Dupin, Holmes, Peirce, ed. U. Eco & T.A. Sebeok, Indiana Uni-
    versity Press, Bloomington & Indianapolis, 1983, pp.198-220.

1984a *Semiotics and the Philosophy of Language*, Macmillan, Houndmills & London; Indiana University Press, Bloomington & Indianapolis.

1984b *Semiotica e filosofia del linguaggio*, Einaudi, Turin. Italian edition of the above.

1986 "Aristotle: Poetics and Rhetoric", in T.A. Sebeok (ed.), *Encyclopedic Dictionary of Semiotics*, Mouton/de Gruyter, Berlin, New York & Amsterdam, pp.54–55.

1987 "Latratus canis", in *Micro Mega*, 1, pp.73-82.

Eco, U., Lambertini, R., Marmo, C., & Tabarroni, A.

1984 "On Animal Language in the Medieval Classification of Signs", in *Versus*, 38/39, pp.3-38.

Eco, U., & Marmo, C. (eds.)

1989 *On the Medieval Theory of Signs*, John Benjamins, Amsterdam & Philadelphia.

Eco, U., & Sebeok, T.A. (eds.)

1983 *The Sign of Three: Dupin, Holmes, Peirce*, Indiana University Press, Bloomington & Indianapolis.

Edelstein, L.

1966 *Plato's Seventh Letter*, Brill, Leiden.

Engels, J.

1962 "La doctrine du signe chez Saint Augustin", in *Studia Patristica*, 6, pp.366-73.

Evans-Pritchard, E.E.

1937 *Witchcraft, Oracles and Magic among the Azande*, Clarendon Press, Oxford.

Fagot, A.M.

1984 "Medicina e probabilità", in *Kos*, 1, 1, pp.24-31.

Ferri, S.A.

1916 "Saggio di classificazione degli oracoli", in *Athenaeum*, 4, pp.396-415.

Festa, N.

1932 *I frammenti degli stoici antichi*, Laterza, Bari.

Fischer, M.H.

1971 "Peirce's Arisbe: The Greek Influence in His Later Philosophy", in *Transactions of the C.S. Peirce Society*, 7, 4, pp.187-210.

Flacelière, R.

1950 "Le délire de la Pythie est-il une légende?", in *Revue des Etudes Anciennes*, 52, pp.306-24.

Fontenrose, J.

1978 *The Delphic Oracle: Its Responses and Operations, with a Catalogue of Responses*, University of California Press, Berkeley, Los Angeles & London.

Frege, G.

1892 "Über Sinn und Bedeutung", in *Zeitschrift für Philosophie und philosophische Kritik*, Vol. 100, pp.25-50. (Englisih translation by Max Black, "On Sense and Meaning", in Peter Geach & Max Black [eds.], *Translations from the Philosophical Writings of Gottlob Frege*, Basil Blackwell, Oxford, 1952, pp.56-78.)

Friedrich, J.
1954 *Entzifferung verschollener Schriften und Sprachen*, Springer Verlag, Berlin. (English translation by F. Gaynor, *Extinct Languages*, Philosophical Library, New York, 1957; Peter Owen, London, 1962.

Frohn, W.
1986 "Hippocrates", in T.A. Sebeok (ed.), *Encyclopedic Dictionary of Semiotics*, Mouton/de Gruyter, Berlin, New York & Amsterdam, pp.308-309.

Gambarrara, D.
1984 *Alle fonti della filosofia del linguaggio. 'Lingua' e 'nomi' nella cultura greca arcaica*, Bulzoni, Rome.

Genette, G.
1976 *Mimologiques. Voyage en Cratylie*, Seuil, Paris.

Gernet, L.
1968 *Anthropologie de la Grèce antique*, Maspero, Paris. (English translation by J. Hamilton and B. Nagy, *The Anthropology of Ancient Greece*, Johns Hopkins University Press, Baltimore & London, 1981.)

Ginzburg, C.
1979 "Clues: Morelli, Freud, and Sherlock Holmes", in U. Eco & T.A. Sebeok (eds.), *The Sign of Three: Dupin, Holmes, Peirce*, Indiana University Press, Bloomington & Indianapolis, 1983, pp.81-118.

Glidden, D.K.
1983a "Epicurean Semantics", in *Syzētētesis. Studi sull'epicureismo greco e romano, offerti a Marcello Gigante*, Gaetano Macchiaroli, Naples, pp.185–226.
1983b "Skeptic semiotics", in *Phronesis*, 28, 3, pp.213-55.

Goldschmidt, V.
1953 *Le système stoïcien et l'idée du temps*, Vrin, Paris.

Goltz, D.
1974 *Studien zur altorientalischen und griechischen Heilkunde*, Franz Steiner Verlag, Wiesbaden.

Graeser, A.
1978 "The Stoic Theory of Meaning", in J.M. Rist (ed.), *The Stoics*, University of California Press, Berkeley, Los Angeles & London, pp.77-100.

Grimaldi, W.M.A.
1980 "Semeion, Tekmerion, Eikos in Aristotle's Rhetoric", in *American Journal of Philology*, 101, pp.383-98.

Grmek, M.D.
1983 *Les maladies à l'aube de la civilisation occidentale, recherches sur la réalité pathologique dans le monde préhistorique archaïque et classique*, Payot, Paris.

Grmek, M.D., & Robert, F.
1977 "Dialogue d'un médecin et d'un philologue sur quelques passages des *Epidémies VII*", in R. Joly (ed.), *Corpus Hippocraticum*, "Actes du Colloque Hippocratique de Mons (22–26 sept. 1975)", Mons, pp.275-90.

Groupe μ

1970 *Rhétorique générale*, Larousse, Paris. (English translation by P.B. Burrell & E.M. Slotkin, *A General Rhetoric*, Johns Hopkins University Press, Baltimore & London, 1981.)

Haller, R.

1962 "Untersuchungen zum Bedeutungsproblem in der antiken und mittelalterlichen Philosophie", in *Archiv für Begriffsgeschichte*, 7, pp.57-119.

Halliday, W.R.

1913 *Greek Divination: A Study of Its Methods and Principles*, Macmillan, London; repr. Argonaut, Chicago, 1967.

Hanke, M.

1986 "G. Weltrings 'SEMEION' in der aristotelischen, stoischen, skeptischen und epikureischen Philosophie", in *Kodikas/Code*, 9, 1/2, pp.7-38.

Heinimann, F.

1945 *Nomos und Physis. Herkunft und Bedeutung einer Antithese im griechischen Denken des 5. Jahrhunderts*, Friedrich Reinhardt, Basel.

Herzfeld, M.

1982 "Divining the Past", in *Semiotica*, 38, 1/2, pp.169-75.
1986 "Divination", in T.A. Sebeok (ed.), *Encyclopedic Dictionary of Semiotics*, Mouton/de Gruyter, Berlin, New York & Amsterdam, pp.212-13.

Hjelmslev, L.

1943 *Omkring sprogteoriens grundlaeggelse*, Munksgaard, Copenhagen. (English translation by F.J. Whitfield, *Prolegomena to a Theory of Language*, University of Wisconsin Press, Madison, 1961.)

Hulser, K.H. (ed.)

1987-88 *Die Fragmente zur Dialektik der Stoiker. Neu Sammelung der Texte mit deutschen Übersetzung und Kommentaren*, 4 vols., Frommann & Holzboog, Stuttgart.

Hurst, M.

1935 "Implication in the Fourth Century B.C.", in *Mind*, 44, pp.484-95.

Irigoin, J.

1983 "Préalables linguistiques à l'interprétation des termes techniques attestés dans la collection hippocratique", in F. Lasserre & Ph. Mudry (eds.), *Formes de pensée dans la Collection Hippocratique*, "Actes du IV Colloque international hippocratique (Lausanne, 21–26 septembre 1981)", Droz, Geneva, pp.173-80.

Irwin, T.H.

1982 "Aristotle's Concept of Signification", in M. Schofield & M. Nussbaum (eds.), *Language and Logos: Studies in Ancient Greek Philosophy Presented to G.E.L. Owen*, Cambridge University Press, Cambridge, pp.241-66.

Jackson, B.D.

1969 "The Theory of Signs in St. Augustine's *De Doctrina Christiana*", in *Revue des études augustiniennes*, 15, pp.9-49.

Jaeger, W.
1934 *Paideia. Die Formung des griechischen Menschen*, de Gruyter, Berlin & Leipzig. (English translation by Gilbert Highet, *Paideia: The Ideals of Greek Culture* [translated from the second German edition], 3 vols., Basil Blackwell, Oxford, 1939–1944.)

Joly, R.
1980 "Un peu d'épistémologie historique pour hippocratisants?", in M.D. Grmek (ed.), *Hippocratica*, "Actes du Colloque hippocratique de Paris (4–9 septembre 1978)", Editions CNRS, Paris, pp.285-98.

Kennedy, G.
1969 *Quintilian*, Twayne, New York.

Kerényi, K.
1953 "Problemi intorno alla Pythia", in *Apollon: Studien über antike Religion und Humanität*, Verlag Franz Leo, Vienna, Amsterdam & Leipzig (1937); 2nd edition, Dusseldorf, 1953.

Kneale, W.C. & M.
1962 *The Development of Logic*, Clarendon Press, Oxford.

Kretzmann, N.
1967 "History of Semantics", in P. Edwards (ed.), *Encyclopedia of Philosophy*, Vol.7, Macmillan & The Free Press, New York, pp.358-406.
1971 "Plato on the Correctness of Names", in *American Philosophical Quarterly*, 8, pp.126-38.

Labat, R.
1948 *Manuel d'épigraphie akkadienne. Signes, Syllabaire, Idéogrammes*, Pane Geuthner, Paris (repr. 1976).
1951 *Traité akkadien de diagnostics et pronostics médicaux*, Paris & Leiden.

Lanata, G.
1967 *Medicina magica e religione popolare in Grecia fino all'età di Ippocrate*, Edizioni dell'Ateneo, Rome.

Lanza, D.
1972 "Scientificità della lingua e lingua della scienza in Grecia", in *Belfagor*, 27, pp.392-429.
1979 *Lingua e discorso nell'Atene delle professioni*, Liguori, Naples.
1983 "Quelques remarques sur le travail linguistique du médecin", in F. Lasserre & Ph. Mudry (eds.), *"Formes de pensée dans la Collection Hippocratique*, "Actes du IV Colloque international hippocratique (Lausanne, 21-26 septembre 1981)", Droz, Geneva, pp.181-85.

Lear, J.
1980 *Aristotle and Logical Theory*, Cambridge University Press, Cambridge.

Le Blond, J.M.
1939 *Logique et méthode chez Aristote. Etude sur la recherche des principes dans la physique aristotélicienne*, Vrin, Paris; 2nd edition, 1970; 3rd edition, 1973.

Leszl, W.
1985 "Linguaggio e discorso", in M. Vegetti (ed.), *Il sapere degli antichi*, Boringhieri, Turin, 1985, pp.13-44.

Lichtenthaeler, C.
1983 "En 1981 comme en 1948: relations de causalité expérimentales et analogies hippocratiques", in F. Lasserre & Ph. Mudry (eds.), *"Formes de pensée dans la Collection Hippocratique*, "Actes du IV Colloque international hippocratique (Lausanne, 21–26 septembre 1981)", Droz, Geneva, pp.383-91.

Lieb, H.
1981 "Das 'semiotische Dreieck' bei Ogden und Richards: eine Neuformulierung des Zeichenmodells von Aristoteles", in Jürgen Trabant (ed.), *Logos Semantikos I*, de Gruyter, Berlin; Gredos, Madrid, pp.137-56.

Littré, E.
1839 *Oeuvres complètes d'Hippocrate*, Adolf M. Hakkert, Amsterdam; new edition 1961.

Liverani, M.
1963 *Introduzione alla storia dell'Asia anteriore antica*, Università de Roma, Centro di Studi Semitici, Rome.

Lloyd, A.C.
1971 "Grammar and Metaphysics in the Stoa", in A.A. Long (ed.), *Problems in Stoicism*, University of London, The Athlone Press, London, pp.58-74.

Lloyd, G.E.R.
1970 *Early Greek Science: Thales to Aristotle*, Chatto & Windus, London.
1979 *Magic, Reason, Experience: Studies in the Origin and Development of Greek Science*, Cambridge University Press, Cambridge.

Long, A.A.
1971a "Language and Thought in Stoicism", in A.A. Long (ed.), *Problems in Stoicism*, University of London, The Athlone Press, London, pp.75-113.
1971b "Aisthesis, Prolepsis and Linguistic Theory in Epicurus", in *Bulletin of the Institute of Classical Studies of the University of London*, 18, pp.114-33.
1982 "Astrology: Arguments pro and contra", in J. Barnes, J. Brunschwig, et al. (eds.), 1982, pp.164-92.

Long, A.A. (ed.)
1971 *Problems in Stoicism*, University of London, The Athlone Press, London.

Lonie I.M.
1981 *The Hippocratic Treatises "On Generation", "On the Nature of the Child", "Diseases IV"*, de Gruyter, Berlin & New York.

Lo Piparo, F.
1988 "Aristotle: The Material Conditions of Linguistic Expressiveness", in *Versus*, 50/51, pp.83-121.

Lorenz, K., & Mittelstrass, J.
1967 "On Rational Philosophy of Language: The Programme in Plato's Cratylus Reconsidered", in *Mind*, 76, pp.1-20.

190   *Bibliography*

Lotman, Ju.M., & Uspenskij, B.A. (eds).
1971 *O Semioticeskom mechanizm kul'tury* "Trudy po znakovym sistemam 5", Tartu,
    Tartuskii Gos. Universitet; *Tipologia della cultura*, Bompiani, Milan, 1975.

Lo Zano-Miralles, H.
1988 "Signs and Language in Plato", in *Versus*, 50/51, pp.71-82.

Lucci, G.
1980 "Filodemo di Gadara e la 'Logica' epicurea", in *Elenchos*, 1, pp.363-72.

Lugarini, L.
1963 "L'orizzonte linguistico del sapere in Aristotele e la sua trasformazione stoica",
    in *Il pensiero*, 8, pp.327-51.

Łukasiewicz, J.
1957 *Aristotle's Syllogistic from the Standpoint of Modern Formal Logic*, Oxford Univer-
    sity Press, Oxford (2nd edition).

Magli, P.
1988 "Ancient Physiognomies", in *Versus*, 50/51, pp.39-55.

Maloney, G., & Frohn, W. (eds.)
1986 *Concordantia in Corpus Hippocraticum/Concordances des oeuvres hippocratiques*,
    Vols. 1–5, Olms-Weidmann, Hildesheim, Zurich & New York.

Manetti, G.
1986a "Cicero", in T.A. Sebeok (ed.), *Encyclopedic Dictionary of Semiotics*, Mouton/de
    Gruyter, Berlin, New York & Amsterdam, pp.107-109.
1986b "Quintilian", in T.A. Sebeok (ed.), *Encyclopedic Dictionary of Semiotics*,
    Mouton/de Gruyter, Berlin, New York & Amsterdam, pp.785-88.
1988 "Perception, Encyclopedia and Language among the Stoics", in *Versus*, 50/51,
    pp.123-44.

Manetti, G. (ed.)
1988 *Signs of Antiquity/Antiquity of Signs*, special number of *Versus*, 50/51.

Manuli, P.
1980 *Medicina e antropologia nella tradizione antica*, Loescher, Turin.
1985 "Medico e malattia", in M. Vegetti (ed.), *Il sapere degli antichi*, Boringhieri,
    Turin, pp.229-45.
1986 "Traducibilità e molteplicità dei linguaggi nel *De placitis* di Galeno", in G. Cam-
    biano (ed.), *Storiografia e dossografia nella filosofia antica*, Tirrenia Stampatori,
    Turin.

Markus, R.A.
1957 "St. Augustine on Signs", in *Phronesis*, 2, pp.60-83.

Marmo, C.
1988 "From Analogical Points of View: On the Use of Analogy in Ancient Greek
    Medical Texts", in *Versus*, 50/51, pp.19-36.

Marquand, A.
1883 "The Logic of the Epicureans", in *Studies on Logic by Members of the Johns Hop-
    kins University*, Little, Brown, Boston, pp.1-11.

Martinelli, R.
1988 "Epicurus, Philodemus and the Theory of Inference", in G. Manetti (ed.), *Signs of Antiquity/Antiquity of Signs*, special number of *Versus*, 50/51, pp.145-74.

Martinet, A.
1960 *Eléments de linguistique générale*, Armand Colin, Paris. (English translation by Elizabeth Palmer, *Elements of General Linguistics*, Faber & Faber, London, 1964.)

Mates, B.
1949a "Diodorean Implication", in *The Philosophical Review*, 58, pp.234-42.
1949b "Stoic Logic and the Text of Sextus Empiricus", in *American Journal of Philology*, 70, pp.290-98.
1953 *Stoic Logic*, University of California Press, Berkeley, Los Angeles & London.

Melazzo, L.
1975 "La teoria del segno linguistico negli Stoici", in *Lingua e Stile*, 10, pp.199-230.

Mignucci, M.
1965 *Il significato della logica stoica*, Patron, Bologna.
1966 "L'argomento dominatore e la teoria dell'implicazione in Diodoro Crono", in *Vichiana*, 3, pp.3-28.

Morpurgo-Tagliabue, G.
1967 *Linguistica e stilistica di Aristotele*, Edizioni dell'Ateneo, Rome.

Morrow, G.R.
1935 *Studies in the Platonic Epistles*, University of Illinois, Urbana; revised edition 1962, Bobbs-Merrill, Indianapolis & New York.

Müller, I.
1978 "An Introduction to Stoic Logic", in J.M. Rist (ed.), *The Stoics*, University of California Press, Berkeley, Los Angeles & London, pp.1–26.

Nagy, G.
1983 "Sema and Noisis: An Illustration", in *Arethusa*, 16, pp.35-55.

Oehler, K.
1986 "Aristotle" in T.A. Sebeok (ed.), *Encyclopedic Dictionary of Semiotics*, Mouton/de Gruyter, Berlin, New York & Amsterdam, pp.52-54.

Pagliaro, A.
1956a *Nuovi saggi di critica semantica*, D'Anna, Florence & Messina.
1956b "Il problema del segno nella filosofia antica", in *Filosofia de linguaggio*, Edizioni dell'Ateneo, Rome.
1957 *La parola e l'immagine*, Edizioni Scientifiche Italiane, Naples.

Parke, H.W.
1967 *The Oracles of Zeus: Dodona, Olympia, Ammon*, Basil Blackwell, Oxford.

Parke, H.W., & Wormell, D.E.
1956 *The Delphic Oracle*, 2 vols., Basil Blackwell, Oxford.

Parker, R.
1983 *Miasma: Pollution and Purification in Early Greek Religion*, Oxford University Press, Oxford.

Peirce, C.S.
1931–58 *Collected Papers*, 8 vols. (ed. Charles Hartshorne & Paul Weiss; vols. 7 and 8 ed. Arthur W. Burks), Harvard University Press, Cambridge, Mass.
1980 *Semiotica. I fondamenti della semiotica cognitiva* (ed. M.A. Bonfantini, L. Grassi & R. Grazia), Einaudi, Turin.
1984 *Le leggi dell'ipotesi* (ed. M.A. Bonfantini, R. Grazia & G. Proni), Bompiani, Milan.

Pellegrini, C.
1984 "Le système divinatoire astrologique: la temporalité en question", in *Actes sémiotiques – Bulletin*, 32, pp.28-32.

Pépin, J.
1985 "SYMBOLA, SEMEIA, OMOIOMATA. A propos de *De Interpretatione*, 1, 16a 3–8 et *Politique* VIII 5, 1340a 6–39", in Paul Moraux (ed.), *Aristoteles – Werk und Wirkung. Band 1. Aristoteles und seine Schule*, de Gruyter, Berlin & New York, pp.22-44.

Perrilli, L.
1991 "Il lessico intelletuale di Ippocrate: *sēmaínein* e *tekmaíresthai*", in *Lexicon Philosophicum*, 5.

Pingborg, J.
1975 "Classical Antiquity: Greece", in T.A. Sebeok (ed.), *Current Trends in Linguistics*, vol. 13, Mouton, The Hague & Paris, pp.69-126.

Plebe, A.
1966 *Introduzione alla logica formale, attraverso una lettura logistica di Aristotele*, Laterza, Bari.

Pohlenz, M.
1948 *Die Stoa*, Vandenhoeck und Ruprecht, Göttingen.

Prantl, C. von
1855 *Geschichte der Logik im Abendlände*, S. Hirzel, Leipzig.

Preti, G.
1956 "Sulla dottrina del *sēmeîon* nella logica stoica", in *Rivista critica di storia della filosofia*, 11, pp.5-14.

Prieto, L.J.
1975 *Pertinence et pratique. Essai de sémiologie*, Editions de Minuit, Paris.

Proni, G.
1981 "Genesi e senso dell'abduzione in Peirce", in *Versus*, 28, pp.24-50.
1988 "Aristotle's Abduction", in M. Herzfeld & L. Melazzo (eds.), *Semiotic Theory and Practice: Proceedings of the 3rd International Congress of I.A.S.S., Palermo, 1984*, Mouton/de Gruyter, Berlin, New York & Amsterdam, pp.953-61.

Ramat, P.
1962 "Gr. *hierós*, scr. *isiráh* e la loro famiglia lessicale", in *Die Sprache*, 8, pp.4-28.

Regenbogen, O.
1930 "Eine Forschungsmethode antiker Naturwissenschaft", in *Quellen und Studien zur Geschichte der Mathematik*, 1, 2, Berlin, pp.131-82; repr. in O. Regenborg, *Kleine Schriften*, C.H. Beck'sche, Munich, 1961, pp.141-94.

Rey, A.
1973 *Théories du signe et du sens*, 2 vols., Klincksieck, Paris.
1984 "What does semiotic come from?", in *Semiotica*, 52, pp.79-93.

Rist, J.M.
1969 *Stoic Philosophy*, Cambridge University Press, Cambridge.
1972 *Epicurus: An Introduction*, Cambridge University Press, Cambridge.

Rist, J.M. (ed.)
1978 *The Stoics*, University of California Press, Berkeley, Los Angeles & London.

Robert, F.
1983 "La Pensée hippocratique dans les *Epidémies*", in F. Lasserre & Ph. Mudry (eds.), *Formes de pensée dans la Collection Hippocratique*, "Actes du IV Colloque international hippocratique (Lausanne, 21–26 septembre 1981)", Droz, Geneva, pp.97-108.

Rohde, E.
1890-94 *Psyche, Seelencult und Unsterblichkeitsglaube der Griechen*, Freiburg. (English translation by W.B. Hillis, *Psyche . . .* [translated from the eighth edition], Kegan Paul, London, 1925; repr. Harper & Row, New York, 1966.)

Romeo, L.
1976 "Heraclitus and the Foundations of Semiotics", in *Versus*, 15, pp.73-90.

Ross, W.D.
1923 *Aristotle*, Methuen, London.

Roux, G.
1976 *Delphes. Son oracle et ses dieux*, Belles Lettres, Paris.

Russo, A. (ed.)
1975 *Sesto Empirico, Contro i logici*, Laterza, Bari.

Sandbach, E.H.
1971a "Phantasia Katalēptikē", in A.A. Long (ed.), *Problems in Stoicism*, University of London, The Athlone Press, London, pp.9-21.
1971b "Ennoia and Prolēpsis in the Stoic Theory of Knowledge", in A.A. Long (ed.), *Problems in Stoicism*, University of London, The Athlone Press, London, pp.22-37.

Santambrogio, M.
1984 "Minima Methodica", in *Kos*, 1, 1, pp.16-18.

Saussure, F. de
1916 *Cours de linguistique générale*, Payot, Paris. (English translation by Wade Baskin, ed. C. Bally & A. Sechehaye, *Course in General Linguistics*, Peter Owen, London, 1960; repr. McGraw Hill, New York, 1966; Fontana, London, 1974.)

194   Bibliography

Schimidt, R.T.
1839 *Stoicorum Grammatica*; repr. Adolf M. Hakkert, Amsterdam, 1967.

Schofield, M., Burnyeat, M., & Barnes, J. (eds.)
1980 *Doubt and Dogmatism*, Clarendon, Oxford.

Sebeok, T.A.
1976 *Contributions to the Doctrine of Signs*, Indiana University Press, Bloomington.
1979 *The Sign and Its Masters*, University of Texas Press, Austin.

Sebeok, T.A. (ed.)
1986 *Encyclopedic Dictionary of Semiotics*, Mouton/de Gruyter, Berlin, New York &
     Amsterdam.

Sedley, D.
1973 "Epicurus, On Nature, Book XXVIII", in *Cronache Ercolanesi*, 3, pp.5-83.
1982 "On Signs", in J. Barnes, J. Brunschwig, J. Burnyeat & M. Schofield (eds.),
     Science and Speculation: Studies in Hellenistic Theory and Practice, Cambridge Uni-
     versity Press, Cambridge, pp.239-72.

Simone, R.
1969 "Semiologia agostiniana", in *La cultura*, 7, pp.88-117.

Sissa, G.
1981 "La Pizia delfica: immagini di una mantica amorosa e balsamica", in *Aut Aut*,
     184/185, pp.127-51.
1985 "Il segno oracolare, una parola divina e femminile", in F. Baratta & F. Mariani
     (eds.), *Mondo classico. Percorsi possibili*, Longo, Ravenna, pp.243-52.

Staiano, K.V.
1982 "Medical Semiotics: Redefining an Ancient Craft", in *Semiotica*, 38, 3/4,
     pp.319-46.

Taylor, A.E.
1912 "The Analysis of EPISTEME in Plato's Seventh Epistle", in *Mind*, 21, pp.347-70.

Thagard, P.R.
1978 "Semiotics and Hypothetic Inference in C.S. Peirce", in *Versus*, 19/20, pp.163-
     72.

Thivel, A.
1975 "Le 'divin' dans la collection hippocratique", in *La Collection Hippocratique et
     son rôle dans l'histoire de la médecine*, "Colloque de Strasbourg (23–27 octobre
     1972)", Brill, Leiden, pp.57-76.

Todorov, T.
1977 *Théories du symbole*, Seuil, Paris. (English translation by C. Porter, *Theories of the
     Symbol*, Oxford, 1982.)
1985 "A propos de la conception augustinienne du signe", in *Revue des Etudes au-
     gustiniennes*, 31, pp.209-14.

Vance, E.
1986 "Augustine", in T.A. Sebeok (ed.), *Encyclopedic Dictionary of Semiotics*,
     Mouton/de Gruyter, Berlin, New York & Amsterdam, pp.62-64.

Vegetti, M.
1967 "Teoria ed esperienza nel metodo ippocratico", in *Il Pensiero*, I, pp.66-85.
1973 "Nascita dello scienziato", in *Belfagor*, 6, pp.641-63.
1979 *Il coltello e lo stilo*, Il Saggiatore, Milan.
1983 *Tra Edipo e Euclide. Forme del sapere antico*, Il Saggiatore, Milan.

Vegetti, M. (ed.)
1976 *Opere di Ippocrate*, Utet, Turin.

Verbeke, G.
1974 "Philosophie et semeiology chez les Stoïciens", in *Etudes Philosophiques présentées au Dr. Ibrahim Madkour*, Gibo, pp.15-38.
1978 "La philosophie du signe chez les Stoïciens", in *Les Stoiciens et leur logique*, "Actes du Colloque de Chantilly" (18–22 septembre 1976), Vrin, Paris, pp.401-24.

Vernant, J.
1948 "La divination. Contexte et sens psychologique des rites et des doctrines", in *Journal de Psychologie Normale et Pathologique*, juillet-septembre, pp.299-325.

Vernant, J.-P.
1974 "Parole et signes muets", in J.-P. Vernant (ed.), *Divination et rationalité*, Seuil, Paris.

Vernant, J.-P. (ed.)
1974 *Divination et rationalité*, Seuil, Paris.

Viano, C.A.
1954 "Studi sulla logica di Aristotele: l'orizzonte linguistico della logica aristotelica", in *Rivista critica della storia della filosofia*, 9, pp.5-37.
1958a "La dialettica di Aristotele", in *Rivista di filosofia*, 49, pp.154-78.
1958b "La dialettica stoica", in *Rivista di filosofia*, 49, pp.179-277.

Volli, U.
1979 *La retorica delle stelle*, L'Espresso Strumenti, Rome.

Wald, L.
1979 "Le rapport entre *signum* et *denotatum* dans la conception d'Augustin", in S. Chatman, U. Eco & J.M. Klinkenberg (eds.), *A Semiotic Landscape/Panorama sémiotique*, Mouton, The Hague, Paris & New York, pp.569-72.

Weidemann, H.
1989 "Aristotle on Inference from Signs (*Rhetoric*, I, 2, 1357b 1–25)", in *Phronesis*, 34, 3, pp.343–51.
1991 "Grundzüge der Aristotelischen Sprachtheorie", in P. Schmitter (ed.), *Sprachtheorien der abendländischen Antike*, Gunter Narr, Tübingen, pp.170-92.

Weingartner, R.H.
1969 "Making Sense of *Cratylus*", in *Phronesis*, 15, pp.5-25.

Weltring, G.
1910 *Das* SEMEION *in der aristotelischen, stoischen, epikureischen und skeptischen Philosophie*, Hauptmann, Bonn; repr. in *Kodikas/Code*, 9, 1/2, pp.39-118.

Wenskus, O.

1983 "Vergleich und Beweis im 'Hippokratischen Corpus' ", in F. Lasserre & Ph. Mudry (eds.), *"Formes de pensée dans la Collection Hippocratique,* "Actes du IV Colloque international hippocratique (Lausanne, 21–26 septembre 1981)", Droz, Geneva, pp.393–406.

Zeller, E.

1865–68 *Philosophie der Griechen in ihrer geschichtlichen Entwicklung,* 3 vols., Tübingen. (English translations by B.F.C. Costelloe & J.H. Muirhead, *Aristotle and the Earlier Peripatetics,* London, 1847; O.J. Reichel, *Socrates and the Socratic Schools,* London, 1868, and *The Stoics, Epicureans and Sceptics,* London, 1870; S.F. Alleyne, *Plato and the Older Academy,* London, 1876, *A History of Greek Philosophy from the Earliest Period to the Time of Socrates,* London, 1881, and *A History of Eclecticism in Greek Philosophy,* London, 1883.)

Giovanni Manetti is a teacher and researcher in the Institute of Communication Studies at the University of Bologna. He is an editor of the journal *Versus – Quaderni di studi semiotici* and has written, in collaboration with P. Violi, *Grammatica dell'arguzia* and *L'analisi del discorso*.

Christine Richardson teaches in the Department of Languages at the University of Bologna.